PATRICIA G. BERMAN

MODERN HIEROGLYPHS: GESTURAL DRAWING AND THE EUROPEAN VANGUARD 1900–1918

DISTRIBUTED BY THE UNIVERSITY OF PENNSYLVANIA PRESS

DAVIS MUSEUM AND CULTURAL CENTER WELLESLEY COLLEGE WELLESLEY MASSACHUSETTS

Published in conjunction with an
exhibition held at the
Davis Museum and Cultural Center
Wellesley College
Wellesley, Massachusetts
January 27 – March 19, 1995
which traveled to
The Equitable Gallery
New York, New York
March 28 – May 6, 1995.
The exhibition and catalogue
were supported in part by a grant from the
National Endowment for the Arts,
a federal agency;
the William T. Kemper Foundation;
the E. Franklin Robbins Charitable Trust;
and the Wellesley College Friends of Art.

Front endpaper: detail of catalogue number 26
Back endpaper: detail of catalogue number 3

ISBN Number 1-881894-06-1
Library of Congress Catalog Card Number 94-068690

Distributed by
University of Pennsylvania Press
13th Floor, Blockley Hall
418 Service Drive
Philadelphia, Pennsylvania 19104

CONTENTS

LENDERS TO THE EXHIBITION

ALLEN MEMORIAL ART MUSEUM
Oberlin College, Oberlin, Ohio

THE BALTIMORE MUSEUM OF ART
Baltimore, Maryland

BUSCH-REISINGER MUSEUM
Harvard University Art Museums
Cambridge, Massachusetts

DAVIS MUSEUM AND CULTURAL CENTER
Wellesley College
Wellesley, Massachusetts

THE DETROIT INSTITUTE OF ARTS
Detroit, Michigan

THE FOGG ART MUSEUM
Harvard University Art Museums
Cambridge, Massachusetts

FRANCEY AND DR. MARTIN L. GECHT
Chicago, Illinois

INDIANA UNIVERSITY ART MUSEUM
Bloomington, Indiana

THE METROPOLITAN MUSEUM OF ART
New York, New York

MUSEUM OF FINE ARTS
Boston, Massachusetts

THE MUSEUM OF MODERN ART
New York, New York

NATIONAL GALLERY OF ART
Washington, D.C.

PHILADELPHIA MUSEUM OF ART
Philadelphia, Pennsylvania

THE PHILLIPS COLLECTION
Washington, D.C.

PRINCETON UNIVERSITY LIBRARIES
Princeton, New Jersey

THE SNITE MUSEUM OF ART
University of Notre Dame
Notre Dame, Indiana

SOLOMON R. GUGGENHEIM MUSEUM
New York, New York

THE UNIVERSITY OF IOWA MUSEUM OF ART
Iowa City, Iowa

THE UNIVERSITY OF MICHIGAN MUSEUM OF ART
Ann Arbor, Michigan

PRIVATE COLLECTION

DIRECTOR'S FOREWORD

MODERN HIEROGLYPHS: GESTURAL DRAWING AND THE EUROPEAN VANGUARD 1900–1918 confirms the Davis Museum and Cultural Center's commitment to scholarly excellence and the support of original research. As the first in-depth analysis of gestural drawing, the exhibition examines the revolutionary introduction to twentieth-century art of a technique central to contemporary practice. The presentation traces the rapidly executed single-line gestural drawing pioneered by Auguste Rodin and then practiced by the first generation of Expressionists in France, Germany, and Austria. Through the study of a studio technique, MODERN HIEROGLYPHS investigates the psychological complexity of early modernist practice.

The Davis Museum and Cultural Center at Wellesley College is a particularly appropriate site for MODERN HIEROGLYPHS. The exhibition's dual emphasis on studio practice and art history reiterates the "Wellesley Method" of art education developed here in the late nineteenth century. This pedagogical system integrates studio and art historical training into a comprehensive program of study. First-hand examination of original works of art continues to be a central focus of the teaching methods used by the faculty and by museum educators. In addition, Wellesley faculty launched the study of modernism early in the century. In 1927, Assistant Professor Alfred Barr pioneered the study of modern art in the Wellesley undergraduate curriculum with the introduction of one of the first courses offered in modern art anywhere. Today modern art continues to hold a central place in the art history curriculum.

Drawing upon the intellectual and cultural resources of the college community, the exhibition provides a singular opportunity to collaborate with colleagues throughout the institution. Exploring the fields of psychology, literature, music, studio art, dance, and theater, the exhibition's programming acts as a catalyst for cross-disciplinary dialogues. Linking the scholarly community and its diverse audiences, the museum provides a space where this ambition can be realized.

The shared interests of Wellesley College faculty and the museum staff are a continuous source of enrichment to the curriculum and to museum programming. The opportunity to present an exhibition conceived by a faculty member is a particularly gratifying experience. It is a pleasure to support the important work of Assistant Professor Patricia Berman, a talented and valued colleague, who has long understood the distinctive opportunities offered by a teaching museum. As a colleague and friend, Pat has enlivened our work together with her intelligence and enthusiasm. After many years of productive and enjoyable discussion, we are delighted to present this innovative exhibition.

I would like to thank the museum staff for their dedication and creativity at every stage of this project. I would especially like to acknowledge Curator Lucy Flint-Gohlke, who brought her formidable expertise in this field to the organization of MODERN HIEROGLYPHS. The efforts of Associate Director Kathleen Harleman ensured the success of many aspects of this exhibition. Curator of Education Corinne Fryhle collaborated fully with Patricia Berman and Lucy Flint-Gohlke in developing the creative interdisciplinary programming for the exhibition. Former Assistant Curator Joseph Giuffre was involved in the early stages of planning for the exhibition. Registrar Lisa McDermott expertly handled the complex loan and shipping agreements as well as logistical arrangements for the exhibition's tour. Assistant Director of Museum Development Nancy Gunn provided invaluable assistance with program activities. Museum Technician John Rossetti brought a creative and sympathetic perspective to the exhibition design. Once again, Anita Meyer has created a catalogue design that reflects the spirit and energy of the subject.

As always, Vice-President for Resources and Public Affairs Peter Ramsey has been a source of support and encouragement. Together with his staff, in particular Rodger Crowe and Christine Atwood, he has assisted the museum in identifying funding sources for the exhibition. I would like to thank Laura Kemper Fields '72 for her important role in obtaining a generous grant from the W.T. Kemper Foundation. The support of the E. Franklin Robbins Charitable Trust through Trustee Joyce Robbins Michaelson '64 and Patricia Ann Michaelson '91, has also been critical to the realization of this project. Once again, we are grateful to the National Endowment for the Arts for providing important support for this exhibition. The Wellesley College Friends of Art have also contributed in crucial ways to its success.

We are delighted to share this exhibition with The Equitable Gallery in New York, where MODERN HIEROGLYPHS will be on view from March 28, 1995 to May 6, 1995. It is both a personal and professional pleasure to work with Director Pari Stave.

Ultimately any exhibition relies on the generosity of its lenders. We are fortunate to collaborate with such a distinguished group of institutions and collectors. To them we extend sincere thanks for their willingness to share these important works with a wide and diverse audience. Their participation has greatly enriched this exhibition and its programming. These drawings, individually and as a group, embody the inventiveness of the early modernist enterprise. Through their freshness and spontaneity, they provide intimate contact between the audience and the artists' working methods.

SUSAN M. TAYLOR
Director
Davis Museum and Cultural Center

ACKNOWLEDGMENTS

This exhibition and catalogue would not have been possible without the assistance of numerous people and institutions, and I am deeply grateful to them for their generosity. First and foremost, I would like to thank the staff of the Davis Museum and Cultural Center for making this exhibition a reality. On both a personal and professional level, I thank Susan Taylor, Museum Director, for supporting this exhibition and catalogue with her substantial energies and resources. It is a pleasure and an honor to work with her and her entire staff. To Curator Lucy Flint-Gohlke, I owe more than can be expressed. Her intelligence, expertise, humor, and integrity enriched this project in every way.

MODERN HIEROGLYPHS, which examines gestural drawing from critical and historical perspectives, traces the emergence of the technique as a pan-European phenomenon and explores several implications for the history of modernism. The drawings included in the exhibition are intended to illustrate a range of responses to continuous-line gestural drawing as a new mode of figuration at the turn of the century. Neither the checklist nor the catalogue is meant to be exhaustive. Rather, they are intended to suggest the notion of gestural drawing as a generational phenomenon and as the starting point for further investigation by other scholars.

The idea for this exhibition was generated during discussions with Kirk Varnedoe, then my dissertation advisor at the New York University Institute of Fine Arts. I am profoundly grateful to him for his unfailing generosity and support. I am equally indebted to Robert Lubar, whose insights and expertise contributed to this project in every way. In addition, he, Lucy Flint-Gohlke, and Nancy DuVergne Smith provided invaluable editorial assistance with this catalogue. I am also indebted to the scholarship of Albert E. Elsen, Kirk Varnedoe, Richard Shiff, and Yve-Alain Bois, which helped me to formulate my approach to this material.

Over the course of several years, my ideas have benefited from the advice and comments of numerous curators and scholars. I would like to thank the scholars from each of the institutions that graciously agreed to lend their works to MODERN HIEROGLYPHS, and who assisted me in innumerable ways in creating the exhibition. Among them I would especially like to thank Ida Balboul, The Metropolitan Museum of Art; Peter Nisbet, Busch-Reisinger Museum, Harvard University; Clifford Ackley and Shelley Langdale, Museum of Fine Arts, Boston; Eliza Rathbone and Elizabeth Turner, The Phillips Collection; Joseph Rishel and Christopher Riopelle, Philadelphia Museum of Art; Hilarie Faberman, The University of Michigan Museum of Art; Jay Fisher and Georgeanna Bishop, The Baltimore Museum of Art; Juliet Nations-Powell, Solomon R. Guggenheim Museum; Nanette Esseck Brewer, Indiana University Art Museum; Robert Smoger, The Snite Museum of Art, University of Notre Dame; Larry Feinberg, Allen Memorial Art Museum, Oberlin College; Wendy Weitman, The Museum of Modern Art; Miriam Stewart, The Fogg Art Museum, Harvard University; Sabine Kretzschmar, The Cleveland Museum of Art; Jane Kallir, The Galerie St. Etienne; Dale Roylance, Princeton University Libraries; Mary Lapides, Christie's; Jo-Ann Conklin, The University of Iowa Museum of Art; and Ellen Sharp, The Detroit Institute of Arts. I would also like to thank Alice Adam, Dita Amory, Robin Akert, Ronni Baer, Barbara Butts, Alan Chong, Joan Croce, Albert E. Elsen, Michelle Facos, Joanna Fink, Judy Fox, Corinne Fryhle, Francey and Dr. Martin L. Gecht, Joseph Giuffre, Nancy Gunn, Kathleen Harleman, Melissa Katz, Jane Kallir, Elissa Koff, Lisa Leizman, Catherine Masson, Suzanne Folds McCullagh, Lisa McDermott, Ann Philbin, Jim Roberts, Serge Sabarsky, Daniel Schulman, and Donald Taglialatella for their time and expertise. I am grateful to my colleagues in the Art Department of Wellesley College, especially Alice T. Friedman, whose support of this project has been invaluable, and to Jennifer Brown '95 and Sarah Betzer '94, for their hard work and excellence. Their assistance was crucial to the completion of the catalogue.

Finally, I am grateful to those institutions which made this exhibition possible: to Wellesley College for providing support for this exhibition in the form of an award from the Class of '61 Humanities Fund, and to the National Endowment for the Arts for funding the exhibition and catalogue. And last, but by no means least, I wish to thank Sam Engelstad for his support and advice from three continents.

PATRICIA G. BERMAN

A NOTE ON THE ILLUSTRATIONS

Works that are included in the exhibition and illustrated in this publication are indicated within the text by catalogue number ("cat. no.") in parentheses, referring to the checklist on 112–117. Illustrations of works not included in the exhibition are noted within the text as figures ("fig.") in parentheses. Works reproduced in color are indicated within the text as "cat. no.; color plate" in parentheses.

MODERN HIEROGLYPHS: GESTURAL DRAWING AND THE EUROPEAN VANGUARD 1900–1918

Gestural figure drawing—the direct recording of a model's movements or contours through rapidly executed line—is today a ubiquitous graphic technique. Practiced in the most elementary of art classes, it is the pedagogical starting point for the study of the human figure. In intervals measured in seconds, art students seek the essence of pose and gesture by establishing unbroken visual contact with the subject's body as it moves through space and across time, and by maintaining the continuous touch of stylus to page. The results of this process are condensed, bold line drawings. Disclosing the changing trajectory of the artist's hand, these works are understood to be subjective traces of the artists themselves. Composed of lines that appear to be unmediated by planning or correction, the drawings register a willful awkwardness that suggests direct expression through spontaneity. Conveyed through this technique are, to borrow Henri Matisse's phrase, "moments of the artist."[1]

At the turn of the century, gestural drawing both revolutionized graphic technique and expanded the notion of figuration. Challenging the authority of academic training, the relationship between sketch and painting, and canonical portrayals of the human figure, these spontaneously executed, continuous-line drawings provided a new representational freedom for avant-garde artists. As an informal practice, gestural drawing had a lengthy history as a sketch aesthetic, a means by which artists could record and understand the motions of their subjects in preparation for more finished works.[2] As independent works, however, gestural drawings were not exhibited by artists before Auguste Rodin (1840–1917). Practiced initially as an aid to his sculpture,[3] Rodin's drawings became ends in themselves by 1900. In such a work as KNEELING MALE NUDE (cat. no. 38), the delicate and agitated trails laid down by the artist's roving stylus record, simultaneously, a summary of the model's shifting positions and traces of the artist's own hand in motion. The pentimenti, anatomical distortions, and pockets of cross-hatching belie the sense of solidity that the watercolor washes impart to the model's body.

When such works were published in the 1890s and exhibited beginning in 1899, they garnered considerable prestige among younger artists who sought formal and psychological alternatives to academic practice, and who staked their artistic and social identities on the notions of individuality and spontaneity. As Jacques Lipchitz recalled: "In our period Rodin has had a great influence on the leading painters. For example, on Matisse in his drawing, as well as his sculpture... in fact on all the *fauves*."[4] For his part, Rodin was cognizant of his position in relation to the younger avant-garde when he stated:

> *I have attained naturalness which carries within itself all the schools molten together. Consequently my drawings are freer, they will cultivate liberty in the artists who study them, not by telling them to do as I do, but by revealing their own genius to them and by pushing them toward its full sway by showing them the immense expanse in which they may evolve.*[5]

The terms which this generation used to define its identity are revealed in the manifesto of *Die Brücke*: "Anyone who renders his creative drive directly and genuinely is one of us."[6] Gestural technique embodied this credo.

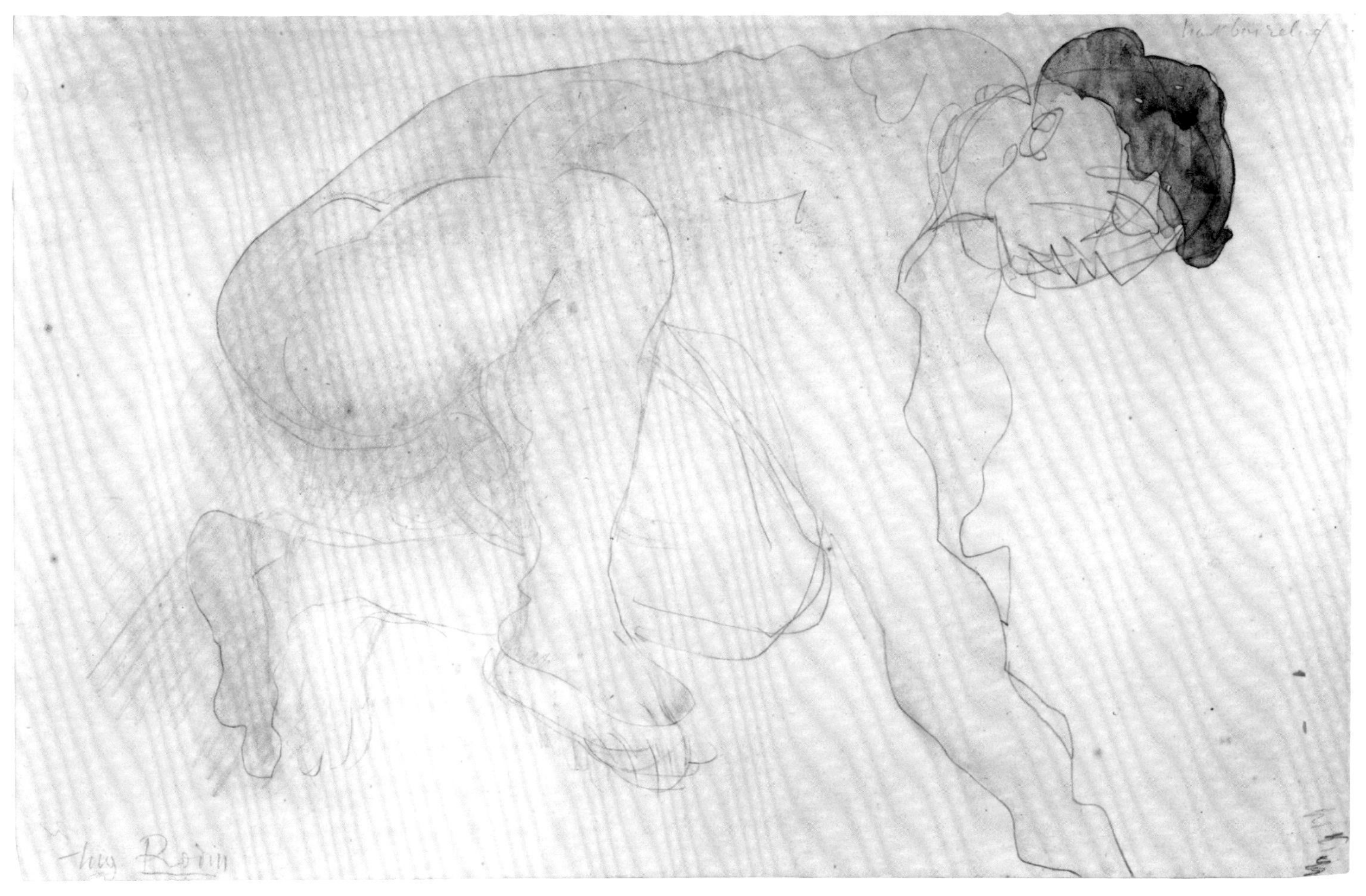

38 Auguste Rodin

KNEELING MALE NUDE, n.d.

The possibilities contained within Rodin's work were assimilated and transformed by a younger generation of artists, including Henri Matisse (1869–1954), André Derain (1880–1954), and Fernand Léger (1881–1955) in France; Gustav Klimt (1862–1918), Egon Schiele (1890–1918), and Oskar Kokoschka (1886–1980) in Austria; and Ernst Ludwig Kirchner (1880–1938), Erich Heckel (1883–1970), and Max Pechstein (1881–1955) in Germany. The works of these artists, illustrated in this publication, suggest the affinities with and legacies of Rodin's innovations, and depict the ways in which gestural drawing converged with the ambitions of early modernism.

This essay explores how gestural technique was pioneered and broadened, and what it signified for the artists who came to maturity between 1900 and 1918. It focuses on the years between 1900, when Rodin began to exhibit his drawings in large numbers, and the end of World War I, by which time the members of this generation were already considered the "historical" avant-garde, and their early practices had entered art academies throughout Europe.

MODERN HIEROGLYPHS

The title MODERN HIEROGLYPHS is a phrase Ernst Ludwig Kirchner used to identify his gestural drawings. Writing under a pseudonym in the 1920s, Kirchner explained that "they are hieroglyphs in the sense that they change nature's forms into simpler two-dimensional shapes and suggest their meaning to the observer much as the written word 'horse' places the image of horse before everyone's eyes."[7] Writing in the third person, the artist commented:

> *Kirchner's drawings perhaps are his purest and most beautiful work. They mirror the feelings of a man of our times, instinctively and without premeditation. Besides, they comprise the formal language of his prints and paintings, that other part of his work in which a conscious will operates. The vital power of this will, however, derives from drawing.*[8]

Here, Kirchner calls attention to the range of intentions held within the gestural line. First, the line is nominative and not mimetic. It acknowledges the formal transformation of three-dimensional space into a two-dimensional surface without the intervention of traditional perspective. By synthesizing objects viewed in nature, the hieroglyph operates on the semiological level as a marker. Second, the line is pure, "unconscious." The line tracks the artist's unmediated response to a motif in nature and functions as the visual equivalent of the artist's will. The line is consequently the equivalent of the artist himself, a consciously crystallized confession. Finally, the unconscious line, as Kirchner suggests, is the generating source for work in other media—printmaking and painting—which often require more conscious interventions. The gestural line returns the artist's hand, and the spectator's gaze, to the spontaneous sources of more formal works. As act, speech, and originating moment, the hieroglyph is positioned as an inherently modern phenomenon.[9]

In addition, as the two-dimensional embodiment of a model moving through space, gestural drawing provides an index of time. Linear recordings of a model's body emphasize the fugitive elements of gesture, tracing motion as it unfolds, and provide a linear pairing or homology between the model's body and the artist's stylus. This imagined simultaneity of the artist's and model's gestures is premised on the continuous line, a line that, instant by instant, appeals to the spectator's sense of psychological and sensual engagement.

By mapping the trajectory of the artist's hand, a new perceptual relationship is established between the viewer's eye and the model's body. This intimacy is enacted through an understanding that the artist and the model intersect in the graphic gesture. Like cardiograms and other graphic models of measure that rationalized invisible or fugitive phenomena for the turn-of-the-century audience,[10] the gestural line recorded the operations of the artist's gaze on a paper surface. In this process, the gestural line embodied art critic and theorist Charles Blanc's notion of *double originalité*—a synthesis of the artist's individuality and the originality of the model[11]—while also providing the viewer with visual evidence of its very production. As a series of practices, in sum, gestural drawing proposes an erotic dialogue with the body that encompasses within its simple and yet profoundly important procedure the aspirations of the first generation of modernists who sought both "essences" in nature and the means to convey them: in Kirchner's words, to create modern hieroglyphs for a contemporary audience.

Gestural drawing was a paradigm shift in the representation of the body in the early years of this century. In this regard, Yve-Alain Bois's description of Matisse's line drawing as a "totem of modernity"[12] may be extended to the gestural drawings of Matisse's contemporaries. Such works, which may be regarded as the products of a generational preoccupation with direct expression, reveal a profoundly self-conscious vanguardism.[13] Richard Shiff has demonstrated that innovative studio techniques at the end of the nineteenth century may be regarded as stylistic tropes for artistic independence. The demands of a competitive market system, in tandem with an increasing emphasis on originality and authenticity in the European art worlds, conditioned the wide experimentation with, and deployment of, signature styles.[14] Following Shiff, I propose that gestural drawing emerged as a trope of authenticity framed as direct expression, and that it reflects the aspirations of early modernism as articulated in 1914 by Karl Schmidt-Rottluff as "an inexplicable yearning to lay hold of what I see and feel and then to find the most direct expression possible for such experience."[15] The spontaneously created line was one of many means by which artists with such aspirations founded their identities in their production.

In his *Foundations of Modern Art*, the artist and critic Amédée Ozenfant noted the widespread impact of Rodin's drawings on the first generation of modernists. Identifying Cézanne and Rodin as fathers of modernism, Ozenfant attributed to them the genesis of Expressionism:

> *It is somewhat surprising that Rodin the revolutionary should almost systematically be ignored in works dealing with Modern Art. Yet his liberating influence was tremendous. His fame was universal just when the Fauves of the new painting were banding together. Indubitably he was the first of them all. He was the model revolutionary.... The freedom with which Rodin treated nature and the human form was added to that of Cézanne liberating himself from the subject. Fauves, Cubists, and all succeeding schools are indebted to these two masters.*[16]

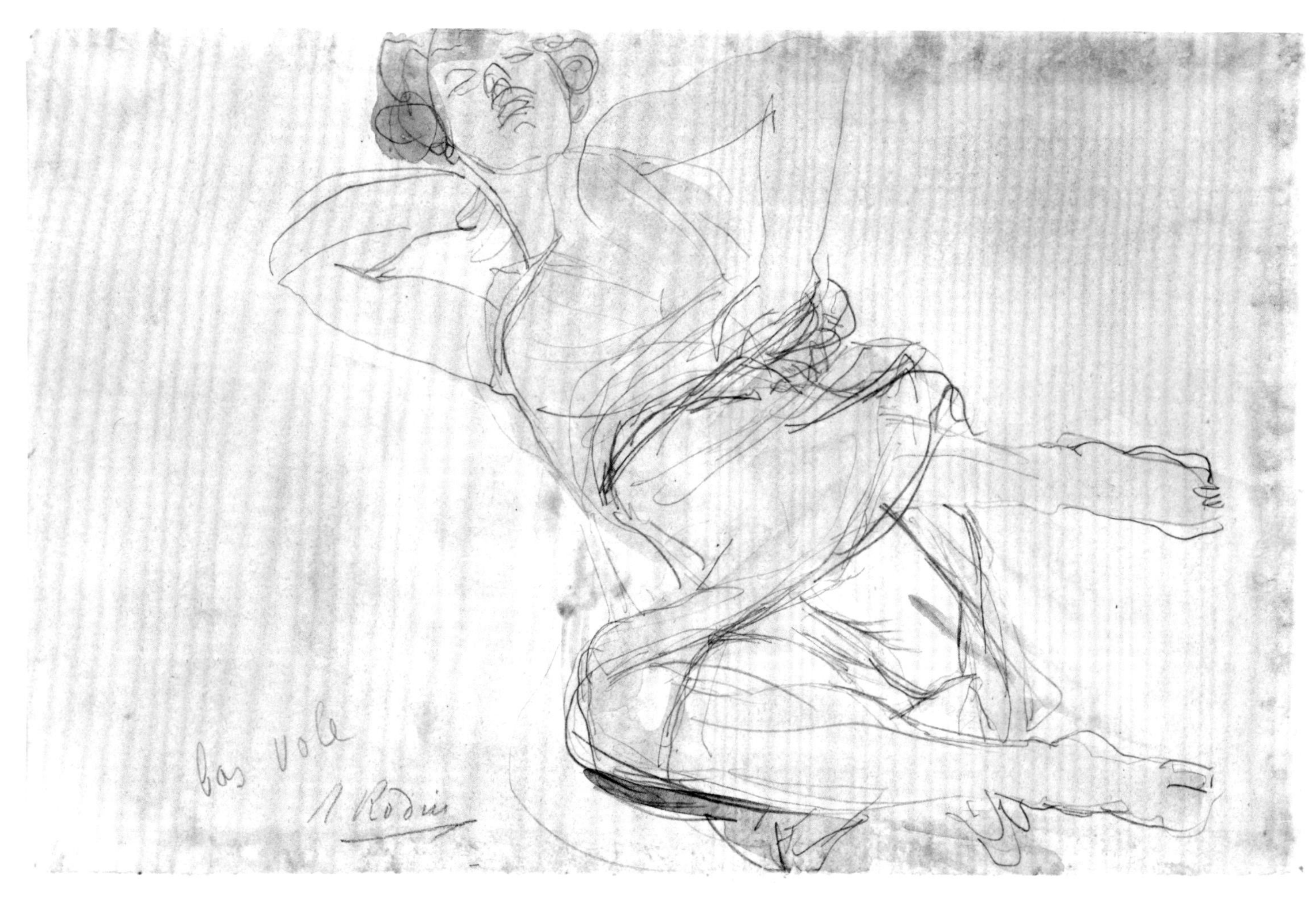

37 Auguste Rodin
RECLINING WOMAN, CLOTHED, n.d.

According to Ozenfant, Rodin had pioneered the tactile and expressionist strains in twentieth-century art, which by 1931, the year in which Ozenfant published his study, were already absorbed into the historical avant-garde. Significantly, Ozenfant illustrated his discussion not with Rodin's sculpture, but with his figure drawings. To examine the foundational vanguard identity that Ozenfant attributes to these drawings, it is important to view the terms in which they were described.

TERMS OF TECHNIQUE

Rodin initiated his later drawing style—the rapid rendering of contour lines—in the mid-1890s. His methods from that time until his death were widely reported in monographs on the artist published between the 1890s and World War I, and have been thoroughly described by Kirk Varnedoe.[17] One contemporary account of the procedure is provided by Rodin's secretary and biographer Anthony M. Ludovici. In this description, Ludovici equated Rodin's technique to a parlor game in order to render familiar the accidents resulting from the artist's procedure of watching the model and not the page:

> *I noticed that he kept his eyes fixed on the model, and never looked down at his pencil, or at the paper on which he was drawing.... I was reminded instantly of those books which used to be produced at evening parties in most English homes some twenty years ago, in which one was expected to draw a pig with one's eyes shut, and I could not help wondering whether Rodin himself, although he was not blindfolded, had the same shock of surprise as we blinded draughtsmen used to have when at last he turned his eyes down to his drawing and saw what his pencil had described. The next thing I noticed was that he seemed under some obligation not to lift his pencil from the paper, after having once begun to draw—another feature which his drawing had in common with the parlor entertainment already referred to—and that he always tried to complete his outline of the figure he was drawing in one wavy and continuous sweep.... Each sheet was covered with one of his characteristic drawings, and each drawing revealed the same kind of mistake or inaccuracy in its final strokes.... Of course, if these kind[s] of strokes were too glaringly wrong, it frequently happened that the drawing was either destroyed or subsequently corrected; but in most drawings that I have seen, the technique of their production—the absence of the guiding eye—is apparent to any careful observer.*[18]

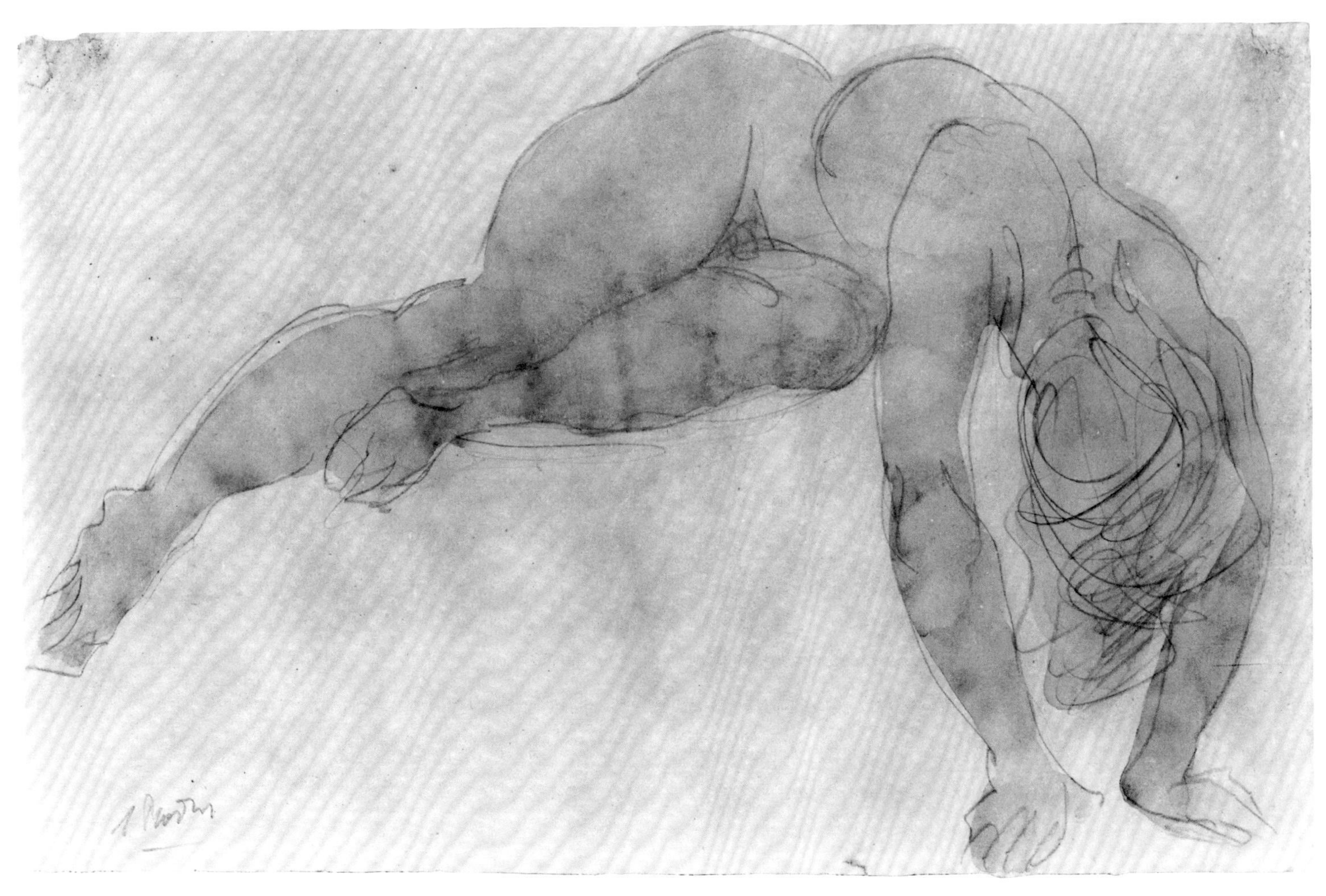

39 Auguste Rodin
SKETCH OF NUDE WOMAN, n.d.

When Clément Janin recounted Rodin's procedure in 1903, he legitimized the stylistic characteristics of the drawings to which Ludovici later alluded when he wrote that "the technique of their production... is apparent." In his description, Janin emphasizes accident and distortion as positive effects of spontaneous production, the lack of control testifying to the artist's ultimate mastery of form:

In his recent drawings, Rodin uses nothing more than a contour heightened with a wash. Here is how he goes about it. Equipped with a sheet of ordinary paper posed on a board, and with a lead pencil—sometimes a pen—he has his model take an essentially unstable pose, then he draws spiritedly, without taking his eyes off the model. The hand goes where it will; often the pencil falls off the page; the drawing is thus decapitated or loses a limb by amputation....
The master has not looked at it once. In less than a minute, this snapshot of movement is caught. It contains, naturally, some excessive deformations, unforeseen swellings, but, if the relation of proportions is destroyed, on the other hand, each section has its contours and the cursive, schematic indication [of] its modeling.
The correction lines are numerous. Often the pencil, in the swiftness of its progress, misses the contour of a breast, the flex of a thigh; Rodin then goes back over this part with hasty strokes which mix together, but in which the just line is found.[19]

These descriptions, and others like them,[20] provided a way of rationalizing Rodin's apparent infelicities—the distorted anatomy and the unconventional placement of the figure on a page—so that the viewer could read them as intentional and innovative. In an undated drawing (cat. no. 35; color plate), Rodin's sweeping lines of the model's torso and upper legs are scaled such that the body has been compressed above and cropped below by the edges of the page. In compensation, Rodin has drawn the missing feet on the lower right of the sheet as a way of completing his observation of the body. In another work (cat. no. 36), the instability of the figure's boundaries can be understood as an index to the motion of the artist's active eye. Tracing the lines point by point, the spectator can reconstruct each spasm, scrawl, wayward movement and, as in the heavier line that circumscribes the model's back, recognize the artist's moments of greater surety.

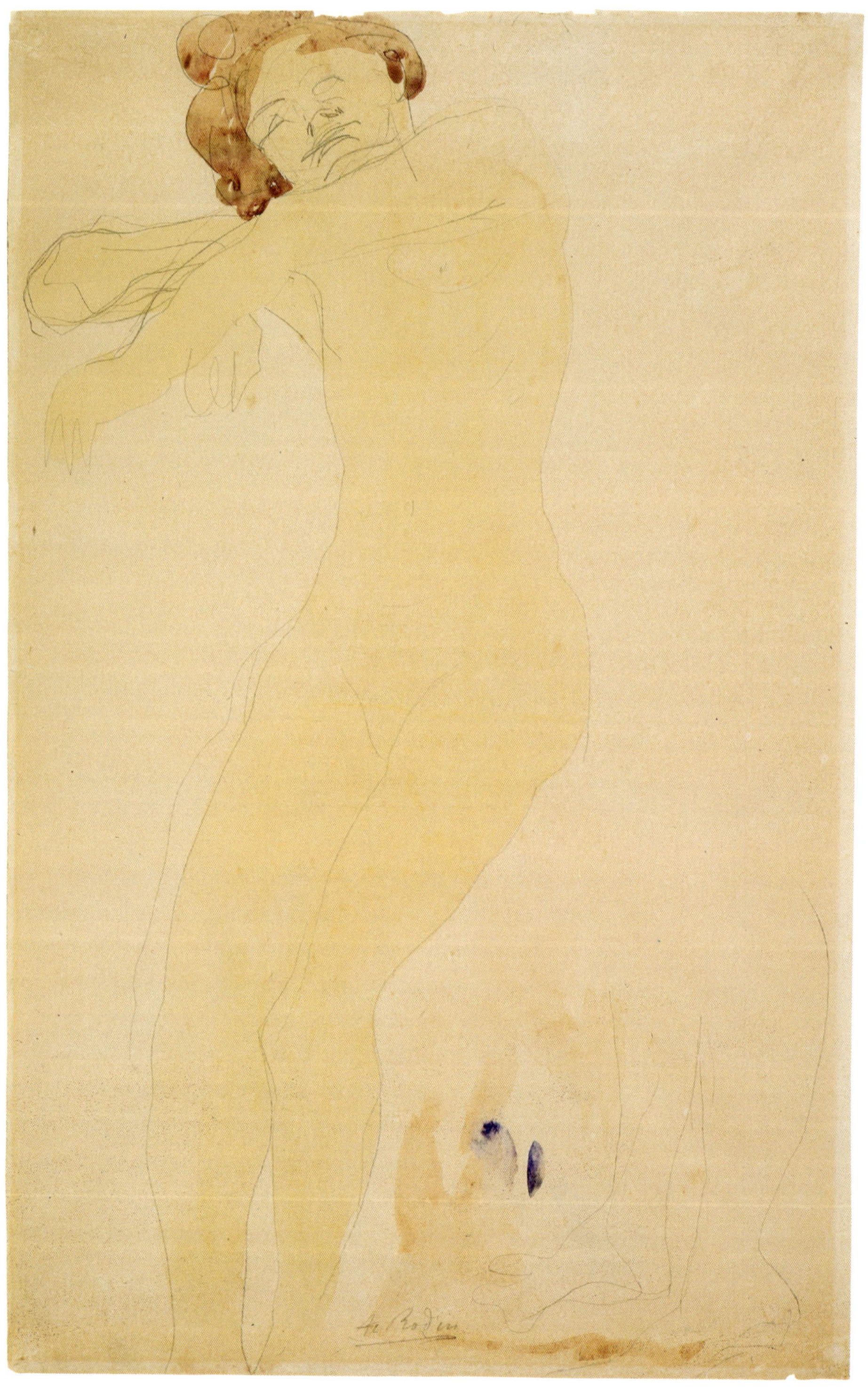

35 Auguste Rodin
STANDING NUDE WOMAN WITH STUDY OF FEET AT LOWER RIGHT CORNER, n.d.

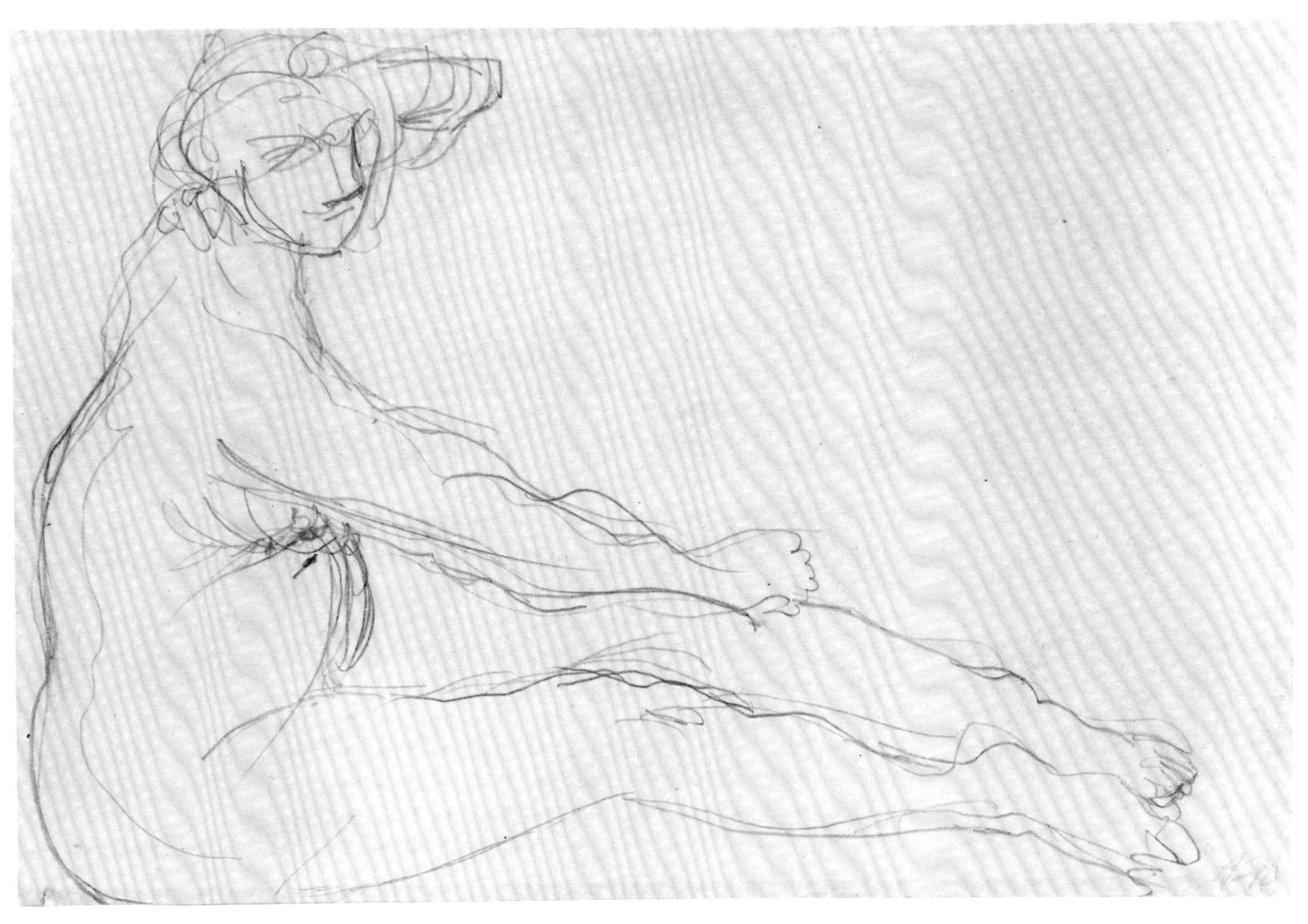

36 Auguste Rodin
WOMAN SEATED, FACING RIGHT, n.d.

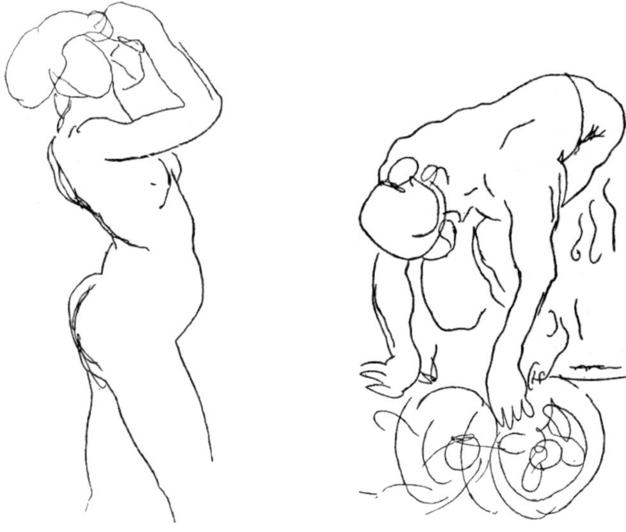

figure 1
After Auguste Rodin, from *La Revue Blanche*, vol. 22, Paris, 1900: 251.
By permission of Harvard College Library, Cambridge.

According to Ludovici, Rodin traced some of his original drawings in an attempt to articulate the stark form of a model's gesture. In the simplified drawing of the image of a seated woman from ca. 1900 (cat. no. 33)—a copy of which was reproduced in a 1900 volume of *La Revue Blanche* (fig. 1) and on the cover of a monograph by Judith Cladel[21]—line appears as silhouette, the continuous containment of a body. In other works, such as the view of a standing figure from behind (cat. no. 40), the continuous line was, perhaps, no longer executed from the model, but may be the result of distillation—a product of the artist's selection and editing. Further intervention occurred in other compositions, when refined drawings, carefully cut out of their supporting sheets, became elements of more complex anatomical grammars. In these cut-out images, which Varnedoe calls "play figures,"[22] Rodin created relationships among disparate figures by moving them across, and then affixing them to, a page (cat. no. 41; color plate).[23] These cut-outs do not seem to have been exhibited in Rodin's lifetime.[24]

Rodin's critics made little distinction between the drawings he made in the presence of the models, those which likely were tracings, and even those copied by someone else for reproduction purposes.[25] As Varnedoe points out, the drawings that appeared in publications, such as the illustration in *La Revue Blanche*, were copies made by other hands after Rodin's original works. The descriptions of Rodin's spontaneous activity thus converged with second-generation drawings, initiating a *de facto* understanding of all of his gestural techniques as spontaneous. This critical merging of spontaneous drawing from nature with drawing that *appeared* spontaneous contributed to the ways in which younger artists began to assimilate gestural technique. In this equation, figural distortion and the untraditional placement of a figure on a page, no matter how carefully planned, were signs of artistic impulse and instinct.

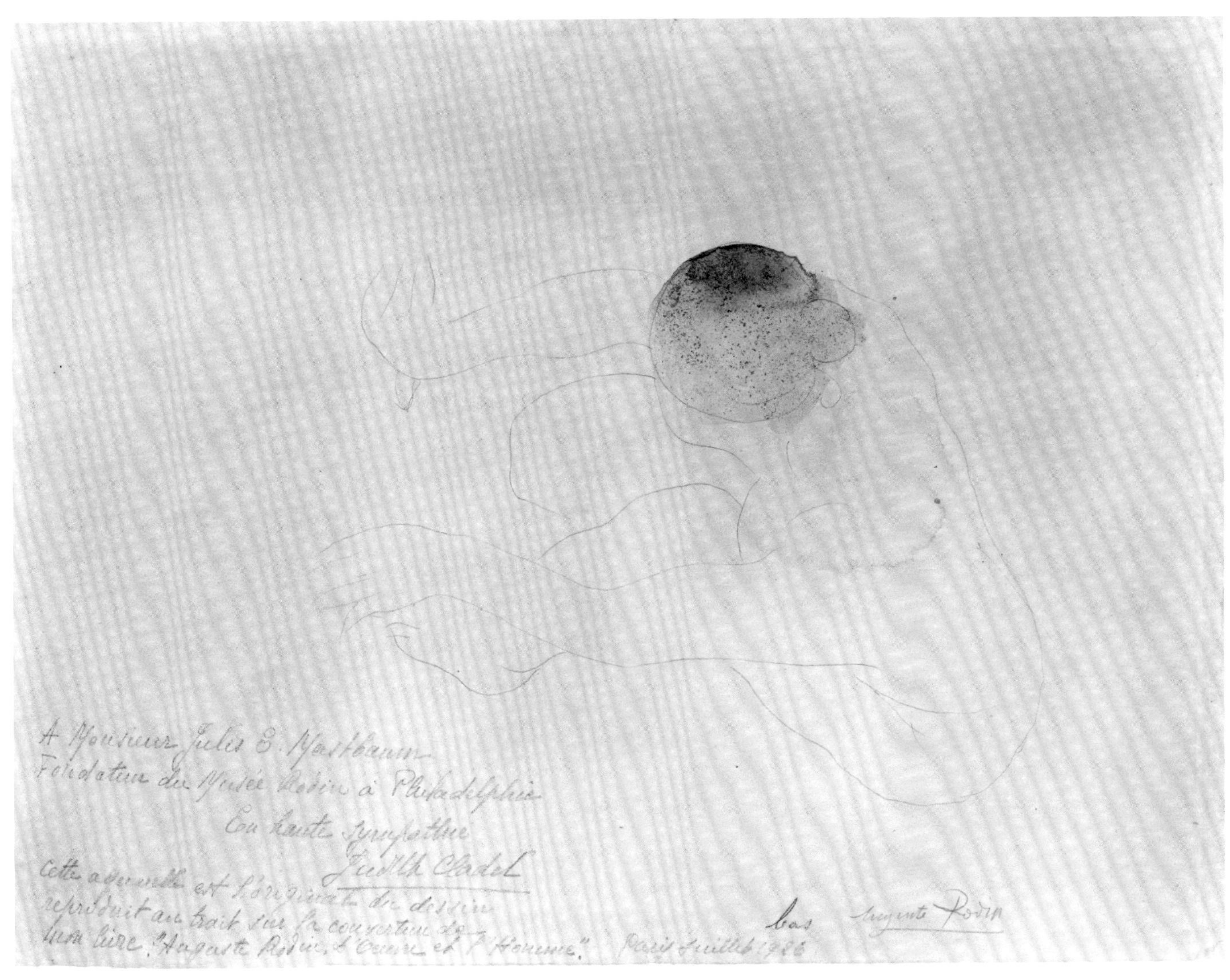

33 Auguste Rodin
SEATED WOMAN, n.d.

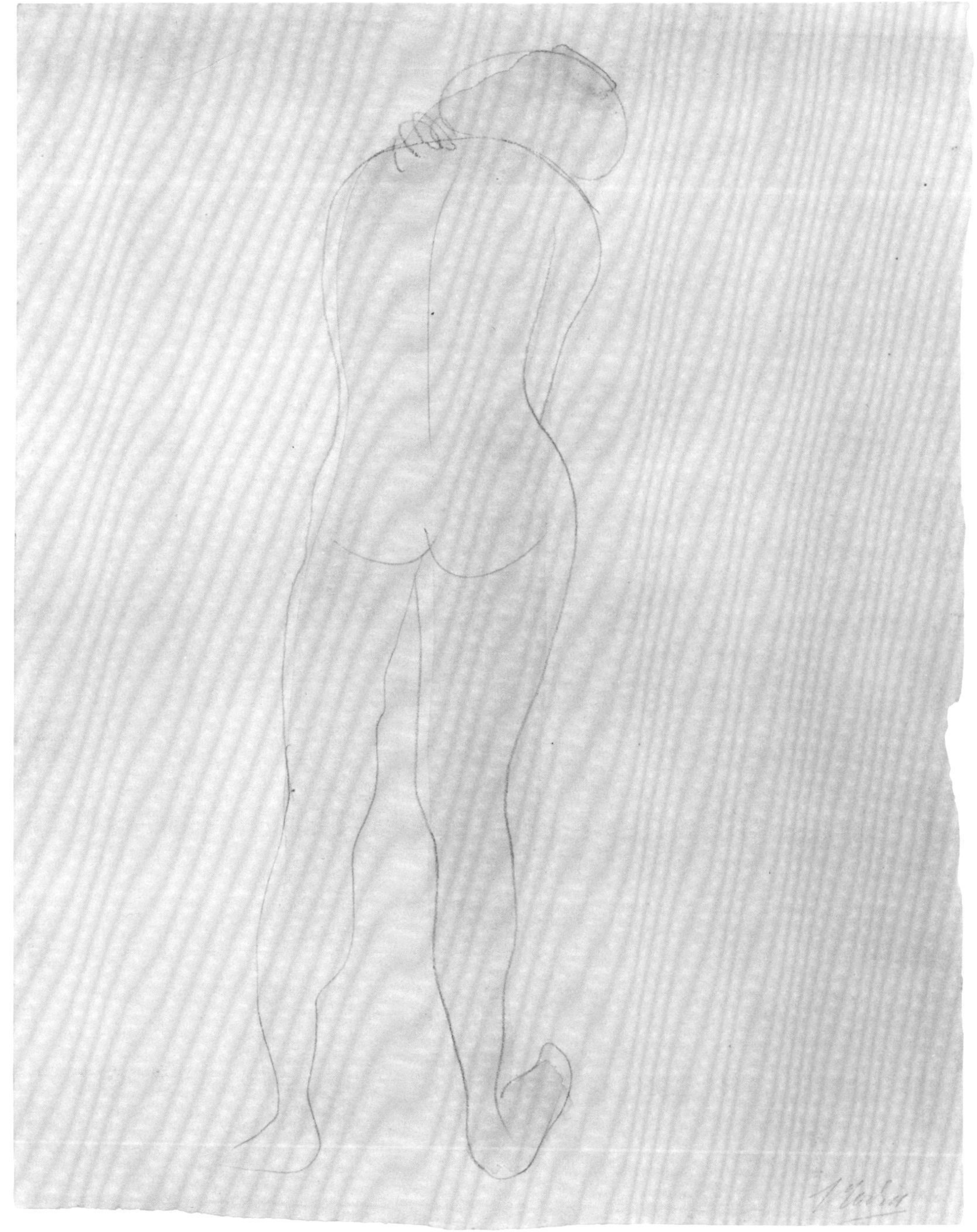

40 Auguste Rodin
STANDING WOMAN SEEN FROM BEHIND, n.d.

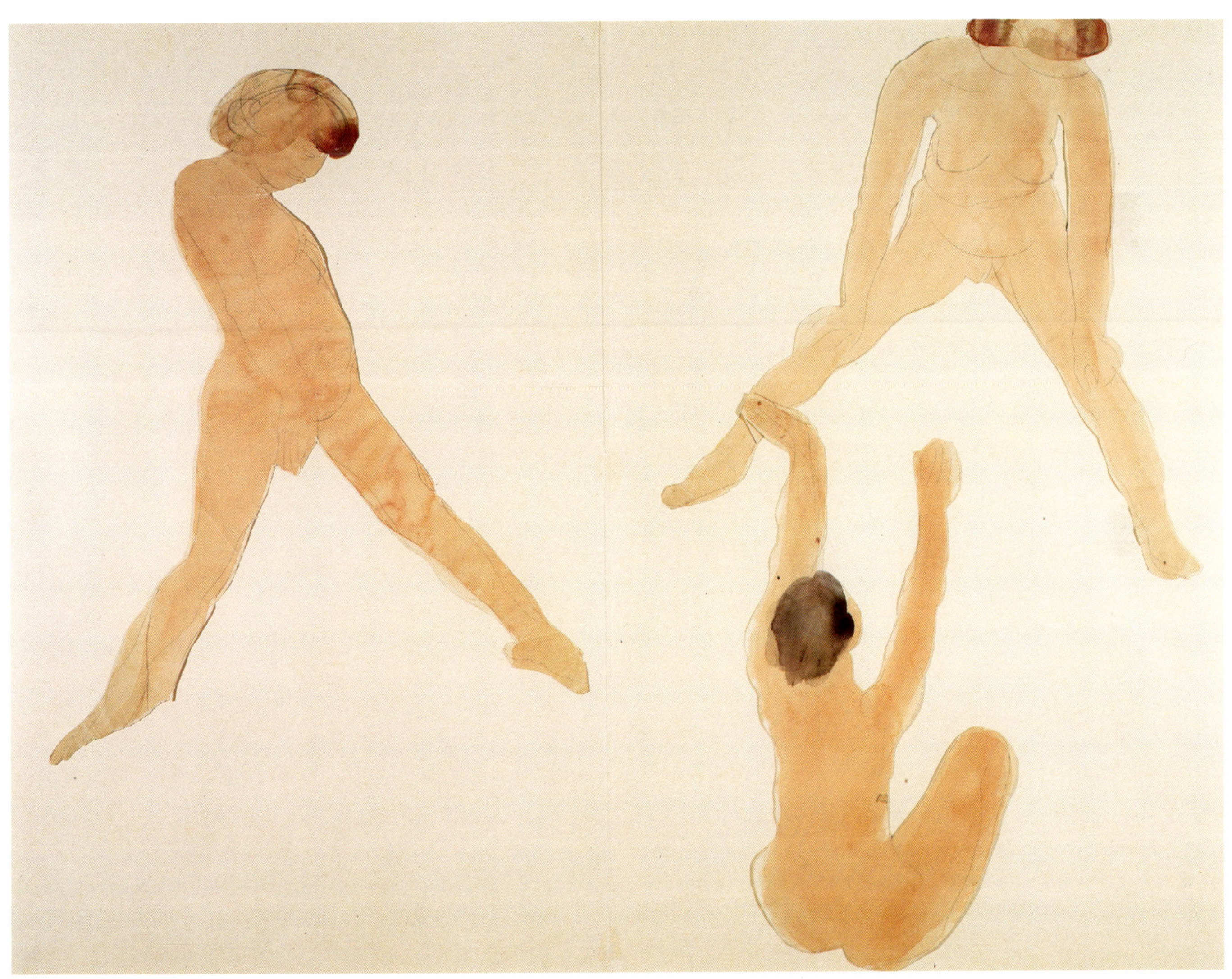

41 Auguste Rodin

MONTAGE SHEET WITH THREE CUT-OUT FIGURES, ca. 1900–05

Ludovici claims that Rodin was initially reluctant to view his drawings as finished works and saw independent meaning in them only after they were validated by others:

> *Thanks to the misguided efforts of enthusiasts, there gradually arose a sort of cult in connection with Rodin's drawings which, I venture to suggest, was as much a surprise to some of his less catholic supporters as it was to the artist himself. Rodin... was not sufficiently alert or self-conscious to perceive the whole meaning of what took place. Baffled though he was at first by the sudden vogue for his drawings, he ultimately bowed his head in resignation before the storm of applause that grew ever louder about him, and accepting the verdict of the very experts who had made his greater work intelligible to the world, he, too, slowly became convinced of the enormous artistic importance of this more trivial side of his productive genius.*[26]

This transformation, says Ludovici, occurred after 1906. He claims, moreover, that the drawings were a means to an end, a sculptor's attempts to investigate human physiognomy by every possible means, and by repetition: "What scales are to the executant musician, so were Rodin's drawings to him, no more and no less, and the fact that they happened to constitute convenient vehicles for his autograph when some unpretentious friend wished to be given a small souvenir, never—at least in my time—modified his view of them in his own mind."[27]

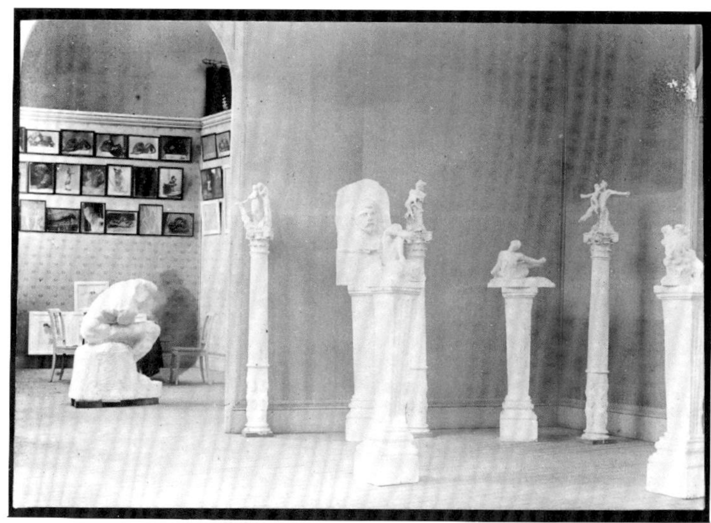

figure 2
Installation of Auguste Rodin's exhibition at the Place de l'Alma, room IV, 1900. Photograph by Bauche, courtesy of the Musée Rodin, Paris.

Despite Rodin's dismissal of the drawings, they played an increasing role in his exhibitions, as Kirk Varnedoe has pointed out,[28] and as Alain Beausire's exhaustive study of Rodin's exhibitions illustrates. Major groupings of his drawings appeared in Brussels and The Netherlands in 1899;[29] Prague in 1902; Düsseldorf, Leipzig, Weimar, and Berlin in 1904; Paris in 1907 and 1908; and in New York at Alfred Stieglitz's Gallery 291 in 1908.[30] Perhaps the most significant large-scale public exhibition of Rodin's drawings was in his own pavilion at the Place de l'Alma during the Universal Exposition of 1900. There Rodin incorporated his gestural drawings into a comprehensive display of his work, which also included his sculpture as well as earlier drawings and other works on paper (fig. 2). As Lampert notes, the number of drawings sent to exhibitions increased in the following years, as did the prominence given to the drawings within the installation designs (fig. 3). Lampert also suggests that Rodin played a major role in the selection and installation design of his works.[31]

From the time that Rodin's gestural drawings were first published and exhibited, critics called attention to their *double originalité*—their traces of the artist's touch and the models' gestures. Camille Mauclair wrote in 1898:

In sacrificing everything to the drawings of movement, *Rodin held to a preoccupation with pure realism, for he [first] intensively studied the instinctive thrust of the personage, without thinking in advance of stylizing it. This double tendency, synthesization of the figure in reducing it to its silhouette and to its value, with a rapid and simultaneous study of movement in all its aspects, Rodin has felt growing in him over the years.*[32]

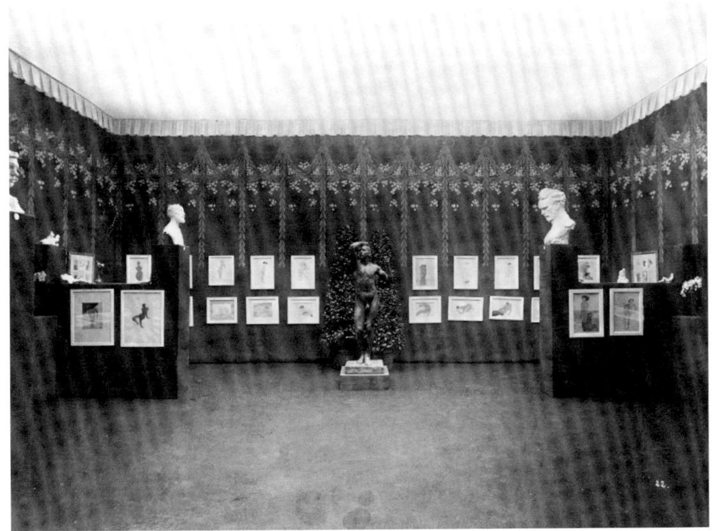

figure 3
Installation of Auguste Rodin's exhibition in Prague, 1902. Photograph by Bruner-Dvorak, courtesy of the Musée Rodin, Paris.

In 1903, Judith Cladel amplified Mauclair's notion of "double tendency" by calling attention to the temporality of the lines as "an attitude, an action rather, seized by an eye as rapid as the movement itself."[33] Quoting from Cladel and other French writers, the German critic Julius Meier-Graefe wrote, "Rodin presents gesture and deed at once."[34] This convergence of act and artifact, moreover, was implicated in what Meier-Graefe described as Rodin's unceasing yearning for an impossible consummation with nature: "His drawings twitch like nerves, and the filling in of the outline with his marvelous aquatint washes seems to exist merely to give resonance to this inarticulate moaning of agony."[35] Meier-Graefe's text also presents a narrative of mastery, in which he equates Rodin with Michelangelo and with a transhistorical notion of genius: in Rodin, "the development of genius in all ages shows itself in a single personality."[36] This dual signification of genius and agonist, as premised on the spontaneously drawn line, was, as Anne Wagner has pointed out, frequently equated with a discourse of hypermasculinity in the Rodin literature. A measure of Rodin's reputation after the turn of the century resided in critical responses to, and uses of, his sexuality as a frame for his art.[37]

Perhaps nowhere else in turn-of-the-century art is there a clearer confluence of the notion of masculine creativity with the expression of sexuality than in Rodin's gestural drawings. Not only do the hundreds of drawings of women masturbating or displaying their genitalia testify to what Varnedoe characterizes as Rodin's "consuming erotic curiosity,"[38] but the hurriedly drawn lines convey the artist's absorption in their activity. Numerous scholars have designated these images of sexual display as Rodin's erotic drawings.[39] I would extend this designation to virtually all of Rodin's gestural drawings. Held within Rodin's freely drawn lines is evidence of an unbroken visual link between the artist's eye and the model's flesh, the expression of what Ludovici termed Rodin's "manu-visual dexterity."[40] If eroticism can be understood as a condition of unfulfilled desire, rather than consummation, then the disjuncture between Rodin's empathic response to his models' bodies and the distance from those bodies implicated in the act of drawing produces an art of profound eroticism. Consummation occurs only in the scopic realm.

The voyeuristic tension inherent in the drawings is a theme that runs throughout the Rodin literature. Arthur Symons articulated this idea in an English-language review of 1902: "He spies upon every gesture, knowing that if he can seize one gesture at the turn of the wave, he has seized an essential rhythm of nature."[41] In the French version of this text, Symons expressed the notion of erotic voyeurism more concretely: "The principle of Rodin's work is sex—a sex aware of itself, an expending energy desperate to reach an impossible goal."[42] Here Pablo Picasso's phrase, "drawing as if to possess" (used as a metaphor by Leo Steinberg),[43] provides insight into Rodin's method. Rodin stated: "Art is nothing else but a sensual voluptuousness. It is only a derivative [of] the power of loving. By creating, the artist deceives his [generative] instinct.... By the lines, the forms, the color, he expresses his idolatry. He caresses her, he adorns her with the most seductive charms. He is the lover. She is the lover."[44] If, as Charles Blanc proposed in *Grammaire des arts du dessin*, line drawing is itself a gendered practice,[45] the assertion of masculine control, then the one-to-one correspondence of the male artist's stylus and the female model's flesh exemplifies this notion: the lines themselves function as signs or markers of female sexual spectacle and male spectatorship. Again, in the words of Picasso, direct linear marking positions "the pencil as delegate of the exploring hand."[46] Such works provide an overt medium for what Martin Jay characterizes as "ocular desire,"[47] a means of closing the gap between spectator and spectacle by making the process of drawing itself an act of displaced touch, of vicarious sexual union.

The number of statements by Rodin and his critics condensing women to Woman, and repeating the convention of Woman as an extension of nature,[48] reinforces the identity of Rodin's gestural drawing as a symbolic practice. The direct and spontaneous representation of active nude bodies was the ultimate form of mastery: "The artist… *sees*; that is to say, that his eye, grafted to his heart, reads deeply in the bosom of Nature."[49] Rodin's studio, which was widely described by his biographers, provided an environment in which eroticism was openly expressed as an extension of nature through the spontaneous movement of his models.[50] In an interview of 1906, Rodin described his studio as a spectacle of nude display: "I am accustomed to having my models wander naked about the studio. They walk, or rest.… I familiarize myself with all of their movements. I constantly note the association of the feelings and the lines of their bodies, and by this observation I accustom myself to discover the expression of the soul, not only in the features of the face, but in the entire human form."[51] In this way, he assured for his drawings an unimpeded view of bodies in motion, detached from the rhetorical poses of academic models and stripped of historical references:[52] "I saw that this movement existed in nature, and that I had only to avoid losing that in my models…that this movement was something natural, not something I could impose artificially; from that point originated my drawings."[53]

Rodin objected to the standard academic practice of directing models' poses:

In my beginnings, when I had a model come I always used to ask her right off what studios she had "worked" in. I saw immediately if she had come from the Academy. As soon as she climbed onto the podium I saw her assume one of those attitudes she had learned there, and it was always wrong. How could it be otherwise? What do they teach you at the Academy? Composition! But composition is theatrics, the dramatic science of lies.[54]

In contrast, Rodin stressed the notion of his studio as a natural environment, and of the models within it as natural embodiments: "I take from life movements I observe, but I do not impose movements on the models.… In everything, I obey nature, and never do I dare give orders to it. My only ambition is servile fidelity to it."[55] Perhaps for this reason, as Ludovici reports, Rodin preferred to use English women, with whom he could scarcely communicate verbally, as models.[56] Their communication was enacted through the movements and responses of their bodies. Lampert notes that Rodin was "the first sculptor to want to make women's sexuality important."[57] This idea was borne out in Rainer Maria Rilke's monograph, in which Rodin's work is credited with presenting female sexuality as an active and conscious force: "The woman is no more the overpowered or willing animal. She is lounging and awake like the man.… To discover in all lusts and crimes, in all trials and all despair, an infinite reason for existence is a part of that great longing that creates poets. Here humanity hungers for something beyond itself."[58] The free movement of Rodin's studio models was introduced within this context.

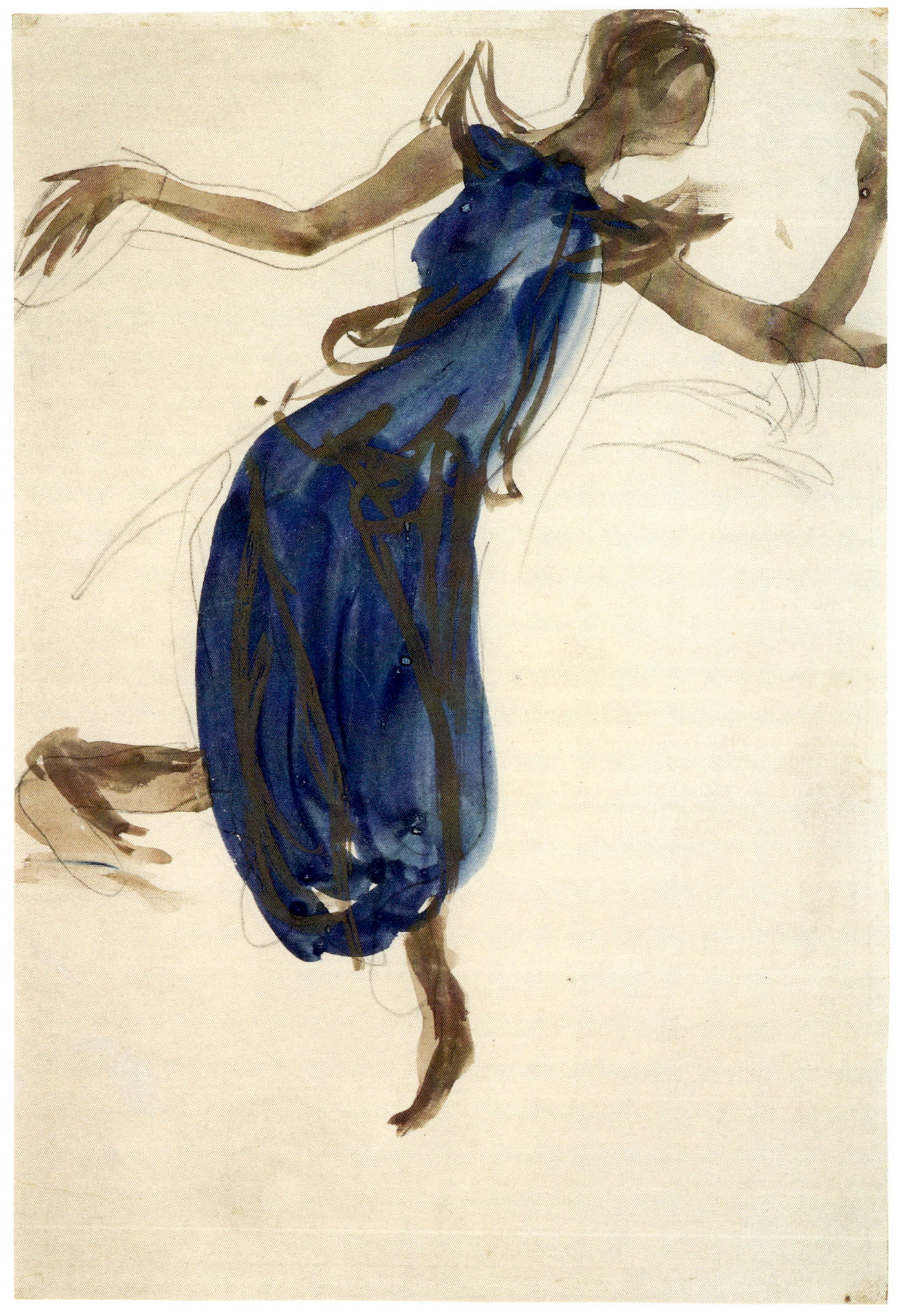

42 Auguste Rodin

CAMBODIAN DANCING GIRL, 1906

DANCE AS METAPHOR

In his later years, Rodin worked with both professional and non-professional models,[59] employing acrobats and cancan dancers,[60] whose muscles were accustomed to movement and not, like professional studio models, trained for stasis. One model recalls Rodin's preference for "vigorous, muscular models with salient whipcord sinews."[61]

Rodin's interest in dance, and in dancers, was also widely acknowledged by his biographers, and was noted in the popular press. In 1906, Rodin was so enthusiastic about a Cambodian dance troupe he had seen in Paris that he followed the dancers to Marseilles, where they performed in a French-sponsored colonial exposition.[62] In an article from the July 28, 1906 issue of *L'Illustration*, George Bois described Rodin sketching the dancers during their practice sessions. A photograph of this procedure was included in the article (fig. 4).[63] Ludovici reported that Rodin was

> *particularly struck with the manner in which... they created the impression of growing on the stage in their hieratic and rhythmic evolutions, a feat impossible [for] our toe-dancers, who reach their utmost height in one spring. He also extolled a particular serpentine movement of their hands and arms, which they caused to pass like an undulating shudder from the tips of the fingers of one hand, up the arms, and across the shoulder blades on to the finger tips of the other hand. He declared that he had learnt movements of the human body which he had not suspected theretofore, and which the ancients had either not known or failed to record; and he pronounced the art of the whole display as more consummate than anything he had ever seen.*[64]

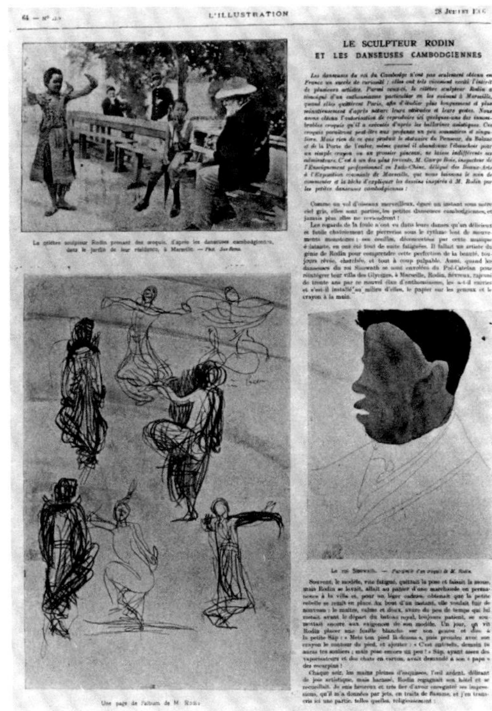

L'ILLUSTRATION

LE SCULPTEUR RODIN
ET LES DANSEUSES CAMBODGIENNES

figure 4
L'Illustration, July 28, 1906, Paris: 64.
By permission of Harvard College Library, Cambridge.

In the article in *L'Illustration*, Bois also reported Rodin's response to non-Western bodies and alluded to the notion that a body habituated to non-Western dance displayed differences in musculature from Western bodies.[65] In Rodin's drawings from that summer, including CAMBODIAN DANCING GIRL (cat. no. 42; color plate), his conception of the body as a site of difference, outside of the Western gestural vocabulary, is expressed through the figures' flowing lines which elide bone and muscle into a generalized flow.[66] Here, the implied masses of Rodin's Western models have given way to almost weightless flesh, to the body as gesture itself.

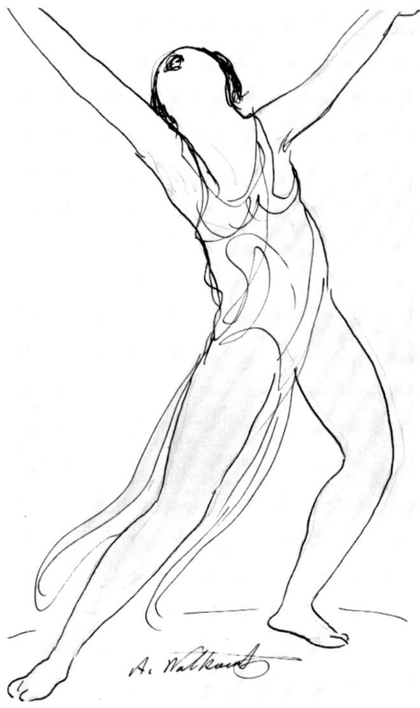

figure 5
Abraham Walkowitz, *Isadora Duncan*, n.d., watercolor, graphite, pen and ink on paper, 14 x 8½". Davis Museum and Cultural Center, Wellesley College. Gift of Ethel R. Slawsby in honor of Sheila Slawsby Kowal, Class of 1959.

The distinction that Rodin made between the gestural conventions of Cambodian dance and the conventionalized gestures of Opéra dancers marks his approach to dance in general. It was well known that his interest in dance was focused on non-canonical and unconventional forms. His contact with Isadora Duncan, Loïe Fuller, and Ruth St. Denis placed him within the most avant-garde dance milieu in Europe.[67] Isadora Duncan had arrived in Paris with aspirations for dance that paralleled Rodin's for sculpture: "I had come to Europe to bring about a great renaissance of religion through the Dance, to bring the knowledge of the Beauty and Holiness of the human body through its expressions and movements."[68] Duncan's technique was premised on the free movement of the body, on allowing the body to move not according to the gestural repertory of the Opéra, but through its own demands: the lungs filling with air conditioned outward movement; the contraction of the diaphragm effected a pulling inward of the limbs and torso.[69] The hundreds of studies that Abraham Walkowitz made of Duncan beginning in 1906 (fig. 5) provide insight into her "natural" vocabulary of the body. Dancing barefoot and wearing only a silk sheath, Duncan presented herself as the embodiment of pure, unmediated expression, a revitalized instinctual classicism.

Ruth St. Denis was received during her first European tour in 1906 with the observation: "There is no forced, artificial stiffness in [her performance], but rather an inner spiritual necessity."[70] This was also the way in which Rodin described Loïe Fuller: "[She] is, to my mind, a woman of genius.... She has reawakened the spirit of antiquity, showing the Tanagra figurines in action."[71] As an embodiment of unconscious urges, sensual liberation, gestural discipline, and the enactment of primal or ancient rhythms, non-academic dance was, for Rodin, a point of intersection with his gestural drawings. Rodin's representations of free movement (cat. no. 34) consequently articulated physical and psychic liberation by bringing together subject, technique and touch. Hand and body, performance and observation, possession and distance, are all inscribed in the trajectory of Rodin's impulsive lines.

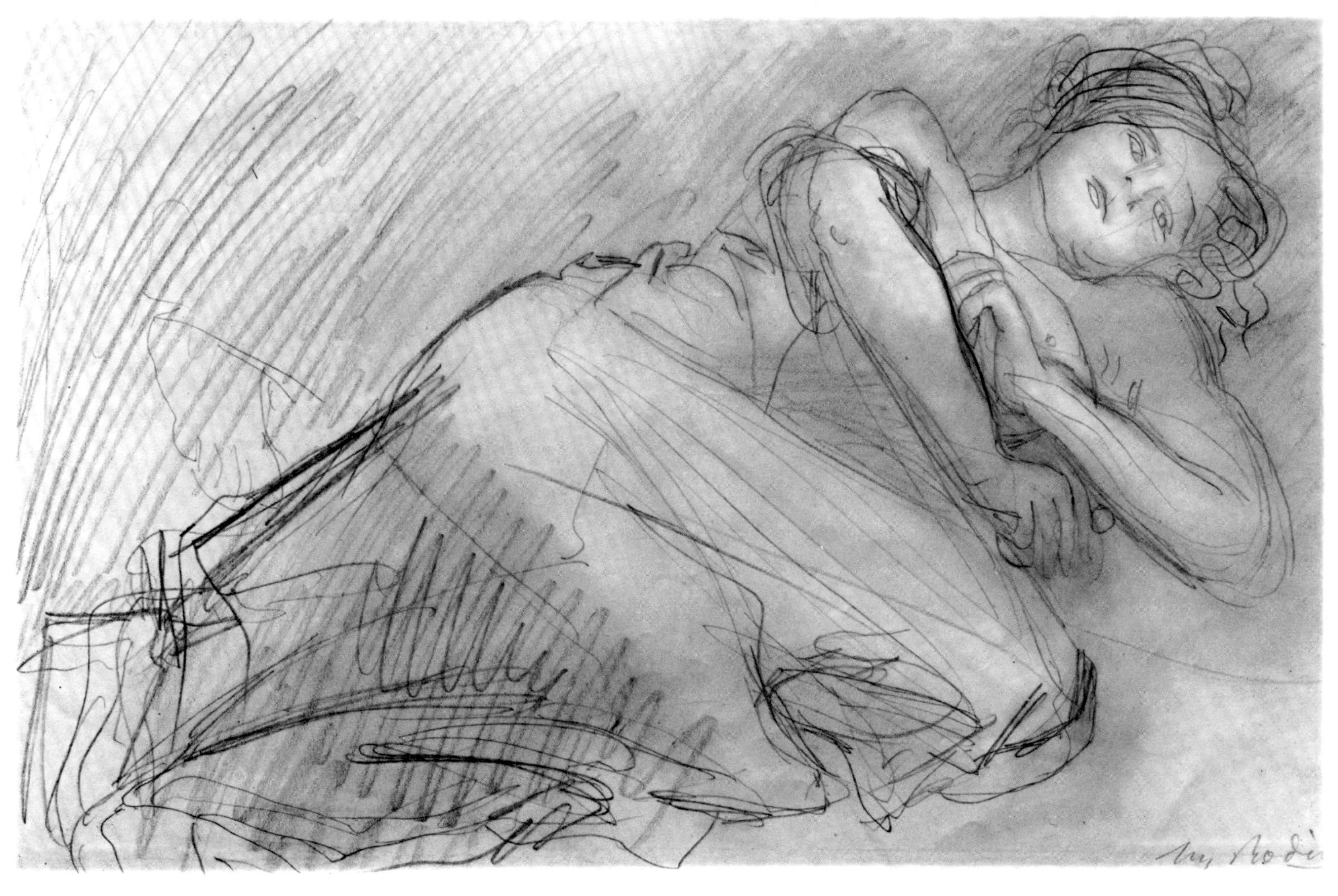

34 Auguste Rodin

L'ABANDONNÉE, ca. 1900

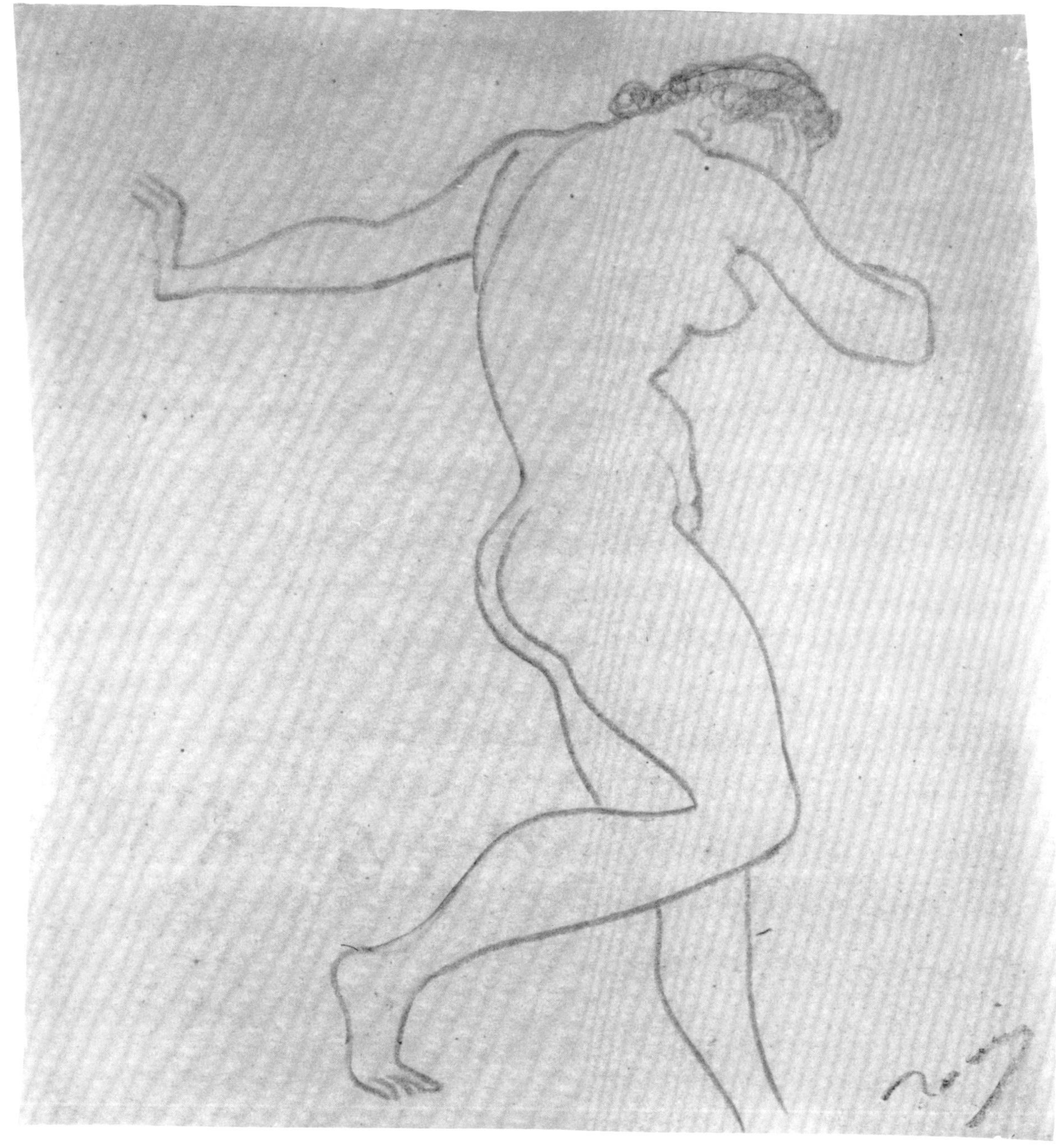

1 André Derain
NUDE, n.d.

figure 6
Théophile-Alexandre Steinlin, *Woman Combing Her Hair*, 1902, soft ground etching, 15 3/4 x 9 7/8". Charles Deering Collection, The Art Institute of Chicago. Photograph © 1994, The Art Institute of Chicago.

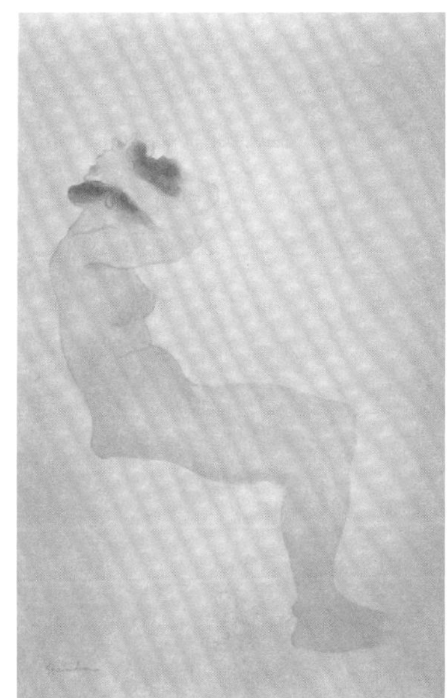

LINEAR STYLE AMONG THE FAUVES

The work of numerous artists living in Paris at the time that Rodin began exhibiting his drawings suggests a rapid assimilation of his technique. Artists as divergent as André Derain and Théophile-Alexandre Steinlin (fig. 6) reflect in their work, if only briefly, a preoccupation with linearity in the wake of Rodin. In particular, Rodin's gestural drawing presented to Matisse, Derain and their colleagues a compelling aesthetic system which contained the implications of eroticism and sensual freedom, and a refiguration of the nude through movement and creative distortion. Through its seeming fusion of the artist's sexual longing with the model's sexual presence, Rodin's drawing suggested a notational system of erotic movement. This notion is reflected in André Derain's 1906 *Bacchic Dance* (fig. 7). In this composition, delicately drawn lines in graphite alternately trace the silhouette and the trajectory of the dancers' limbs and provide receptacles for the layers of watercolor wash. As in Derain's condensed linear nude (cat. no. 1), an affinity with Rodin is apparent.

For Derain's colleague Henri Matisse, the exploitation of gestural drawing occasioned a radical new direction in his work. As many of Matisse's biographers have observed, direct drawing was at the heart of Fauve theory and practice. Numerous sources have been proposed for Matisse's transformation in style in 1905–1906; rarely is Rodin mentioned in this regard. One exception is Albert Elsen, who demonstrated that the impact of Rodin's work on Matisse occurred as early as 1900.[72] Despite the fact that Matisse never admitted the influence,[73] Matisse's key Fauve works suggest both stylistic and procedural affinities with Rodin's drawings.[74]

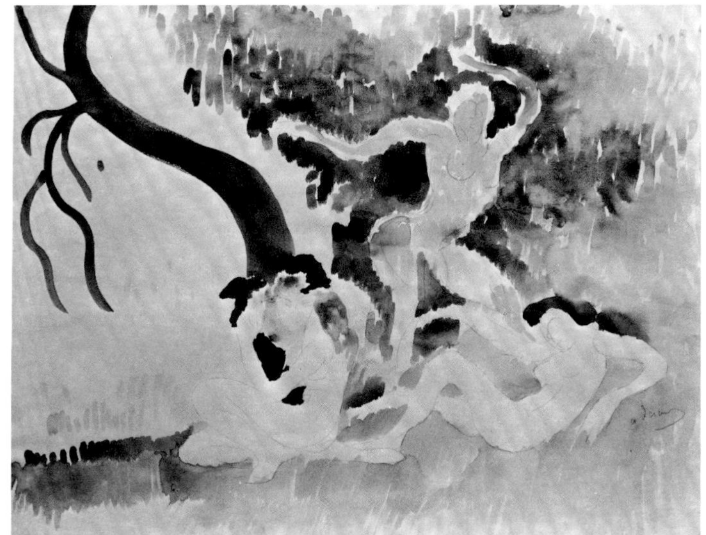

figure 7
André Derain, *Bacchic Dance*, 1906, watercolor and pencil on paper, 19 1/2 x 25 1/2". The Museum of Modern Art, New York. Gift of Abby Aldrich Rockefeller.

The issue of precisely when and how Matisse viewed Rodin's gestural drawings is beside the point.[75] The question is how he could not have seen them. At the turn of the century in France, Rodin was considered one of the greatest living artists, and Matisse's interest in his work is well known. In 1899, Matisse purchased the original plaster for Rodin's portrait *Henri Rochefort*,[76] and in 1900 he was persuaded by the painter Eugène Carrière to visit Rodin in his studio.[77] Matisse then studied for several months with Rodin's student and colleague, Antoine Bourdelle.[78] In that year, Matisse was hired to decorate the interior of the Grand Palais in preparation for the Universal Exposition. It would have been surprising, given Matisse's interest in Rodin's work, if Matisse did not visit the Place de l'Alma during the exhibition. Over the course of three years, beginning in 1900, Matisse used "Bevilaqua," Rodin's model for his sculpture *Walking Man* (1877), as he worked on his own sculpture *The Slave*.[79] Considering Matisse's interest in Rodin as a sculptor, it seems unlikely that Matisse would not have been aware of the numerous publications on Rodin's drawings, such as his colleague Roger Marx's articles in an 1897 issue of *L'Image* and a 1902 issue of *Gazette des Beaux-Arts*.[80] As a member of the hanging committee at the Salon des Indépendants[81] and a participant in survey exhibitions which included Rodin's works,[82] Matisse had ample opportunity to view the full range of Rodin's work. Finally, in 1908, when Matisse moved to the Hôtel Biron, he became Rodin's neighbor.[83] Although Pierre Schneider remarks that the artists' proximity was accidental, he acknowledges Matisse's debt to Rodin and notes the possibility of other encounters.[84]

In 1906, the same year in which Derain created *Bacchic Dance*, Matisse adopted what Yve-Alain Bois calls "drawing as a generative category."[85] As Bois has pointed out, Matisse began to explore gestural drawing at a decisive moment in 1905–1906 when the artist sought a way of extending, and then moving out of, Neo-Impressionism. By dispensing with laborious preparatory sketches and recording his visual impressions of nature through rapidly executed line, Matisse painted and drew directly. The results of Matisse's new approach first appeared in two exhibitions of 1906. At the Salon des Indépendants, Matisse exhibited as his only submission *Le Bonheur de Vivre* (fig. 8), the monumental and manifesto-like announcement of his new vocabulary and procedure;[86] and at the Galerie Druet, he exhibited three woodcuts and twelve lithographs.[87] All these works suggest, through their flowing linearity, a striking sense of spontaneity. Taken together, these works initiated Matisse's exploration of what he later called

> *my purest and most direct translation of my emotion.... I have never considered drawing as an exercise of particular dexterity, rather as principally a means of expressing intimate feelings and describing states of mind, but a means deliberately simplified so as to give simplicity and spontaneity to the expression which should speak without clumsiness, directly to the spectator.*[88]

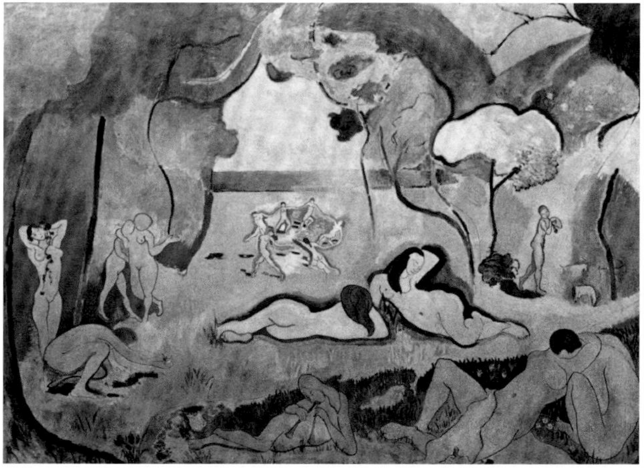

figure 8
Henri Matisse, *Le Bonheur de Vivre*, 1905–06, oil on canvas, 68 1/2 x 93 3/4".

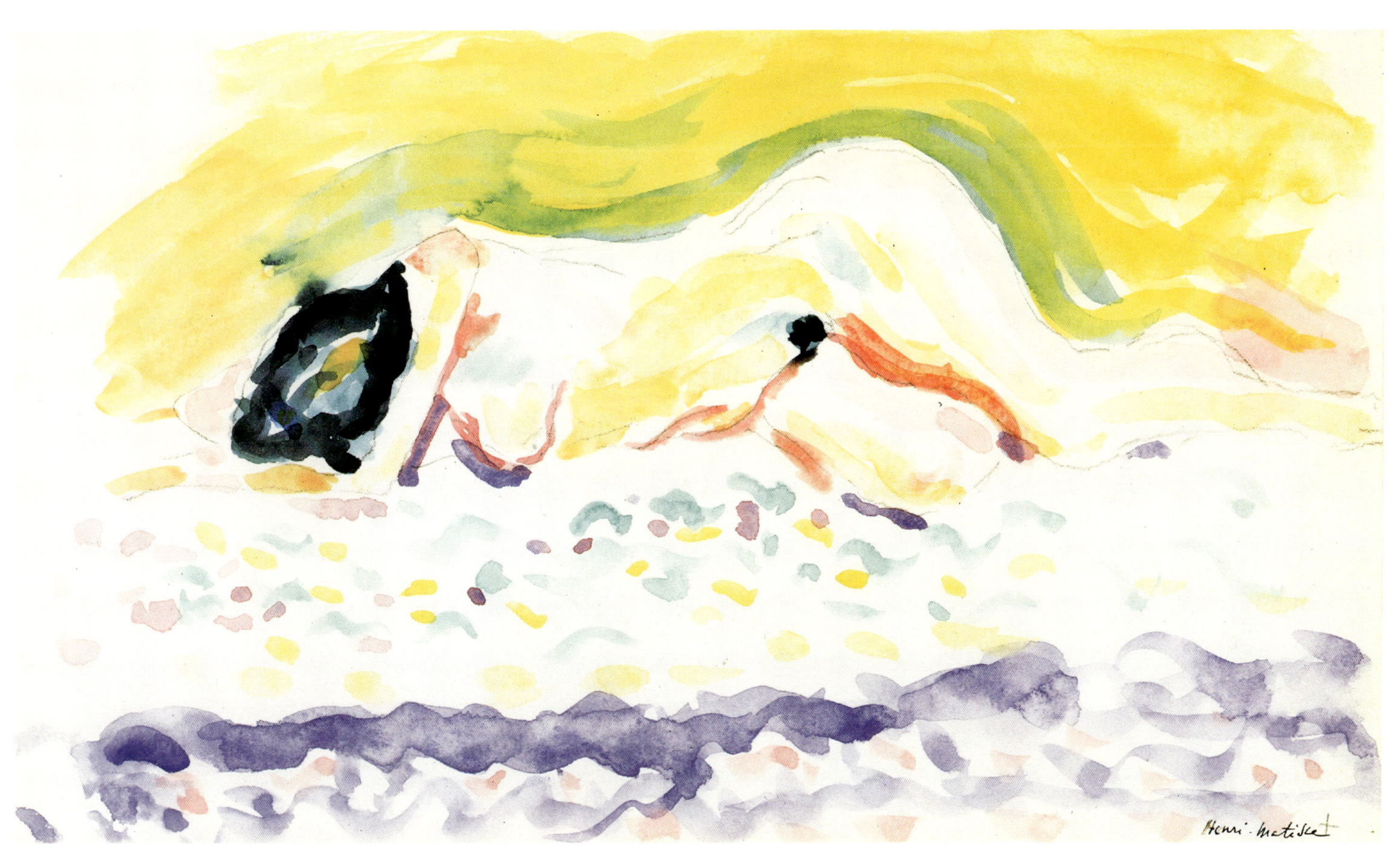

22 Henri Matisse
AT THE SEASIDE (BATHER), ca. 1905

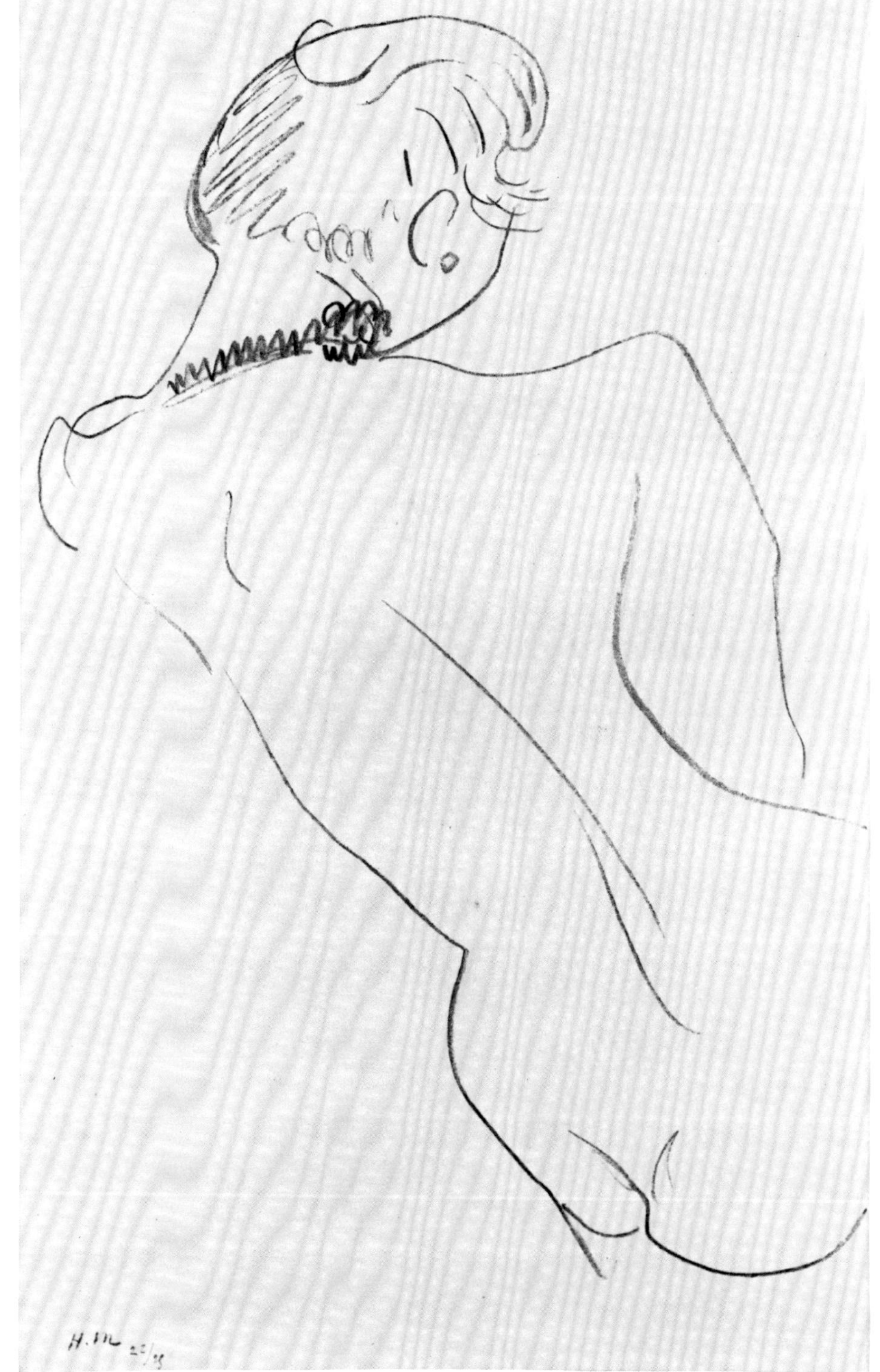

A pencil-and-watercolor drawing (cat. no. 22; color plate) from 1905 suggests Matisse's transition from a reliance on isolated areas of jewel-like color to orchestrate and organize his composition to his exploitation of continuous line to mark and measure space. Here, the touch and delicacy of the graphite gesture bear strong formal similarities to Rodin's works. Even the watercolor wash that lends volume to the model's body suggests Matisse's scrutiny of Rodin's procedure of filling in his lines with veils of wash. The lithographs and woodcuts from 1906 reveal a break from Rodin's concern with movement and instead provide exercises in what Ludovici called Rodin's manu-visual dexterity—the operations of vision as touch. In BACK VIEW OF A NUDE WITH NECKLACE (cat. no. 25), Matisse records his model as she leans slightly back and to her left. The exaggerated and asymmetrical description of her shoulders and the displacement of her neck and head convey the subtle torsion of her movement. Matisse has emphasized the counterpoise of her torso by extending her right shoulder and then directing his crayon downward, detouring around the area of her upper arm that suggests a slight swelling or tension of muscle. Wiry, overlapping lines defining the left shoulder suggest Matisse's visual engagement with the model's contours rather than with his paper.[89] Although in PENSIVE NUDE IN A FOLDING CHAIR (cat. no. 23) he incorporates greater anecdotal detail into the composition, the volume of the seated model has similarly been extracted into a series of sweeping, continuous lines. Matisse attributed his procedure to intuition as expressed by the hand:

25 Henri Matisse
BACK VIEW OF A NUDE WITH NECKLACE, 1906

42

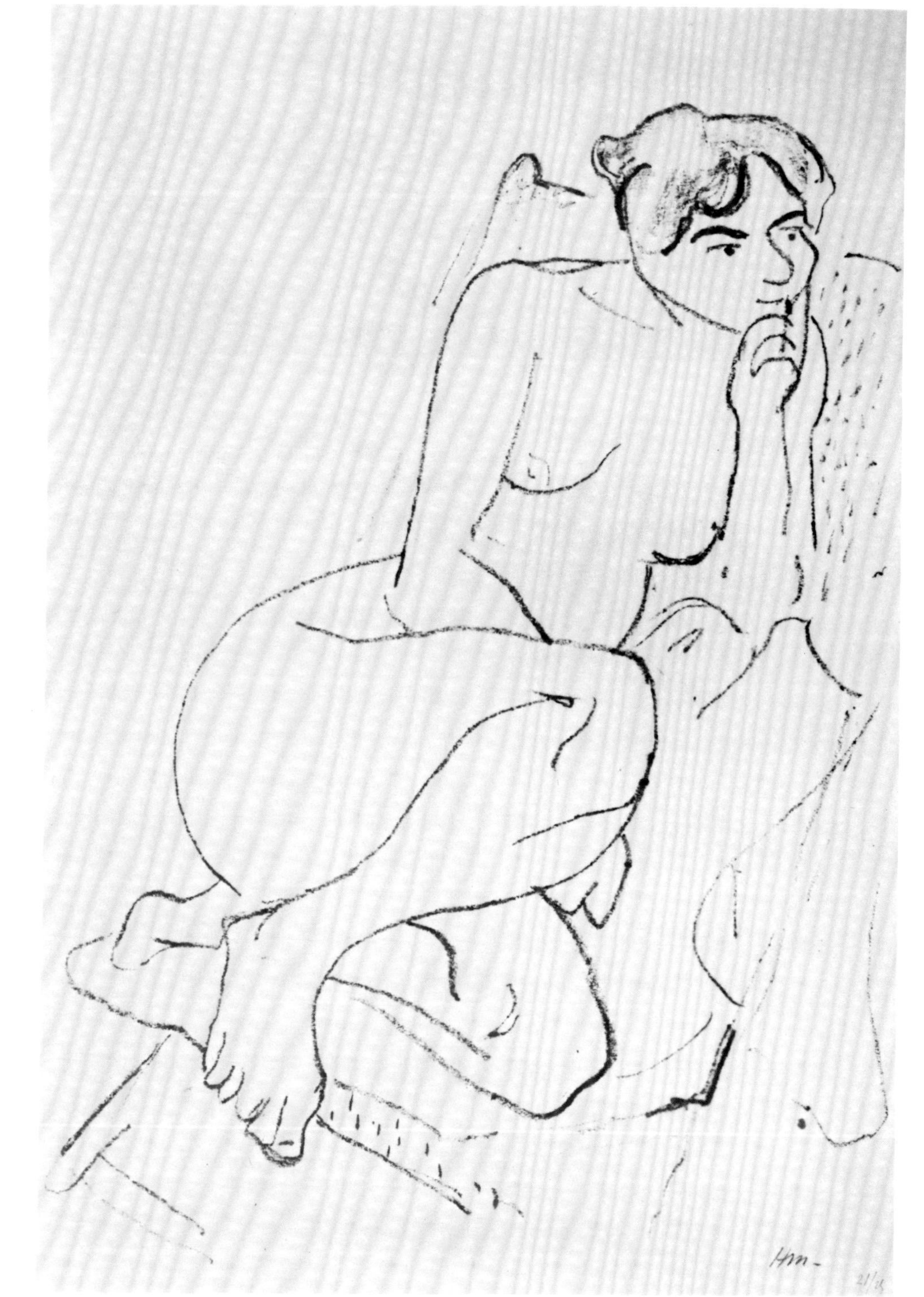

When I make my drawings—"variations"—the path traced by my pencil on the sheet of paper is, to some extent, analogous to the gesture of a man groping his way in the darkness. I mean that there is nothing foreseen about my path: I am led. I do not lead. I go from one point in the thing which is my model to another point which I always see in isolation, independent of the other points towards which my pen will subsequently move.... Just as the spider throws out (or fastens?) its thread to some convenient protuberance and thence to another that it perceives, and from one point to another weaves its web.[90]

The directness of this technique,[91] in which distortions of anatomy and perspective accompany the freely drawn line, suggests an affinity with Rodin. As Elsen notes, there are few other precedents for such a direct and spontaneous production.

23 Henri Matisse
PENSIVE NUDE IN A FOLDING CHAIR, 1906

Matisse's three woodcuts of 1906 (cat. nos. 27, 28, and 29) provide an important insight into Matisse's intentions in regard to the notions of instinct and spontaneity. Unlike the transfer lithographs, which incorporate accident and discovery in their arching lines, the woodcuts were painstakingly rendered to appear accidental. Like Rodin's traced drawings, they bear the constructed mark of the artist's hand. The fact that Mme Matisse was charged with the task of carving the lines in accordance with her husband's drawings[92] suggests how deliberately planned and *un*spontaneous the actual execution was. A comparison between SEATED NUDE (PETIT BOIS CLAIR) (cat. no. 29) and the brush-and-ink drawing on which it was based (fig. 9) reveals the extent to which Matisse wished to maintain the fiction of original spontaneity. In the woodcut, nuances in the width and density of line, implying variations in the pressure that the artist's hand exerted on his brush, have been translated faithfully to the woodcut medium. Only the variations between wet and dry brush strokes in the original have defied translation. Such visual cues as the cropping of the model's hands and right foot, the precarious placement of the model on the page, and the suggested variations in touch define the woodcut as a gestural drawing.

UNTITLED (SEATED NUDE), a pen-and-ink drawing from ca. 1906 (cat. no. 26), incorporates similar croppings, distortions, and traces of unpremeditated touch. As Riva Castleman observes, the work serves as a stylistic link between the linearity of the lithographs and the density of the woodcuts.[93] Retaining the decorative patterning of the woodcuts, which Yve-Alain Bois links to a kind of vestigial Neo-Impressionism, the drawing articulates, like Rodin's gestural drawings, the marks of its making. These marks fuse both gesture and perception, touch and vision.

In this drawing, as in the woodcuts, the active eye of the artist is announced by virtue of the skewed perspective imposed on the model. The willful distortion of the model's body positions the viewer above and in close proximity to it. Through Matisse's emphasis on distortion as signifying the operations of a subjectively perceiving eye, the artist establishes a physical intimacy with the model. The direct tracings of his hand condition the terms of this intimacy, and those terms are allied with the notion of subjective expression.

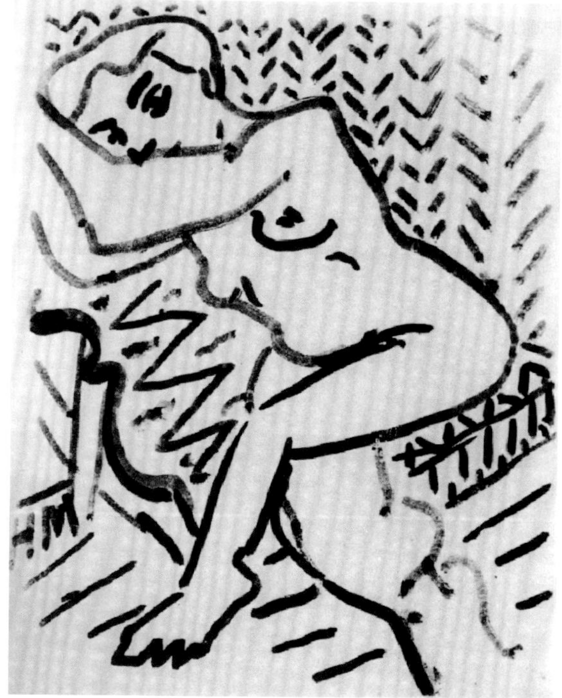

figure 9

Henri Matisse, from Waldemar George, *Dessins de Henri Matisse*, Paris, 1925, plate 17. By permission of Harvard College Library, Cambridge.

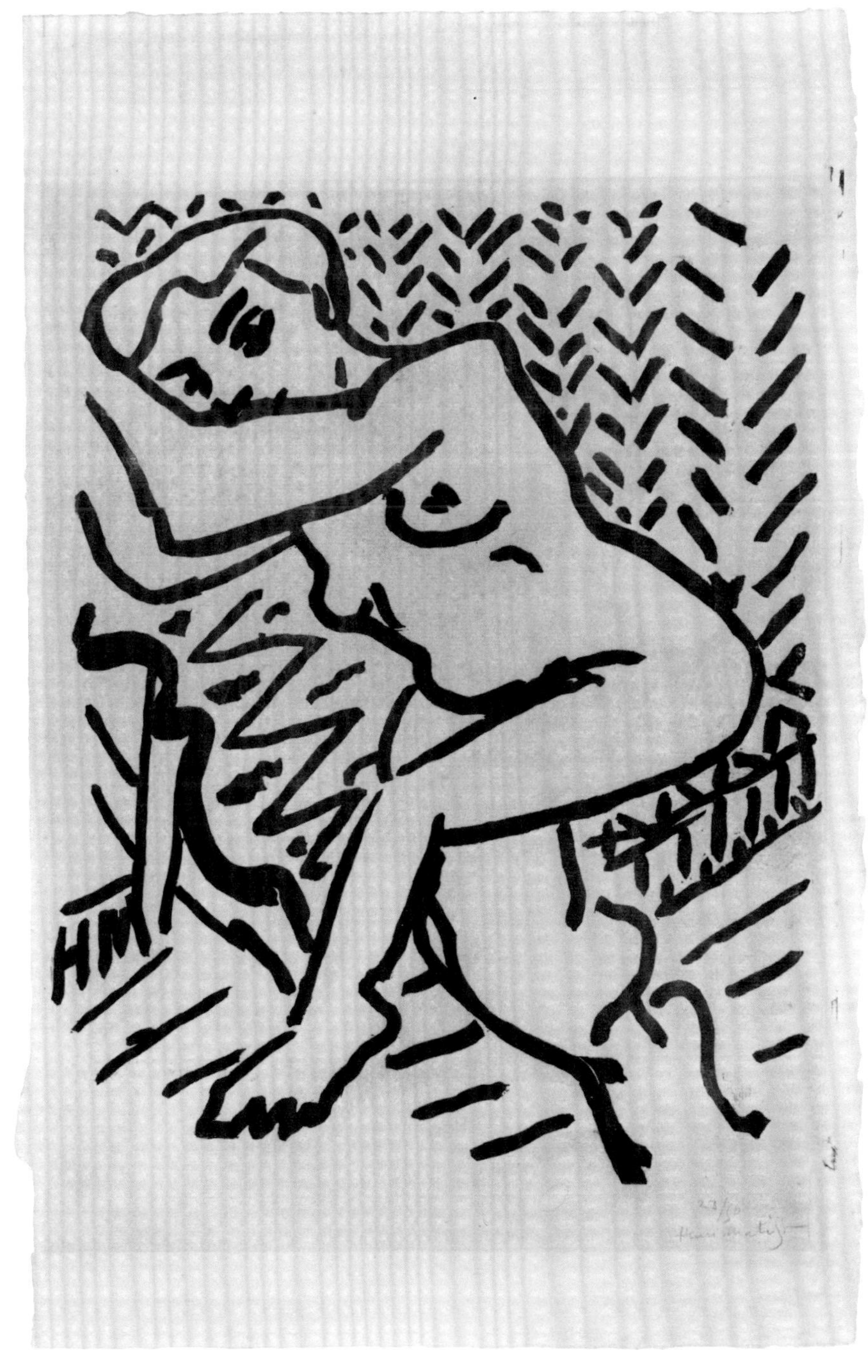

29 Henri Matisse

SEATED NUDE (PETIT BOIS CLAIR), 1906

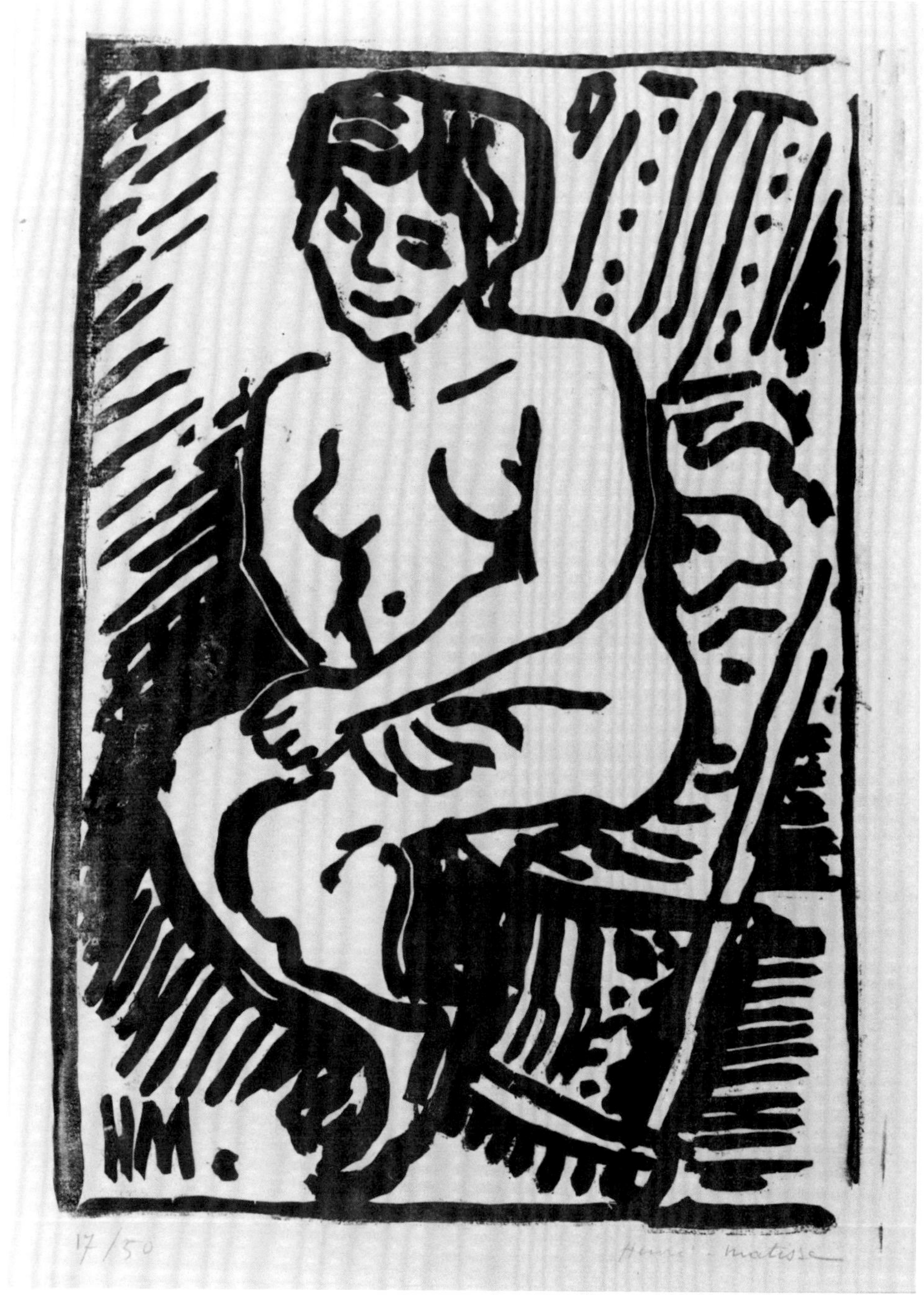

28 Henri Matisse

ÉTUDE DE NUE (PETIT BOIS NOIR), 1906

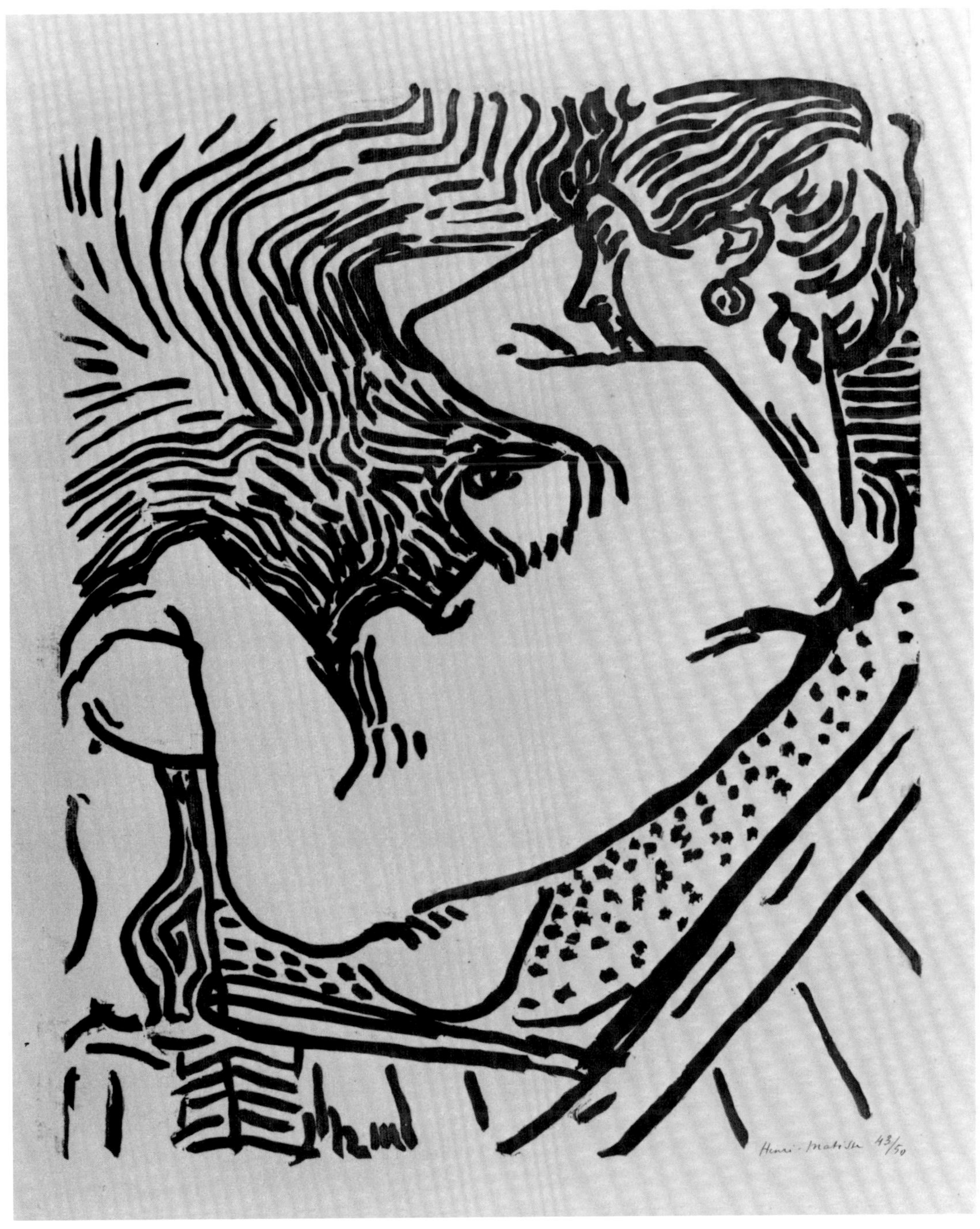

27 Henri Matisse
ÉTUDE DE NUE (LE GRAND BOIS), 1906

Richard Shiff has noted that, for the turn-of-the-century avant-garde, one way of suggesting spontaneity was through formal and stylistic irregularity.[94] This notion was explored throughout theories of perception and representation in the late nineteenth century. In Giovanni Morelli's notions of connoisseurship, irregularities in technique proclaim the signature of the artist, funneling the personality of the artist through the unique gestures of the individual hand.[95] Ludovici repeated this idea in relation to Rodin's drawings, identifying his anatomical distortions and agitated lines as the natural outpouring of his hand: "Inaccuracies... followed naturally from the way in which they were produced."[96] The pairing of creativity and formal distortion ran throughout Matisse's 1908 credo, "Notes of a Painter,"[97] as well as through his pedagogy. As Sarah Stein recorded in 1908, Matisse instructed his students to filter the perception of the visual world through the veil of temperament: "But proportions according to correct measurement are after all but very little unless confirmed by sentiment, and expressive of the particular physical character of the model.... Therefore exaggerate according to the definite character for expression."[98] In this regard, Matisse's and Rodin's cultivation of idiosyncratic proportions in their drawings recalls Jean Moréas's manifesto of Symbolism, in which "a unique character moves through an environment deformed by his own hallucinations, his temperament; the only *reality* lies in this distortion [*déformation*]."[99]

In the late 1870s, this emphasis on distortion served as a theme that recurred throughout the influential treatise *Aesthetics*, by philosopher Eugène Véron. Véron asserted that "expressive art... has nothing to do with beauty, whatever we may consider that to be...."[100] Rather, expression is predicated on contortions, irregularities of touch;[101] exaggeration and deformity are the measure of "a superior artistic realism."[102] Paralleling William James's metaphor of consciousness as a stream[103]—the notion that successive moments blend into the perception of continuous time, a mapping of the successive "nows"[104]—Véron noted that artistic perception occurs over time. The representation of movement as a continuum was a direct communication of the artist's perceptual faculties or consciousness. The challenge to the artist, therefore, was to find the formal means by which time, motion, and sensibility could coalesce.[105] Confirming this idea, particularly as it was expressed by philosopher Henri Bergson,[106] Matisse stated in "Notes of a Painter":

Underlying this succession of moments which constitutes the superficial existence of beings and things, and which is continually modifying and transforming them, one can search for a truer, more essential character, which the artist will seize so that he may give to reality a more lasting interpretation.... Movement seized while it is going on is meaningful to us only if we do not isolate the present sensation either from that which precedes it or that which follows it.[107]

When, in turn, Matisse stated that "drawing is like an expressive gesture, but it has the advantage of permanency,"[108] he anchored his lines within advanced perceptual theory. This territory was, in part, based on the notion that modern vision is tactile and not purely optical.

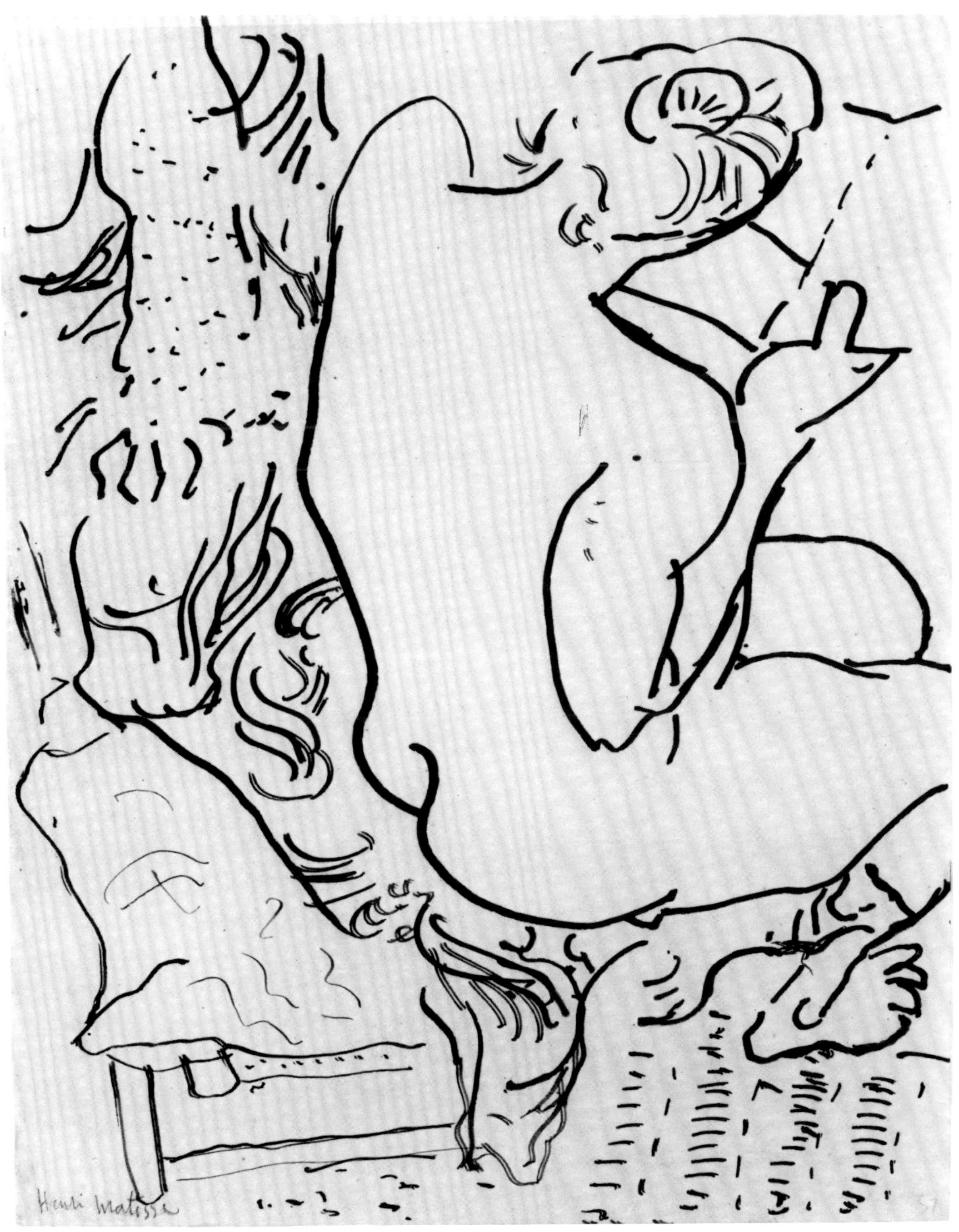

26 Henri Matisse
UNTITLED (SEATED NUDE), ca. 1906

In his highly influential 1893 treatise, *The Problem of Form in Painting and Sculpture*, the artist and theorist Adolf von Hildebrand proposed that the senses of both touch and sight are implicated in spatial perception.[109] These Hildebrand defined as "near" and "far" vision,[110] what Alois Riegl would later characterize as the "haptic" and the "optic."[111] Hildebrand claimed that the eye has the ability to integrate the two modes of perception and that artistic accomplishment is premised on their integration: "An artistic talent consists in having these two functions precisely and harmoniously related."[112] In fact, he proposed that the mission of art is "to reestablish and make felt the sound and natural relations between our thought and sense activities."[113] Rodin reflected this idea when he said of his drawings: "My object is to test to what extent my hands already feel what my eyes see."[114] Hildebrand also proposed the notion that "the specifically artistic force and talent of the painter rest on his ability to discover the visual values of space in nature . . ."[115]—that expressive art is constituted by the recognition of the perceiving eye.[116]

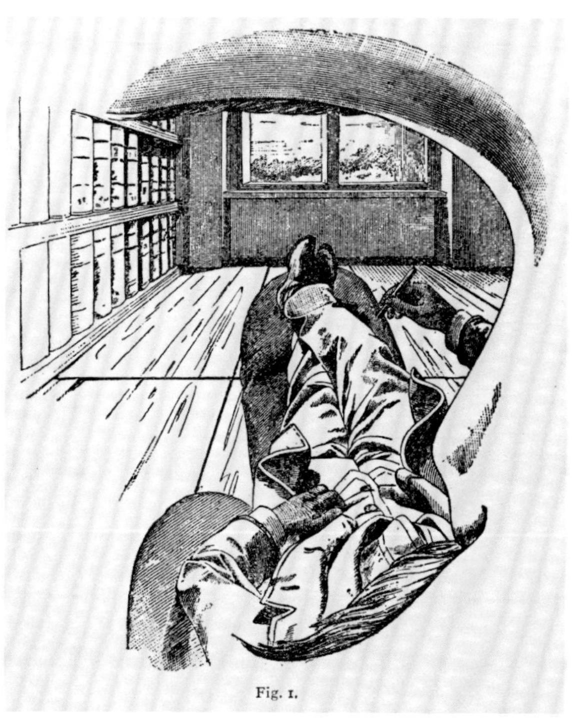

figure 10
Ernst Mach, *Contributions to the Analysis of the Sensations* [1885], Chicago, 1897, figure I: 16. By permission of Harvard College Library, Cambridge.

PERCEIVING EYE, PERCEIVING HAND

When Matisse began to explore the technique of gestural drawing as a generative category, he reconfigured vision as representation. The disjunctive proportions within his figures from 1906, in particular those represented in pen-and-ink drawings (cat. no. 26) and woodcuts (cat. nos. 27, 28, and 29), may be understood to articulate perception, especially in regard to the operations of stereoscopic vision. The figural distortions he presents are, in part, the exaggeration of the distances he maps between each point of the models' bodies and his eye, the result of what the Prague- and Vienna-based philosopher, physicist, and psychologist Ernst Mach termed "relational viewing."[117] In a lecture from 1867, which was published in the 1890s, Mach traced the disparities between the operations of the two eyes that constitute stereoscopic vision and noted that the eyes compensate for one another in the measurement of distance.[118] In his most widely circulated text, *Contributions to the Analysis of the Sensations* (1885), Mach proposed that by closing one eye and thus removing the relational balance of stereoscopic vision the perceptual field is not only flattened, but it becomes distorted and framed by the viewer's body (fig. 10). Despite the lack of subtlety with which he illustrated this observation, Mach's notion that the body is inscribed on the visual field is of fundamental importance here. Reflecting the notion proposed by Hermann von Helmholtz that perception is mediated by memory and unconscious inference,[119] Mach implicated perception in the corporeal presence of the viewer.

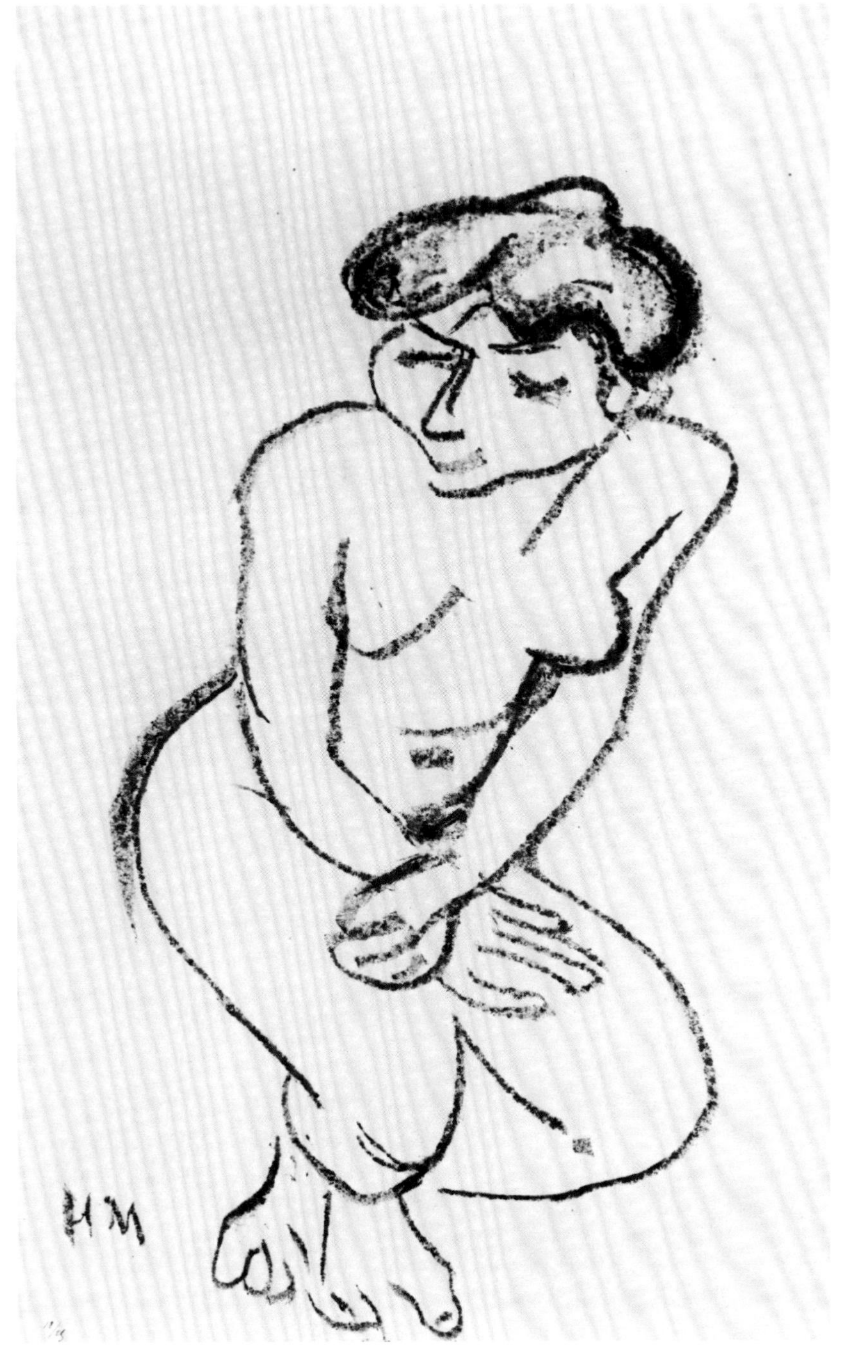

24 Henri Matisse

CROUCHING NUDE WITH EYES LOWERED, 1906

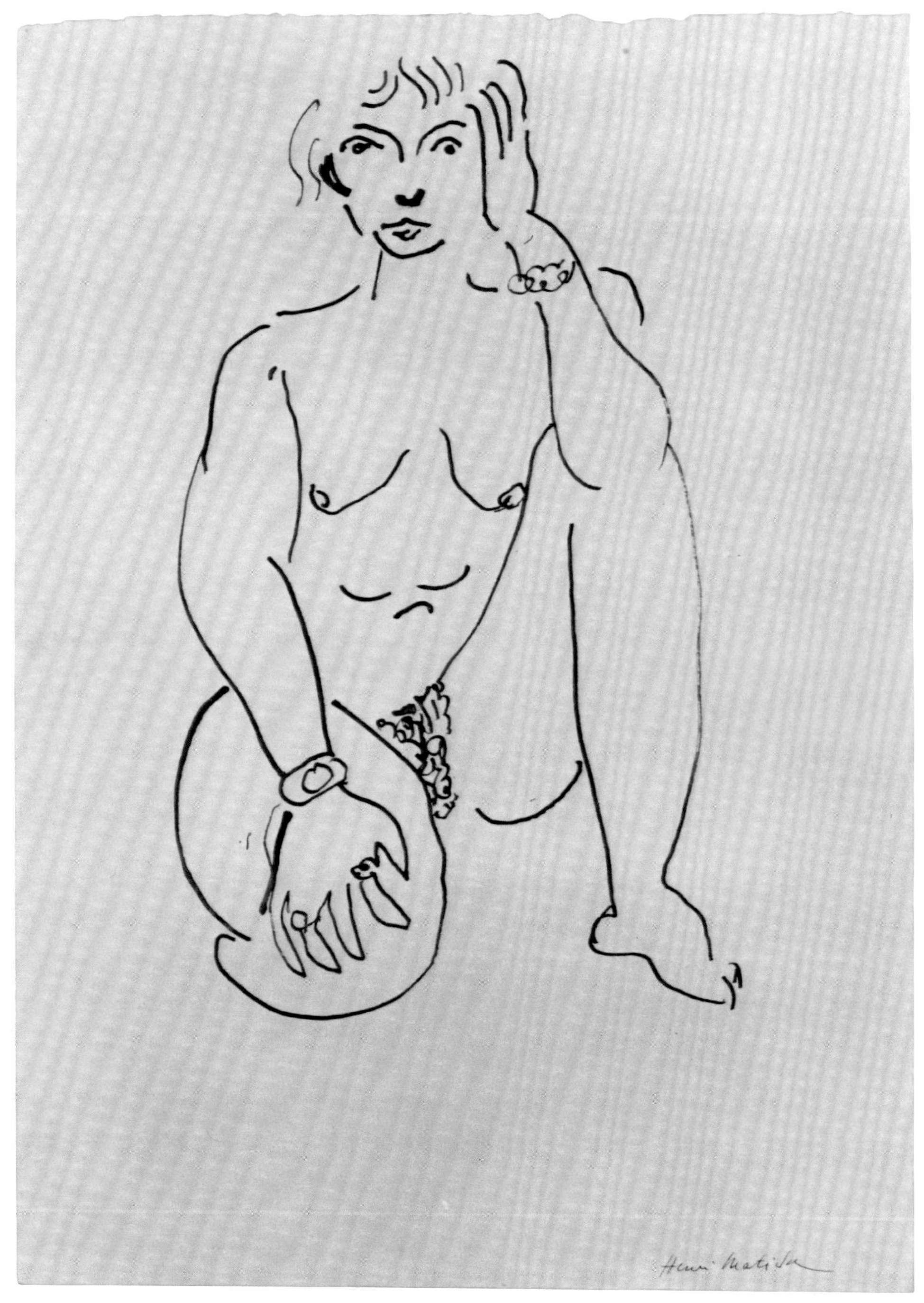

30 Henri Matisse
NUDE WITH BRACELETS, ca. 1909

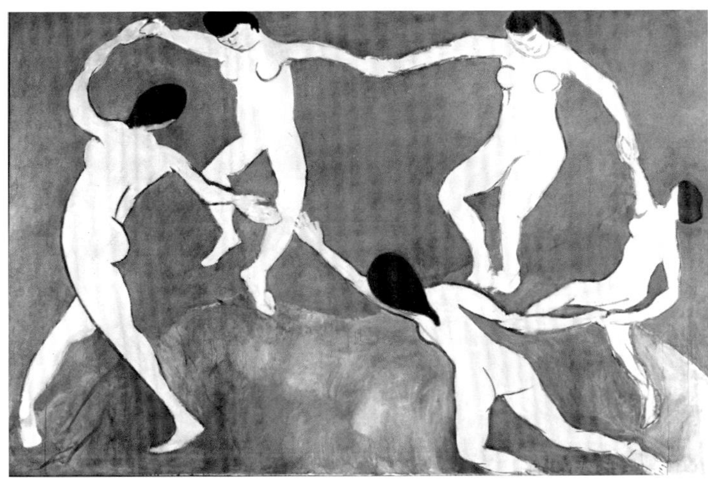

figure 11
Henri Matisse, *The Dance (First Version)*, Paris, March 1909, oil on canvas, 102 1/2 x 153 1/2". The Museum of Modern Art, New York. Gift of Nelson A. Rockefeller in honor of Alfred H. Barr, Jr.

The exaggerated anatomies and assertive, reductive lines of Matisse's gestural drawings may, in this light, be understood to thematize perception. As a negotiation between haptic and optic vision, they equate opticality with tactility. As references to the artist's proximity to the model, they convey spatial perception, and, as traces of the artist's hand in motion, they are material markers of temporality. Unlike Rodin's gestural drawings, the motion suggested by Matisse's figural works from 1906 is not founded in the movements of his models, but instead conveyed through irregularities of touch and distortions in scale.

Matisse's *The Dance* (fig. 11), however, comes closest to Rodin's synthesis of the artist's hand and the model's gesture communicated by the continuous, distorting line.[120] Here, Matisse locks the fundamental instability of movement and gesture into the cursive rendering of bodies in space—the externalization of psychic drives, the dialogue between visuality and eroticism. In this and in the breakthrough works of 1905–1906, gestural drawing provides the terms by which the artist's expression may be read.

LINEAR STYLE IN AUSTRIAN EXPRESSIONISM

Mach's work on perceptual theory had a direct bearing on the German and Austrian Expressionists. In 1916, the Viennese critic Hermann Bahr cited Mach, along with Alois Riegl, Josef Maria Obrist, Gustav Klimt, and Otto Wagner, as generative influences on the Expressionist movement.[121] In his treatise *Expressionismus* Bahr defined the movement as a dialogue or passage between the artist's direct perception of nature and the articulation of an inner vision. According to Bahr, the act of drawing transacts this passage,[122] binding perception and intuition in "a kind of touchsight, *eine Art Tastsehen*."[123] Described in this context, touchsight—haptic vision, tactile viewing—represents the terms by which the visible world can be filtered through the artist's consciousness. The term acknowledges the artist's separation from corporeal reality, the desire for fusion with it and, at the same time, the impossibility of such fulfillment. This is also the way in which Oskar Kokoschka described his approach to perception. Kokoschka defined the consciousness of the artist as contingent upon an inner vision: "The state of awareness of visions is not one in which we are either remembering or perceiving. It is rather a level of consciousness at which we experience visions within ourselves.... Visions seem actually to modify one's consciousness."[124] It is this vision or veil of sensibility that reconstructs the visual world as a fourth dimension of perception, the mediation of the artist's vision by his other perceptual apparatus: "Painting, you know, isn't based on just three dimensions, but on four. The fourth dimension is a projection of myself.... The other three dimensions are based on the vision of both eyes (not just one); the fourth dimension is based on the essential nature of vision, which is creative."[125]

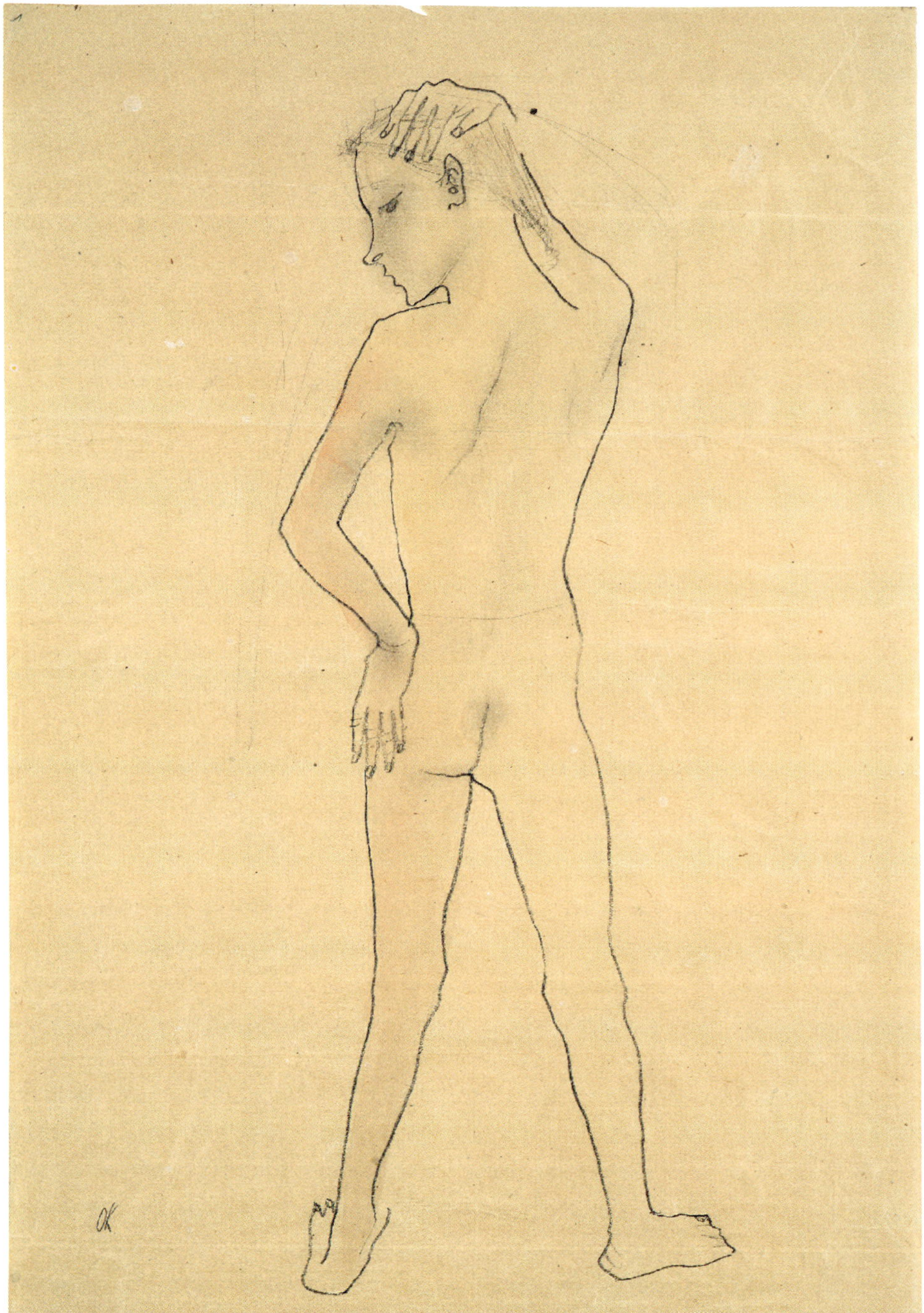

18 Oskar Kokoschka

NUDE YOUTH SEEN FROM THE BACK, 1906–07 (possibly 1905)

KOKOSCHKA'S GESTURAL DRAWINGS

Kokoschka's figure drawings, beginning in 1907, symbolize the dialogue between inner vision and outer perception through the exploration of the continuous gestural line. In such works as NUDE YOUTH SEEN FROM THE BACK (cat. no. 18; color plate), Kokoschka seems to have followed Rodin's procedure of translating a model's contours to his paper surface without removing his eyes from the figure. The body, rendered in a few long trails of the artist's pencil, displays the altered proportions and distortions that result from the artist's sustained gaze at the model; his continuous, unitary, circumscribing line announces the presence of the artist's hand at each of its breaks and junctures. Jane Kallir has suggested a link between Kokoschka's technique and the unorthodox teaching practices of Alfred Roller at the Kunstgewerbeschule, where Kokoschka was enrolled between 1905 and 1908. Roller instructed his students to make quick action sketches of the human body in order to represent motion as an inherent quality of the model's body.[126] Kokoschka's memories of life drawing classes at the school were of more conventional uses of stationary models,[127] and he claimed to have invented the rapid, simplified drawing style in his own teaching.[128] In addition, the isolation of his figures on the page, his visualization of eroticism, and his imprecise filling-in of the pencil contours with watercolor wash, all point to a dialogue with Rodin's gestural drawings.[129] Between 1907 and 1910, Kokoschka also produced a series of simplified outline drawings of street urchins, acrobats, and studio models[130] using both the style and procedure of Rodin: the models assume unorthodox poses as though they have been rendered in mid-movement, uninstructed by the artist regarding pose and comportment. By using non-professional models and rendering them in such cursive fashion, Kokoschka achieved a freedom in his drawings that bears a strong relation to that of Rodin and Matisse.

RODIN AS MODEL

Perhaps both Kokoschka and Roller became aware of Rodin's drawings when they were exhibited at the IV Vienna Secession exhibition of 1899. As Elsen points out, Kokoschka probably saw the 1908 exhibition of 120 drawings and prints by Rodin at the Viennese gallery of Hugo Heller and Company, the exhibition for which Rainer Maria Rilke delivered a lecture on Rodin.[131] Rilke's lecture, which was later incorporated into a short monograph on the artist, suggested that Rodin's later drawings were the climax of his work: "These drawings of the last ten years are not, as so many take them to be, rapid jottings, preparatory and transitory studies; they contain a final statement of long, uninterrupted experience.... Never have drawings, even the rarest of Japanese drawings, possessed such a power of expression and at the same time been so innocent of purpose."[132] This presentation repeated the interpretations of the drawings already available in German-language publications[133] and posed the drawings, like all of Rodin's work, as the point at which the artist's memory and experience merge with his direct sense perceptions.

As Elsen and Alessandra Comini have noted, Rodin was considered a hero among members of the Vienna Secession at the turn of the century.[134] Included in the first exhibition of the Secession, Rodin was received as an artist whose work embodied the Secessionists' objectives.[135] His one-man exhibition at the Universal Exposition in Paris had commanded the attention of a number of the most important vanguard Austrian and German critics, among them Rilke, Georg Simmel, Stefan George, Stefan Zweig,[136] and, perhaps, the painter Gustav Klimt.[137] A strong admirer of Rodin's work, Klimt had been instrumental in including Rodin in the first Secession exhibition[138] and in introducing single-line gestural drawing as a central technique of Viennese modernism.

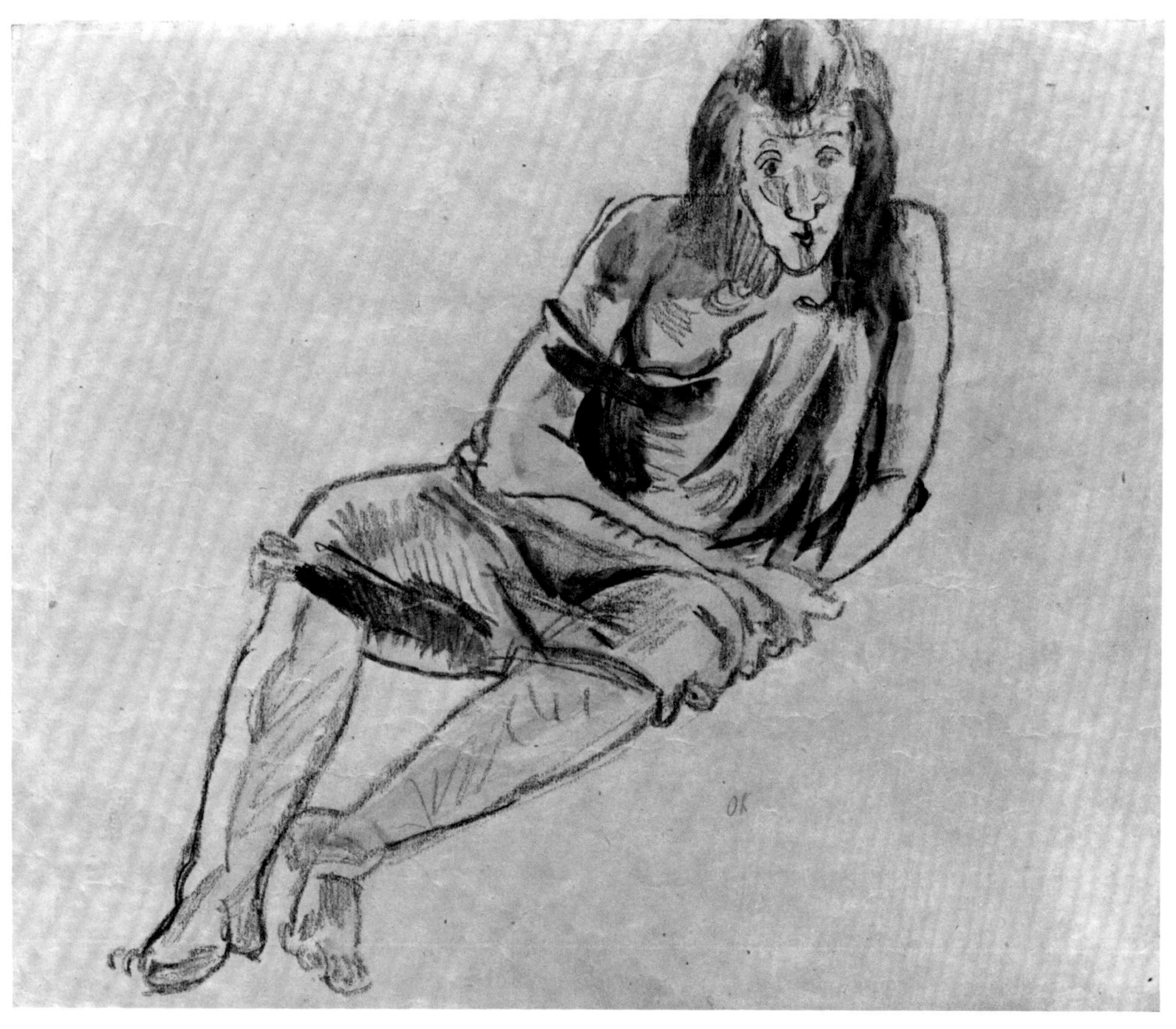

19 Oskar Kokoschka

SEATED WOMAN, 1912–13

Klimt's figure drawings recall Rodin's in their reliance on simplified, nominative line as the dual signifier of both silhouette and volume (cat. no. 14). Paralleling Rodin's procedure, Klimt often represented his models in awkward positions or at acute viewing angles (cat. no. 16) in order to capture a sense of their free movement and their vitality and to clarify the artist's physical relationship to the model. In his sheets of independent nude figure studies and in sketches related to his portraiture (cat. no. 13) Klimt used the rapidly drawn line to summarize volume, placement, and the artist's direct erotic engagement with the model. The drawings depicting overt sexual activity—renderings of his female models masturbating or displaying their vaginal areas—were, like Rodin's, popular with Viennese collectors of erotica.[139] Although many hundreds of Klimt's drawings are studies for his monumental commissions, the majority of post-1905 works are independent compositions that illustrate and manifest erotic possession through the use of a febrile line. Jane Kallir proposes that the public scandal surrounding Klimt's allegorical paintings intended for the University of Vienna was a turning point in his career, initiating his more private work.[140] His reception and emergence as an oppositional figure in Vienna was premised, in part, on the sexual content of these works. In fact, as Peter Vergo notes, erotic desire seems to have been at the heart of Klimt's production. As a way of characterizing his work, Klimt displaced his identity as an artist onto his subjects: "I am more interested in other people, above all, women."[141] This displacement is evoked symbolically through the deployment of his line as the delegate of his hand.

Klimt acted as a mentor to the young, emerging artists Oskar Kokoschka and Egon Schiele,[142] and clearly their own graphic work is indebted in theme and technique to his example.[143] In turn, Klimt felt that "the young follow their own path and will probably go far beyond me. That is as it should be, for no one taught me how or what to paint. Only one kind of teacher is any good, and that is the one who can liberate true genius... perhaps that is what I have been able to do for Kokoschka."[144] The assumption of gestural drawing as a generative activity, to use Yve-Alain Bois's phrase, corresponded to the moment when each artist expressed his most urgent desire to break away from academic training. In 1907 Kokoschka complained that "the Werkstätte are still handmaking the same old culture,"[145] and in the winter of 1907–1908 he wrote: "I can't stand it here any longer, it's all as ossified as if the screaming had never been heard." In a manifesto-like statement of 1909, Schiele proclaimed himself to be "a creator... entirely alone without recourse to anything in the past that has been handed down."[146]

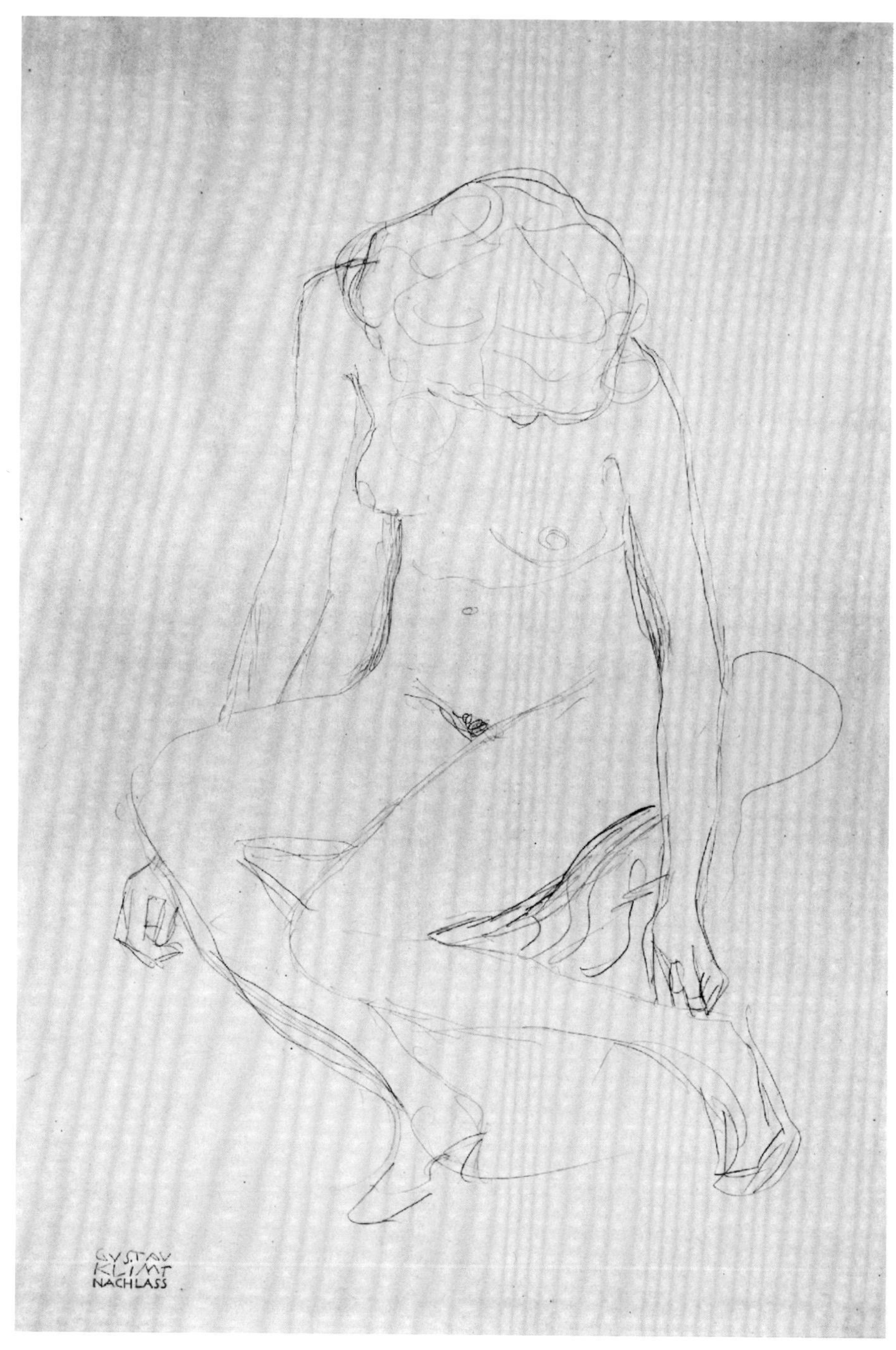

14 Gustav Klimt
SEATED NUDE, n.d.

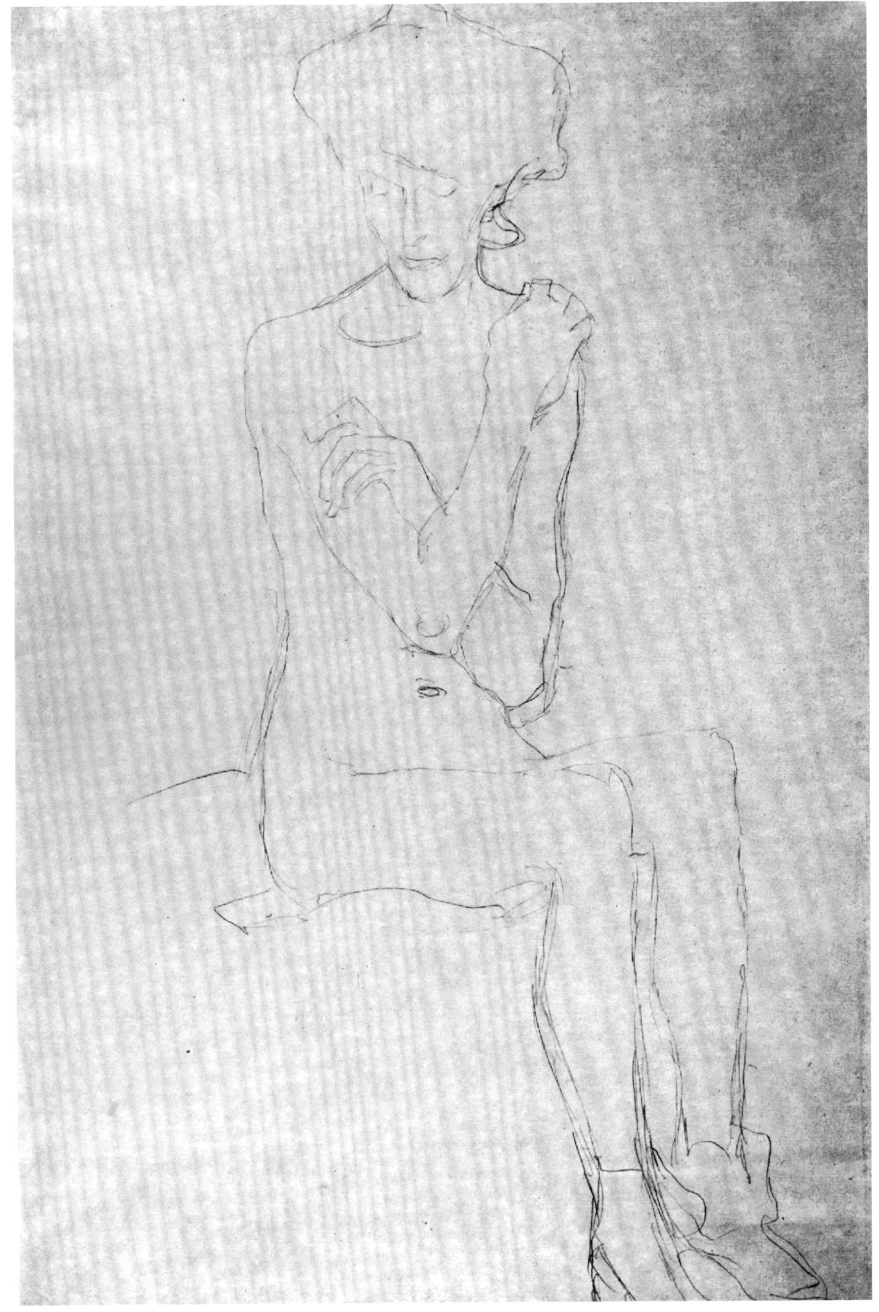

15 Gustav Klimt

SEATED NUDE WITH ARMS CROSSED, 1910–12

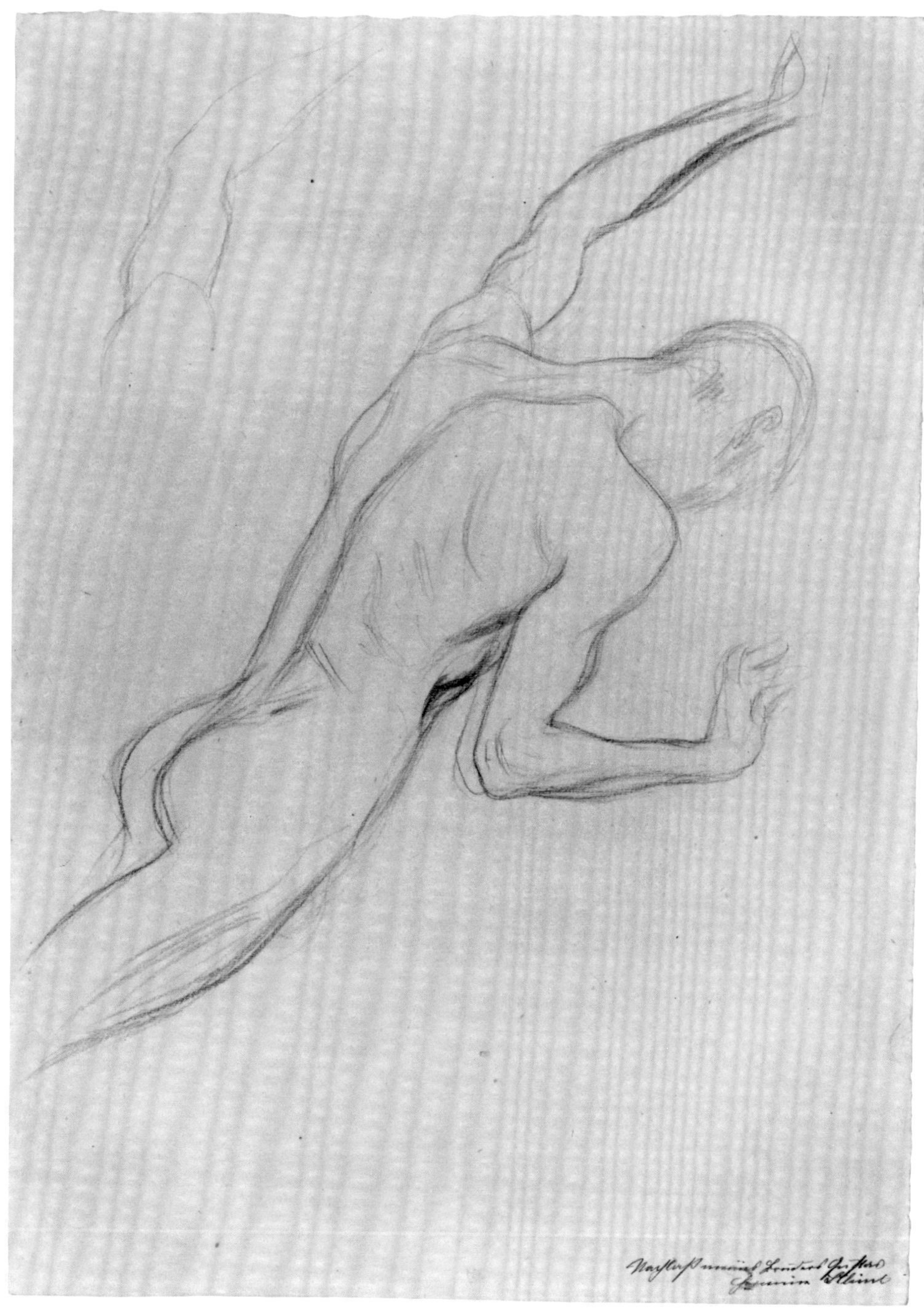

16 Gustav Klimt

STUDY OF A MALE FIGURE, n.d.

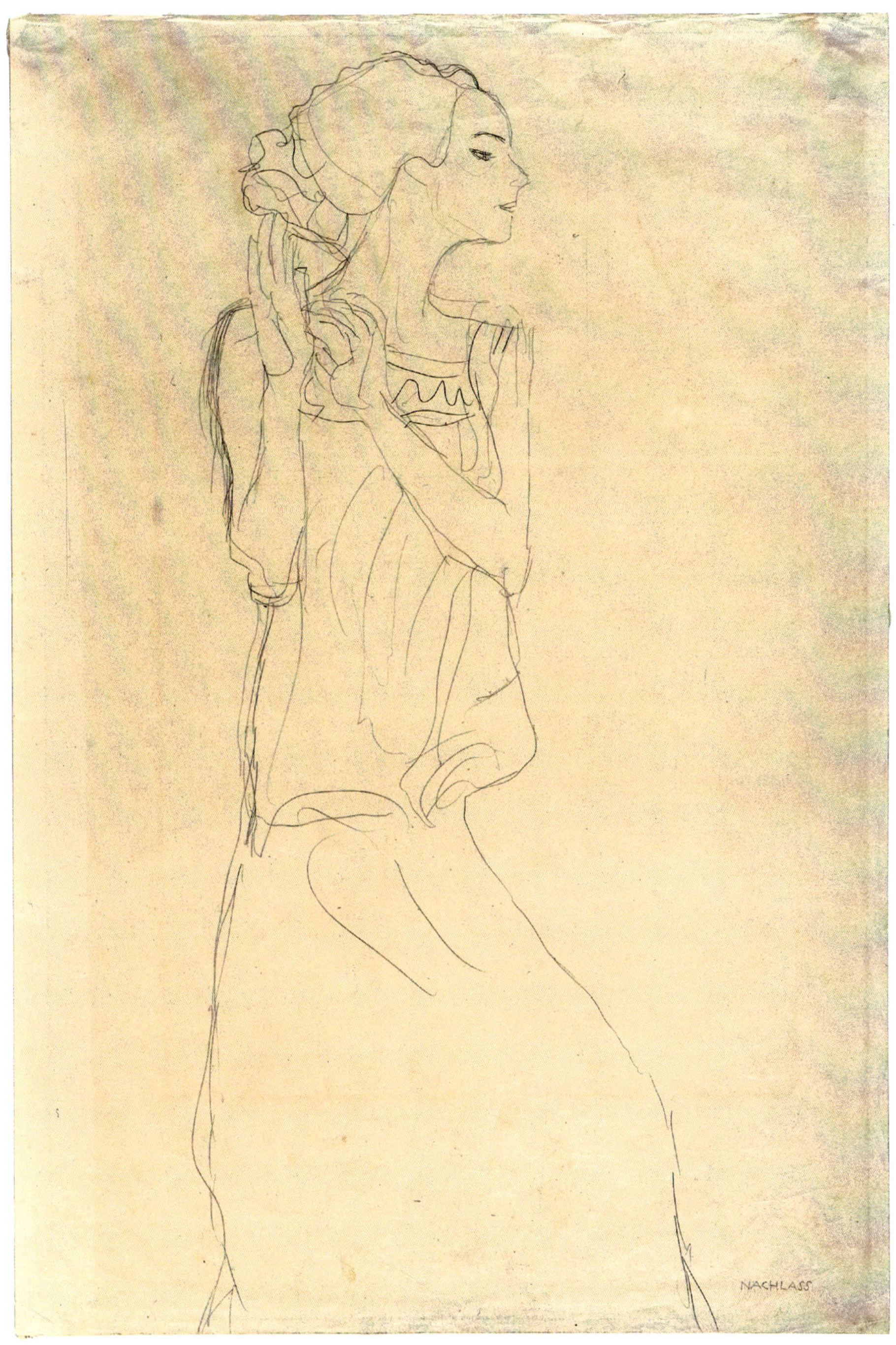

11 Gustav Klimt

STRIDING FIGURE WITH ARMS RAISED TO THE RIGHT, n.d.

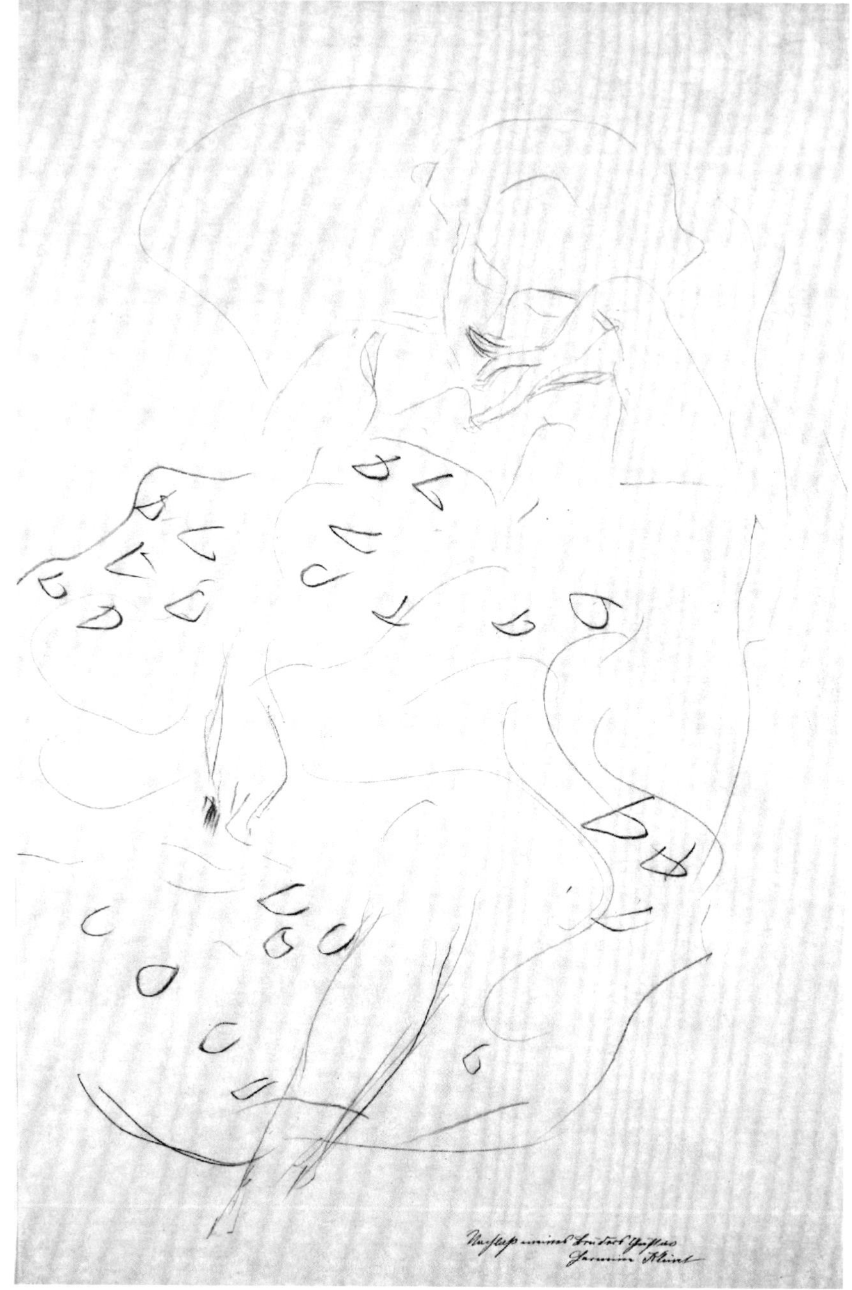

12 Gustav Klimt

GIRL SEATED IN A CHAIR, ca. 1904

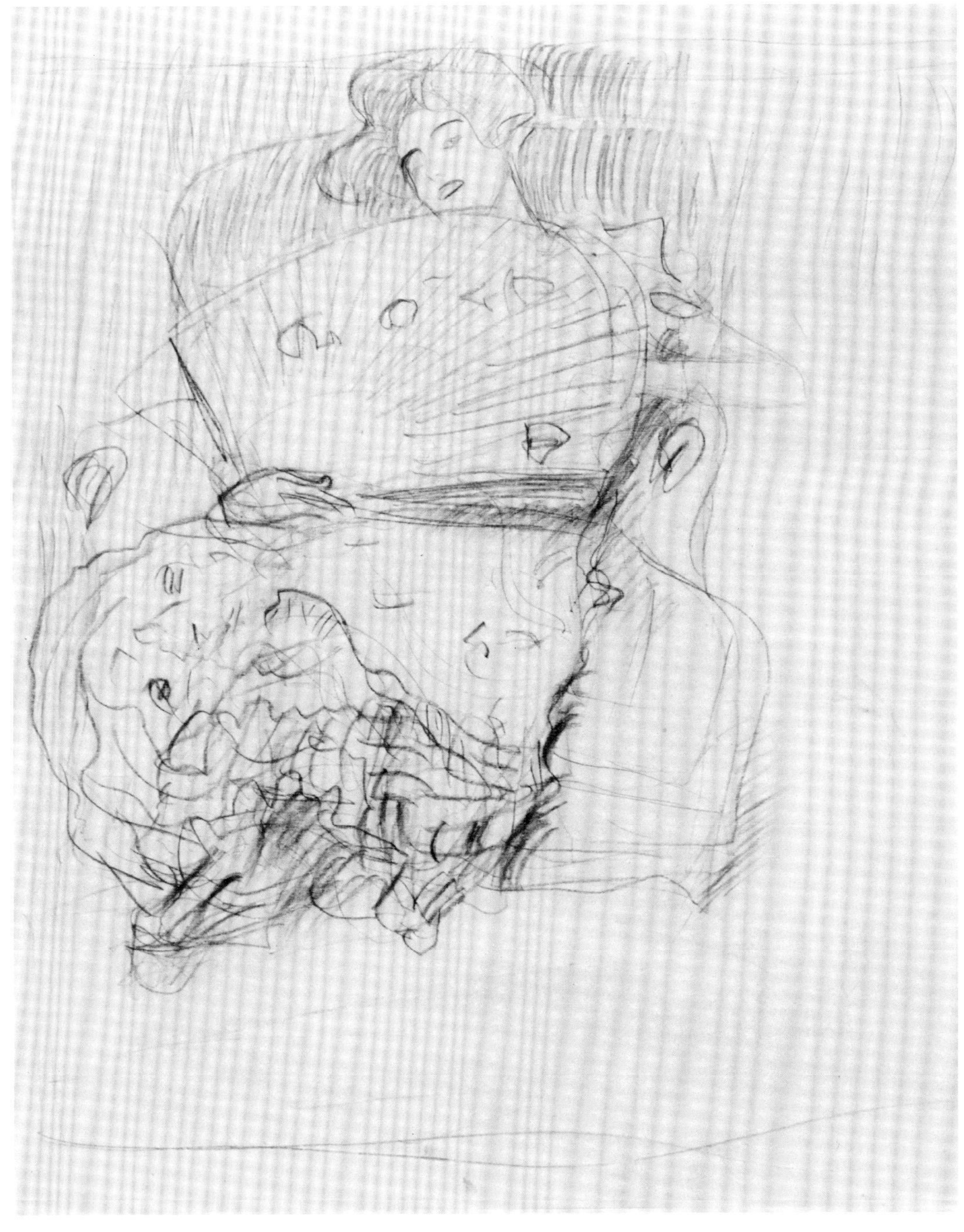

13 Gustav Klimt
LADY WITH A FAN, n.d.

REPRESENTATION OF THE SEXUAL SELF

In asserting their dissatisfaction with historical pedagogy, Schiele and Kokoschka were also reacting against the psychological distance that they were forced to maintain between themselves and their subjects. Enacting the process of absorption in what Wilhelm Worringer defined as empathy,[147] Schiele expressed "the craving to experience everything" in his work.[148] Such a desire for fusion and direct experience reiterates the impetus behind Rodin's and Matisse's gestural drawing.

Rodin defined his technique as a means of anchoring empathy in process through his direct visual engagement with the model:

I have, as it were, to incorporate *the lines of the human body, and they must become part of myself, deeply seated in my instincts. I must become permeated with the secrets of all its contours, all the masses that it presents to the eye. I must feel them at the end of my fingers. All this must flow naturally from my eye to my hand. The moment I stop my eyes that flow stops. That is why my drawings are only my way of testing myself. They are my way of proving to myself how far this incorporation of the subtle secrets of the human form has taken place within me.*[149]

Matisse repeated the notion, instructing his students to imagine depicting their model as if they inhabited his or her body: "Close your eyes and hold the vision, and then do the work with your own sensibility. If it be a model assume the pose of the model yourself; where the strain comes is the key of the movement."[150]

The notion of inhabiting the model through the gestural line inserts the artist into the drawing through empathic projection. Schiele, in particular, articulated his empathic projection onto his models through the overt sexuality expressed in his drawings. Schiele's technique, which reflects Rodin's process, is described by Otto Benesch:

Schiele drew quickly. The pencil skated over the white surface of the paper as though led by some ghostly hand . . . and he sometimes held the pencil in the manner of a painter from the Far East. He never used an eraser. If the model changed position, then new lines were placed beside the old with the same infallible certainty. Each sheet of paper followed the next without pause. . . . Inevitably a few drawings went wrong—there was always a heap of rubbish on the studio floor. . . . But the greatest masterpieces were produced as though in a game—from the most relaxed, nonchalant and, yes, even from the most uncomfortable position taken by the artist. But how Schiele's eyes bored into his model! How he perceived every nerve and muscle.[151]

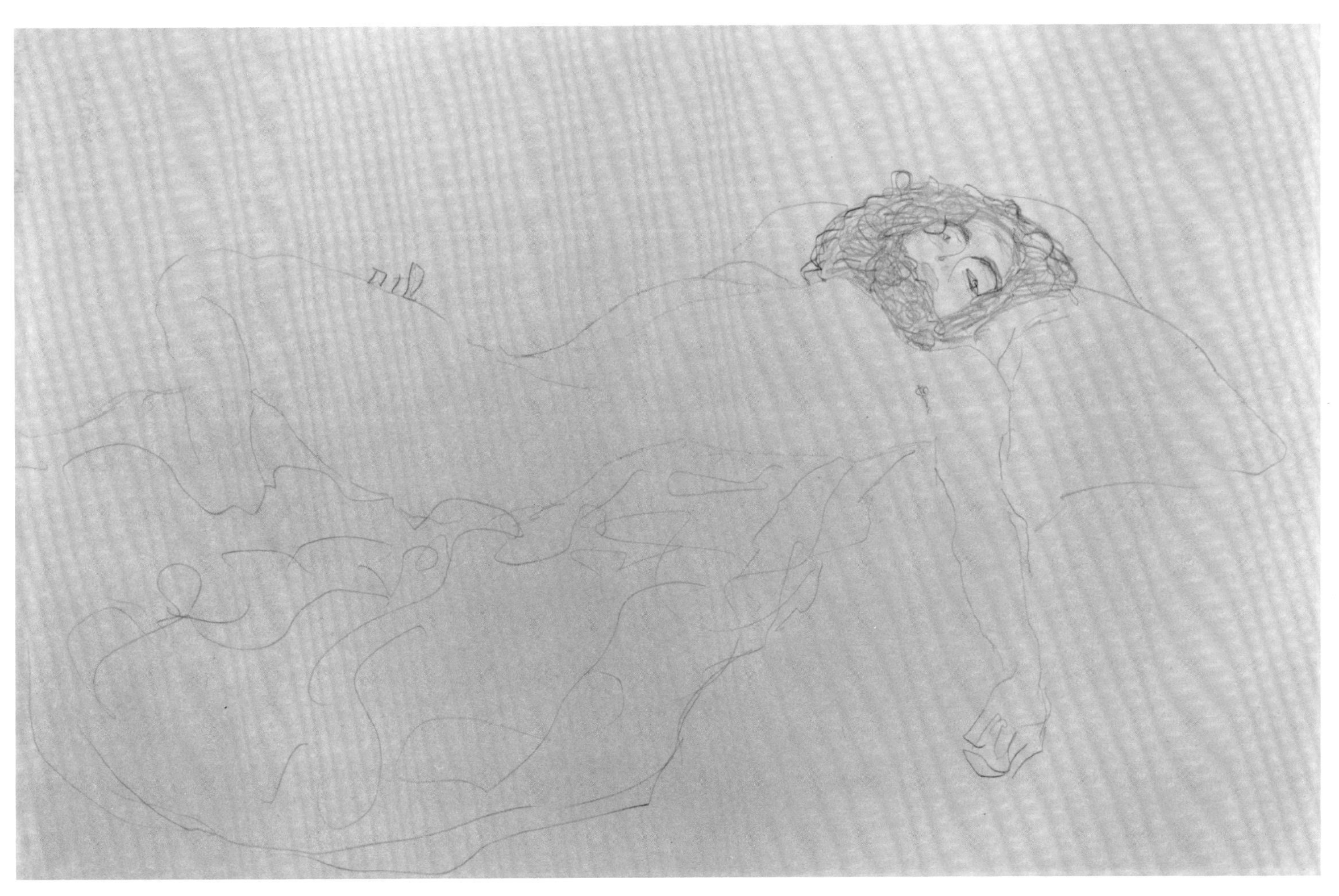

17 Gustav Klimt

RECLINING NUDE, n.d.

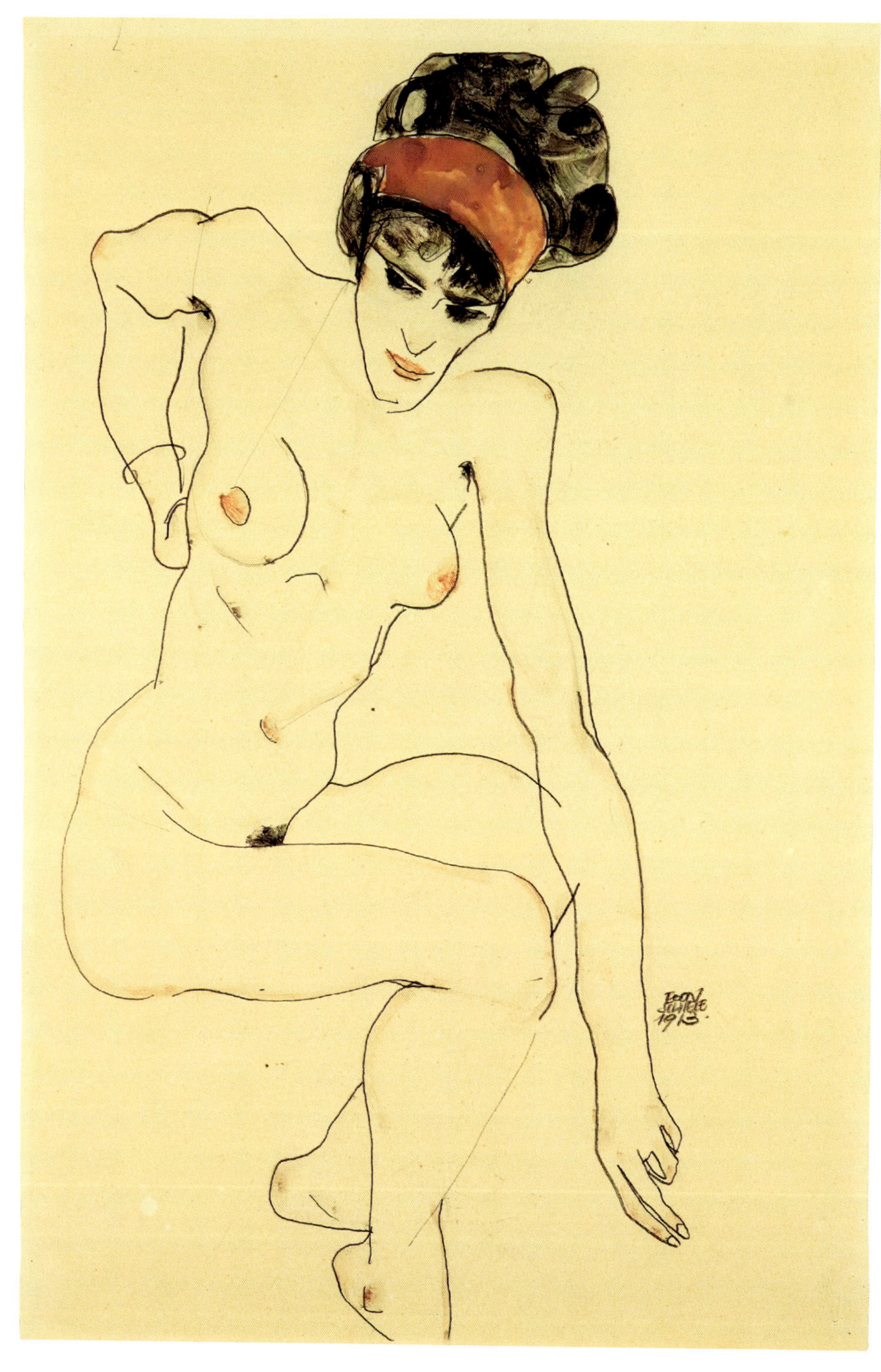

A 1910 drawing by Schiele, *The Artist and His Model* (fig. 12), illustrates his practices and provides a paradigm for the approach to gestural drawing as it emerged throughout Europe around 1910: the male artist, dressed and seated, is reflected in a mirror that also discloses the body of his partially nude female model viewed from both front and back, near and far. The model is represented in an act of self-scrutiny, her exaggerated and elongated *contrapposto* pose the focus of her own gaze; the position is assumed both for herself and for Schiele. The artist's gaze is likewise directed at the model and his lips are pursed in concentration as he reproduces the contours of her body on his drawing pad without removing his eyes from them. However, his gaze seems subtly bifurcated, one eye registering his own reflection, and the other, the mirrored body of his model. Such a suggestion of dual self-absorption and outward perception, of the inscription of the self onto the body of another, manifests the gendered and sexualized identity of Schiele's gestural technique and illustrates the process of empathy through visuality.

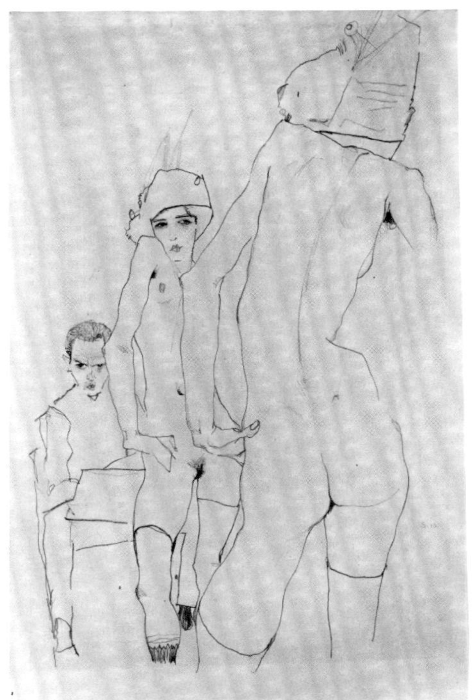

figure 12
Egon Schiele, *The Artist and His Model*, 1910, pencil on paper. Graphische Sammlung Albertina, Vienna.

48 Egon Schiele

SEATED NUDE WITH ORANGE HEADBAND, 1913

In 1910, the year in which the drawing was produced, Schiele adopted the wiry, responsive lines that came to characterize his work. In SEATED NUDE (cat. no. 43) the seismographic rendering, skewed perspective, and suggestion of intimate visual engagement with the model's flesh reveal an affinity with, if not a direct interest in, Rodin's drawings. In that year, in fact, Schiele expressed a desire to have Rodin included in the International Kunstschau in the Künstlerhaus in Vienna.[152] The delicate and almost nervous linearity of the works from 1910–1915 repeats the texture of Klimt's looser single-line compositions (cat. nos. 44 and 45). The distortions and abrupt repositionings of the pencil, alternating with meticulously observed variations in surface texture (cat. no. 46) are allied with Rodin's and Kokoschka's single-line works. In his final years, Schiele made his lines heavier and represented his models with more solidity (cat. no. 49). Like Rodin's drawings, many of these works were intended to be filled in later with paint. Like Rodin and Kokoschka, Schiele created a studio environment in which he worked with non-professional models whom he encouraged to move freely. Paris von Gütersloh described the milieu in which Schiele hired proletarian Viennese children as his models:

There were always two or three small or large girls sitting about in his studio, brought there from the immediate neighborhood, from off the street or picked up in the Schönbrunn park that was nearby. They were ugly and pretty, washed and unwashed, and they did nothing—at least to the layman they might have seemed to do nothing.... They slept, recovered from beatings administered by parents, lazily lounged about... like animals in a cage which suits them, they were left to their own devices, or at any rate believed themselves to be.... With the aid of a little money and much charm [Schiele] had managed to lull these little beasts into a false sense of security.... They feared nothing from the sheet of paper which lay by Schiele on the divan.[153]

43 Egon Schiele
SEATED NUDE, ca. 1910

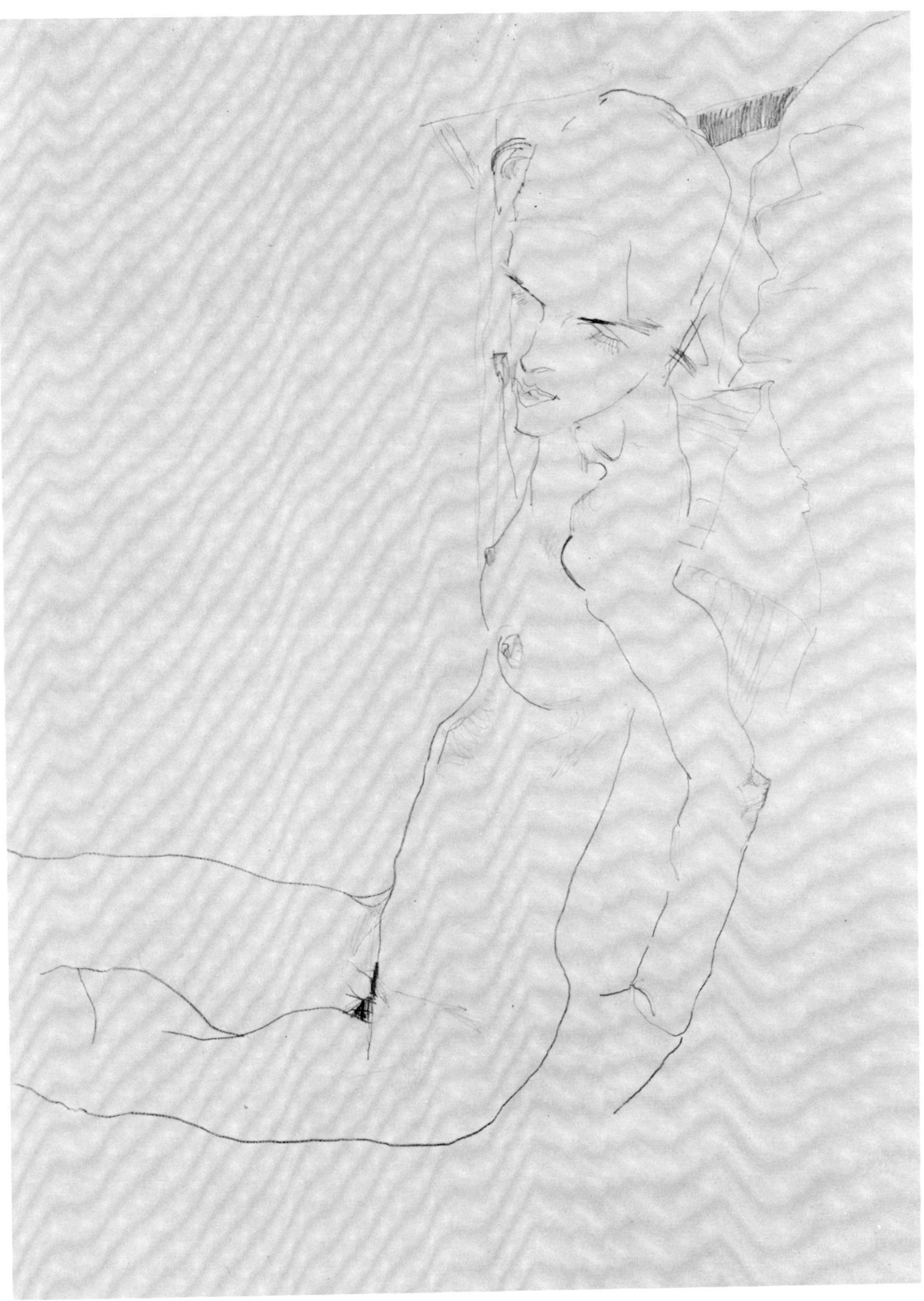

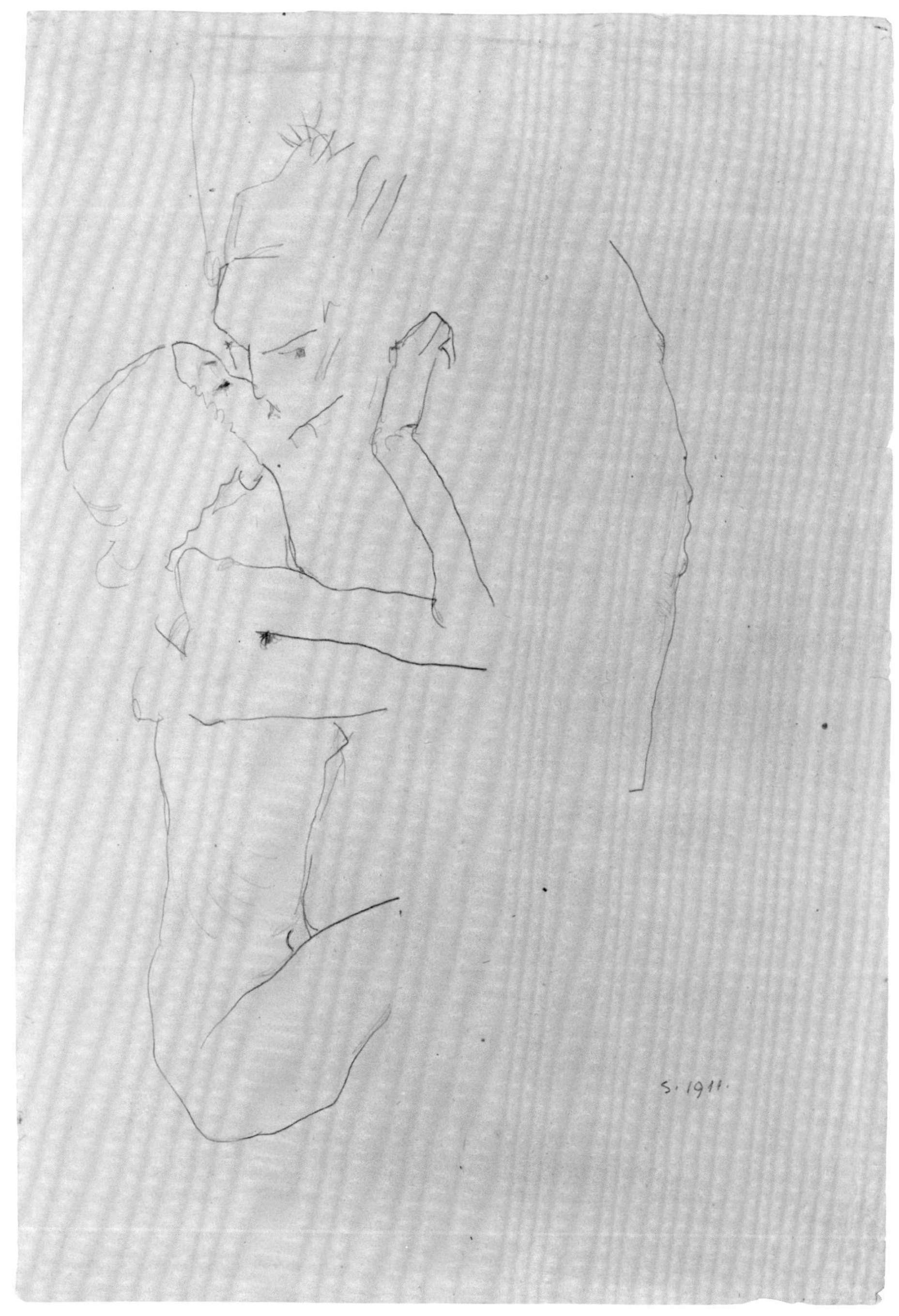

44 Egon Schiele

THE KISS, 1911

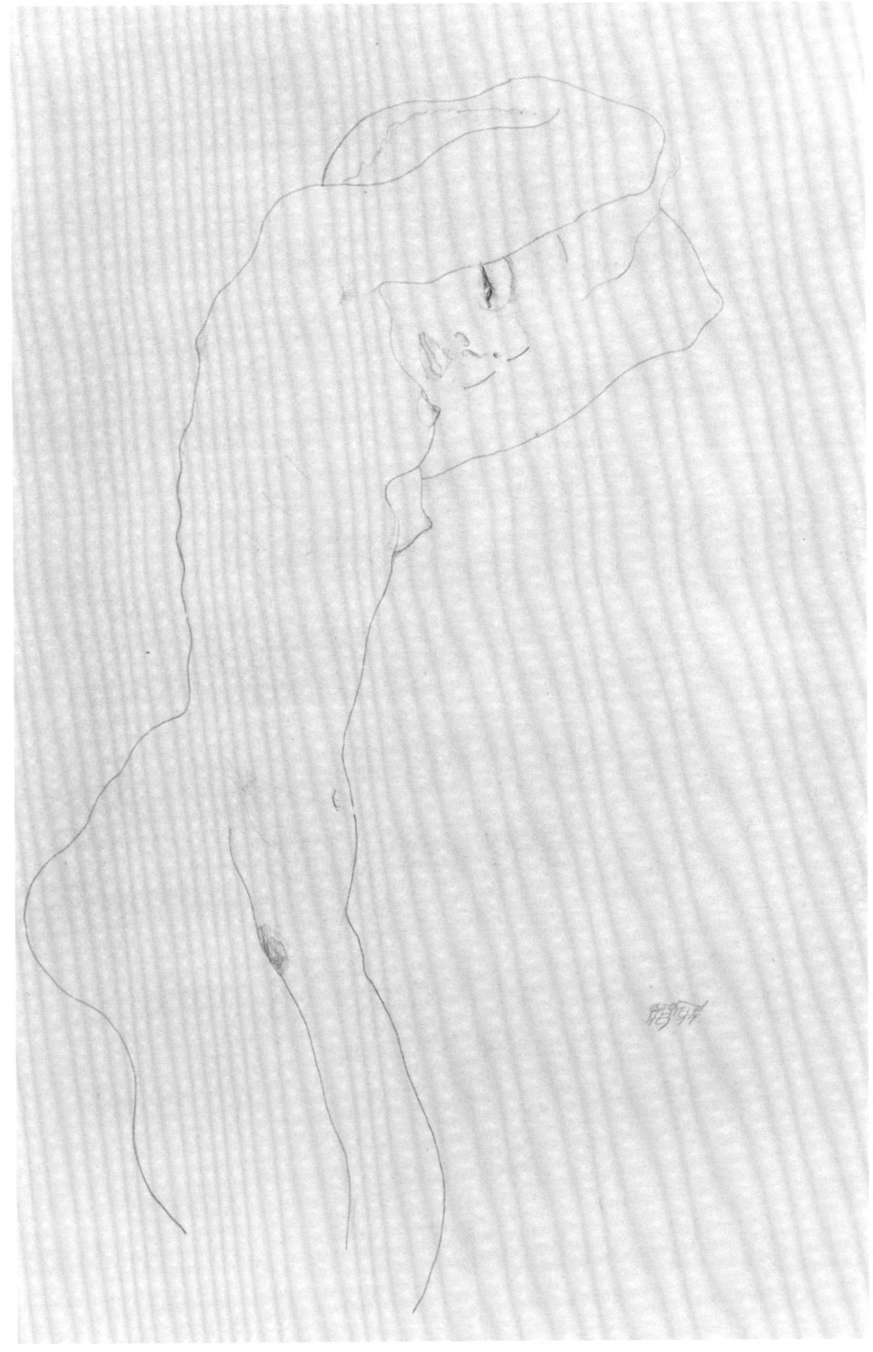

45 Egon Schiele

FEMALE NUDE WITH HANDS CLASPED BEHIND HEAD, 1911

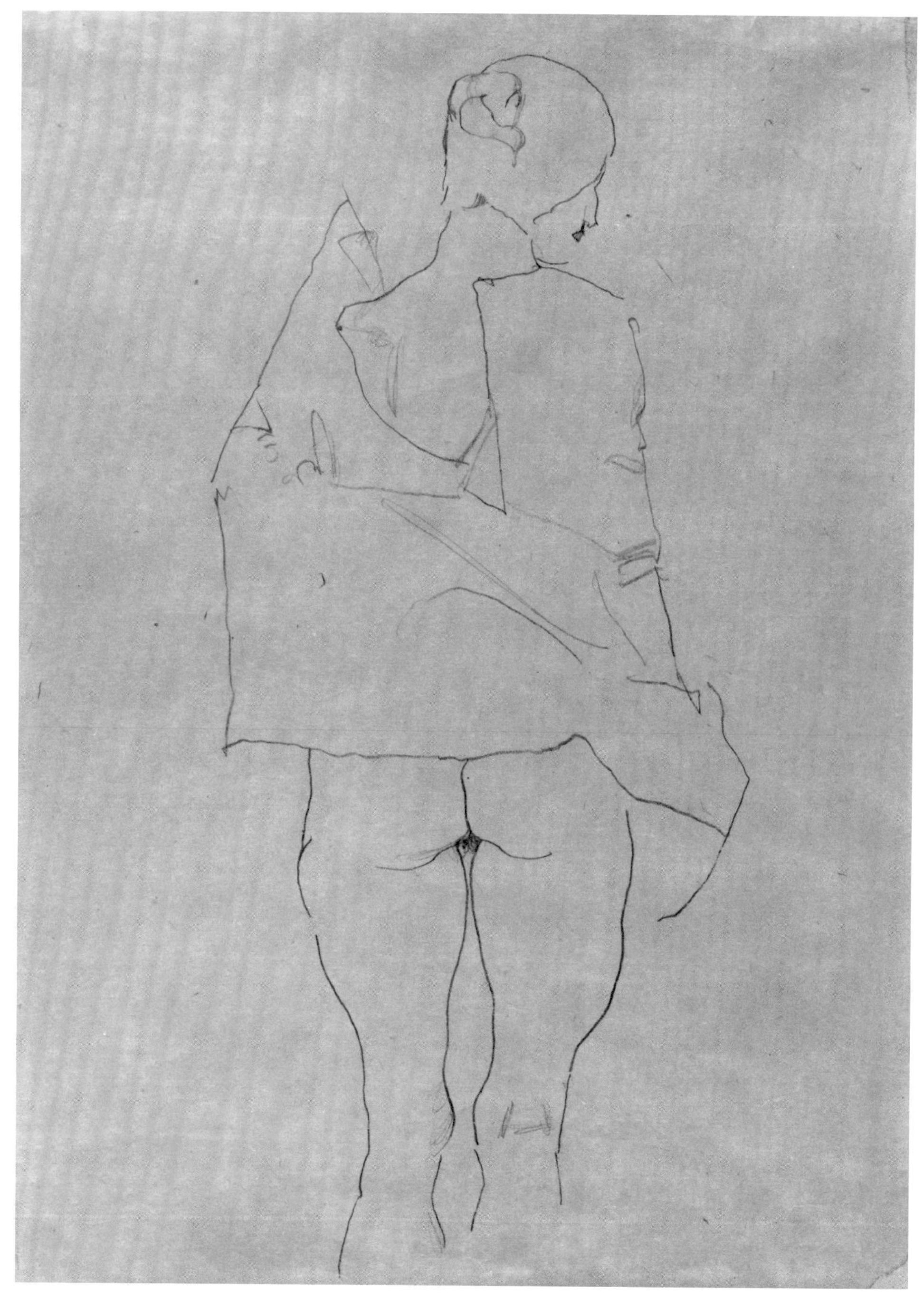

46 Egon Schiele
STANDING SEMI-NUDE FROM THE BACK, 1912

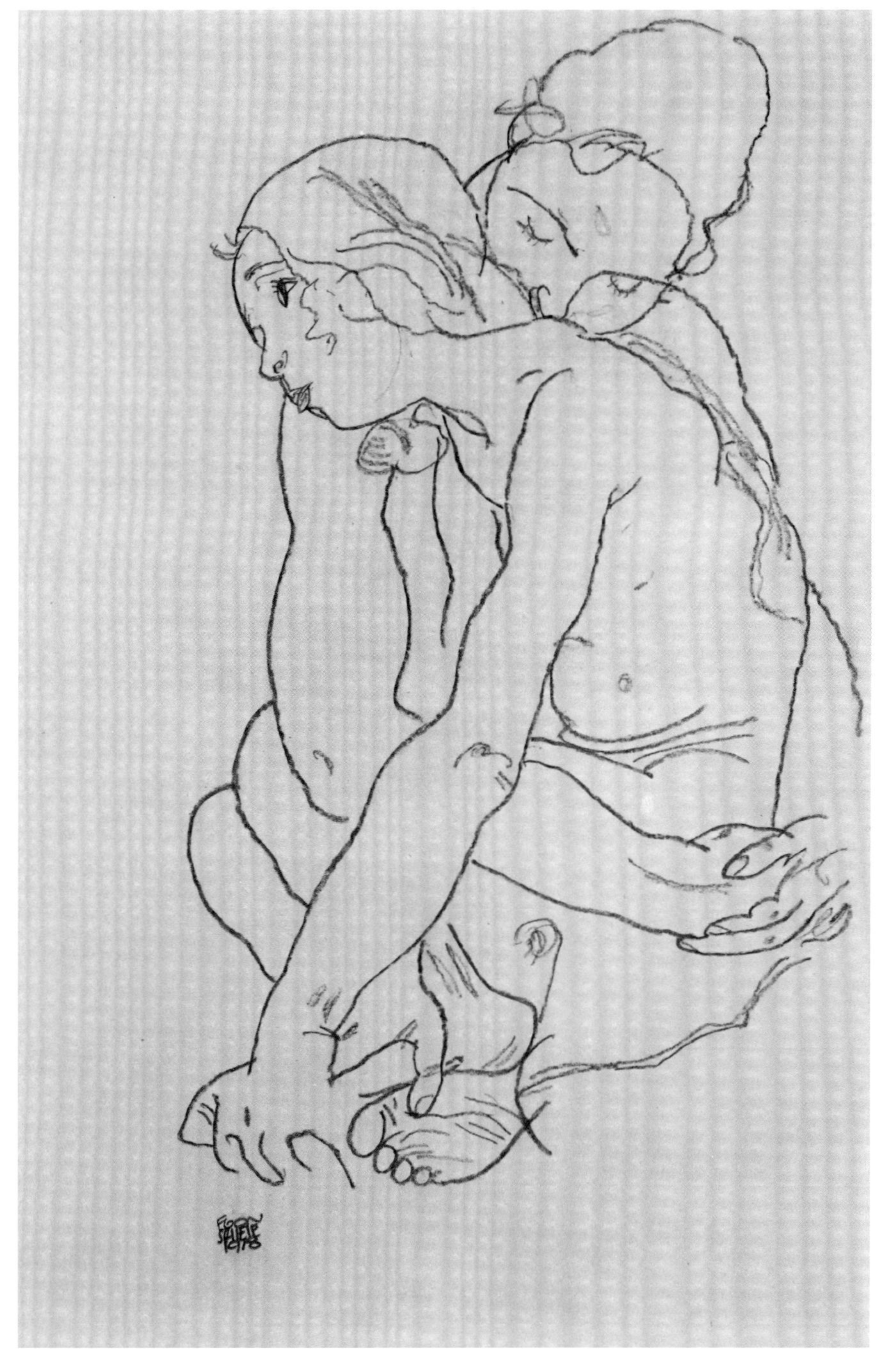

47 Egon Schiele

WOMAN AND GIRL EMBRACING, 1918

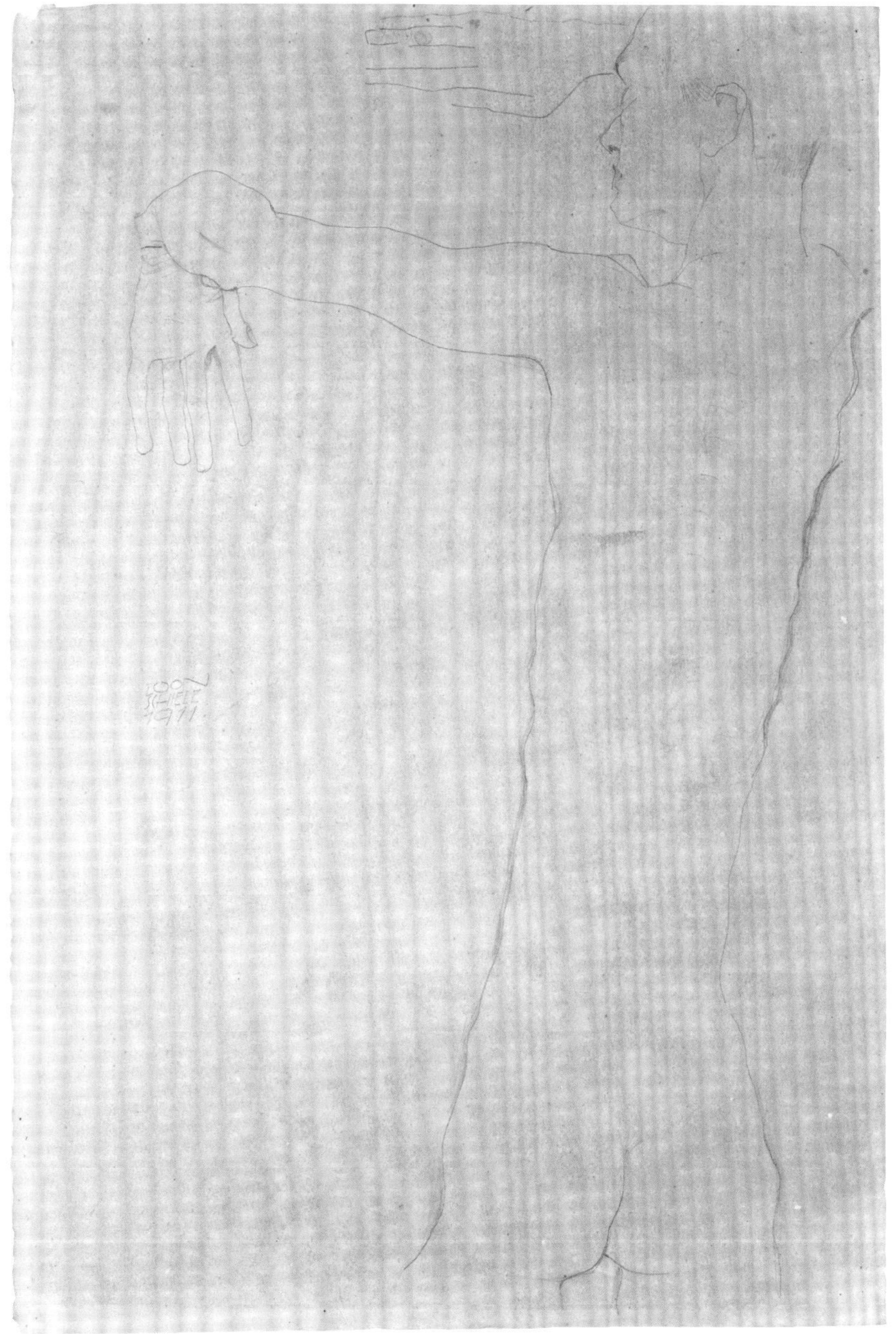

figure 13

Egon Schiele, *Nude Man with Raised Arms*, 1911, pencil on paper, 18 15⁄16 x 12 9⁄16".
The Cleveland Museum of Art. Gift of Severance and Greta Millikin, 59.304.

When Schiele moved to the rural town of Neulungbach in 1911, this studio practice and the rumor that he had had physical relations with a minor led to the artist's incarceration, his trial for indecency, and the burning of one of his drawings.[154] The themes of voyeurism and domination provided by Gütersloh's description, articulated in the drawings, and embedded in Schiele's reputation after his arrest, converge with these issues in Rodin's and Klimt's works to confirm the erotic identity of the artists' gestural drawing. However, unlike the other artists who pioneered the gestural line in the early twentieth century, Schiele applied this technique to numerous self-representations in the nude (figs. 13 and 14). These self-portraits express erotic convergence and sexual candor far more directly than Rodin's or Klimt's works. By cataloguing and extracting the gestures and movements of his own distorted and attenuated body, Schiele reinscribes the erotic activity of gestural drawing onto himself, at once spectator and spectacle, the viewer and the viewed. Reducing his own body to the most weightless kind of linear notation, Schiele replaces other, surrogate, models, and negotiates empathy through the direct confrontation with erotic desire as he both embodied and experienced it.

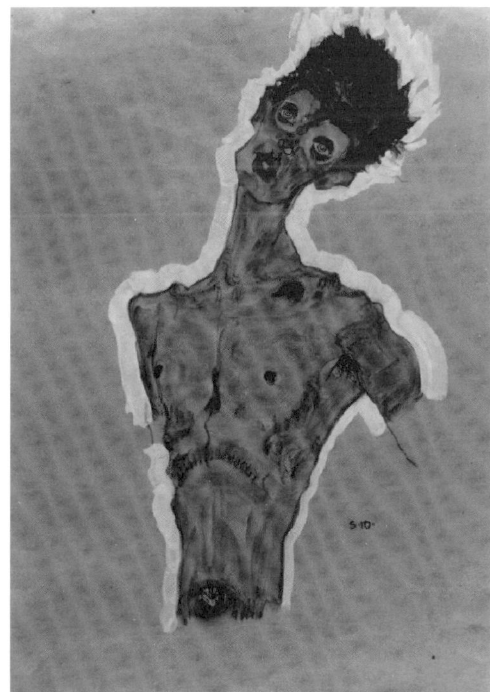

figure 14
Egon Schiele, *Self-Portrait with Head Bent to Right*, 1910, crayon, gouache, and watercolor on paper, 17 13/16 x 12 9/16". Indiana University Art Museum.

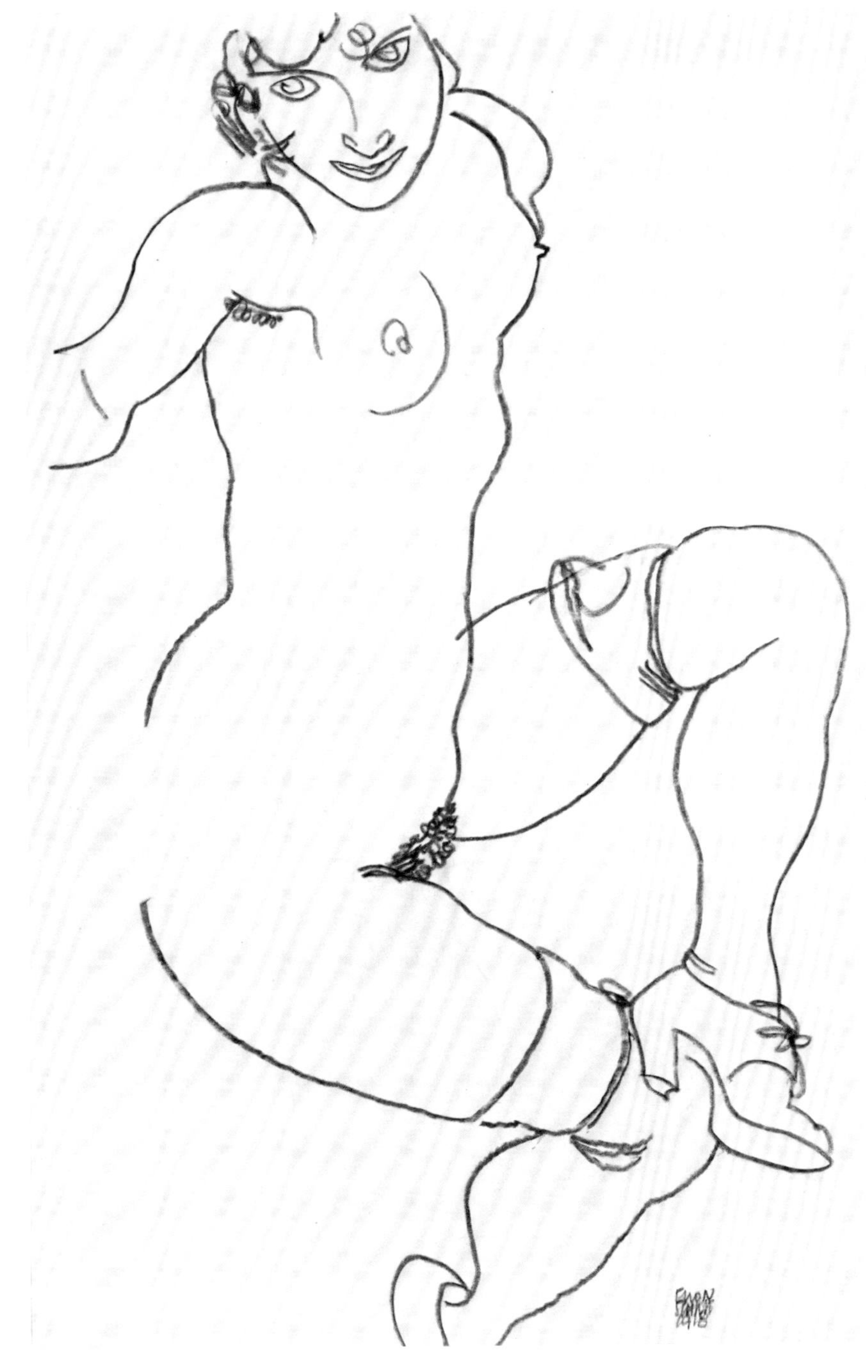

49 Egon Schiele

SEATED NUDE IN SHOES AND STOCKINGS, 1918

As it did in Austria, gestural drawing offered the German avant-garde a process of direct engagement with the physical world. Just prior to 1910, German artists pioneered gestural drawing as a vehicle to record and manifest their responses to the vital forces of nature. For the artists of *Die Brücke*, rapid sketching from life was a fundamental activity informing their work in other media.[155] Their direct, spontaneous recording of nature as both erotic and spiritual activity is at the very root of Expressionism.

The reception of Rodin's gestural drawings in Germany paralleled the early years of *Die Brücke*'s collective activity. Rodin's German reputation was in part enhanced by the overt eroticism of his subjects and technique. In 1904, Rodin exhibited hundreds of his drawings in Dresden, Berlin, Leipzig, and Düsseldorf.[156] In the following year, Harry Graf Kessler, the director of the Ducal Collection at Weimar, helped to arrange the donation of fifteen of Rodin's drawings to that collection.[157] In 1906, Kessler was forced to leave his position when the exhibition of Rodin's drawings drew hostile criticism for their perceived immorality and offensiveness.[158] Rodin's sexualized style and subject matter were also acknowledged in the other cities,[159] but the high critical regard for Rodin's drawings by Rilke, Meier-Graefe, and Georg Simmel suggested that the eroticism of the drawings was a positive expression of a modern genius.

Ernst Ludwig Kirchner began to use freely drawn gestural lines in his work in 1908. The technique seemed to fulfill his own desire for direct, spontaneous, and emotionally honest work. As has been widely noted, Kirchner's confrontation with Matisse's works at Paul Cassirer's gallery in Berlin occasioned a transformation in his approach,[160] just as contact with advanced French art had helped to redirect Max Pechstein's work that same year.[161] In Kirchner's charcoal rendering of a figure reclining on a studio couch (cat. no. 4), the continuous, meandering line that breaks self-consciously across the shoulder and in the back of the left knee marks the beginning of Kirchner's assimilation and transformation of Matisse's 1906 works. The cropped feet, misshapen swelling limbs, the body thrown into an awkward perspective, and the meandering lines of the bedclothes, all reflect Matisse's effects. However, Kirchner has drawn a shadow thrown by the left side of the model's body in an awkward attempt to buttress the figure's corporeal presence. The disjunction between this attempted illusion of three-dimensional space with a single light source and the condensed lines with which Kirchner defined the rest of the composition only calls attention to the reductive quality of the gestural contour lines.

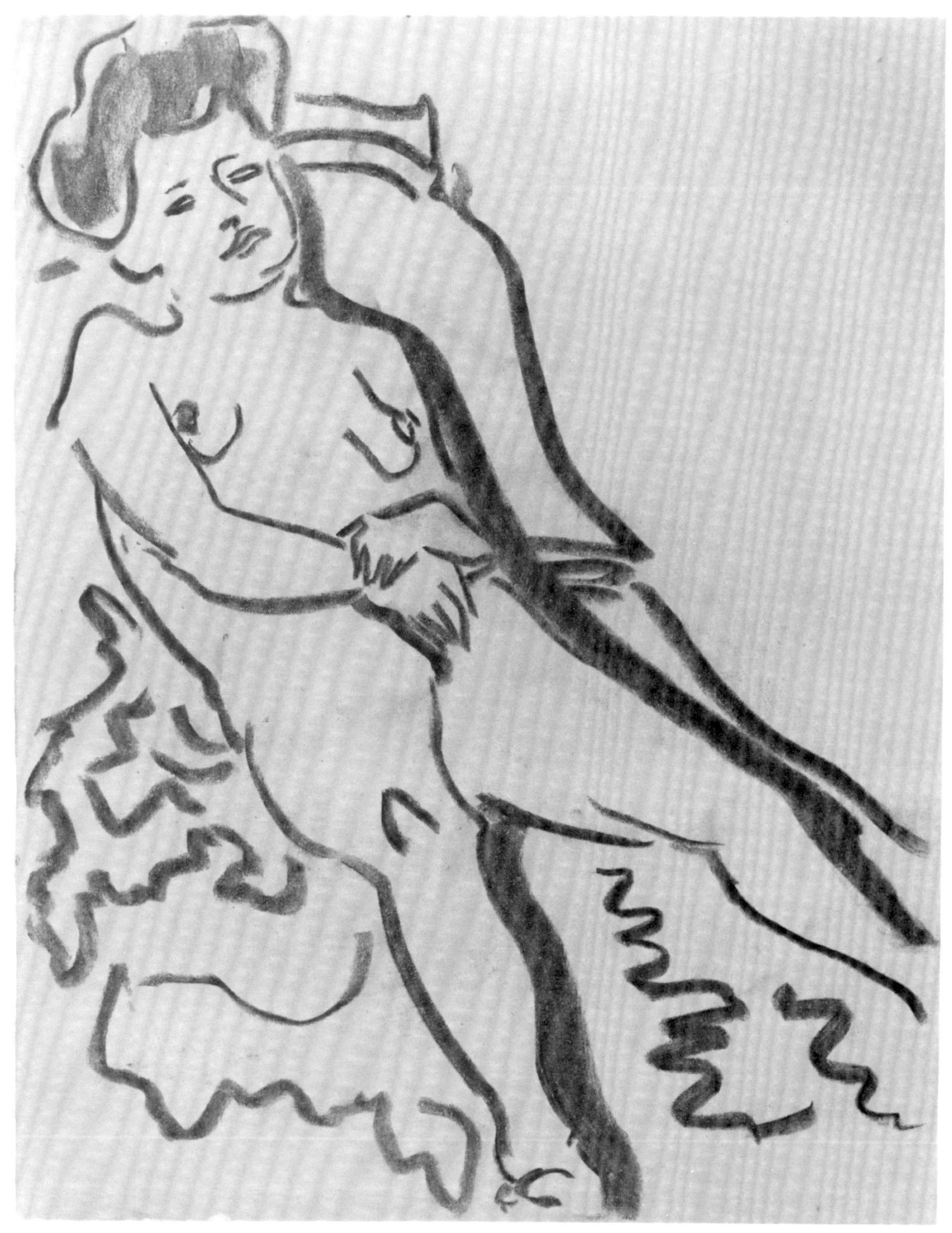

4 Ernst Ludwig Kirchner
MODEL ON A DIVAN, ca. 1908

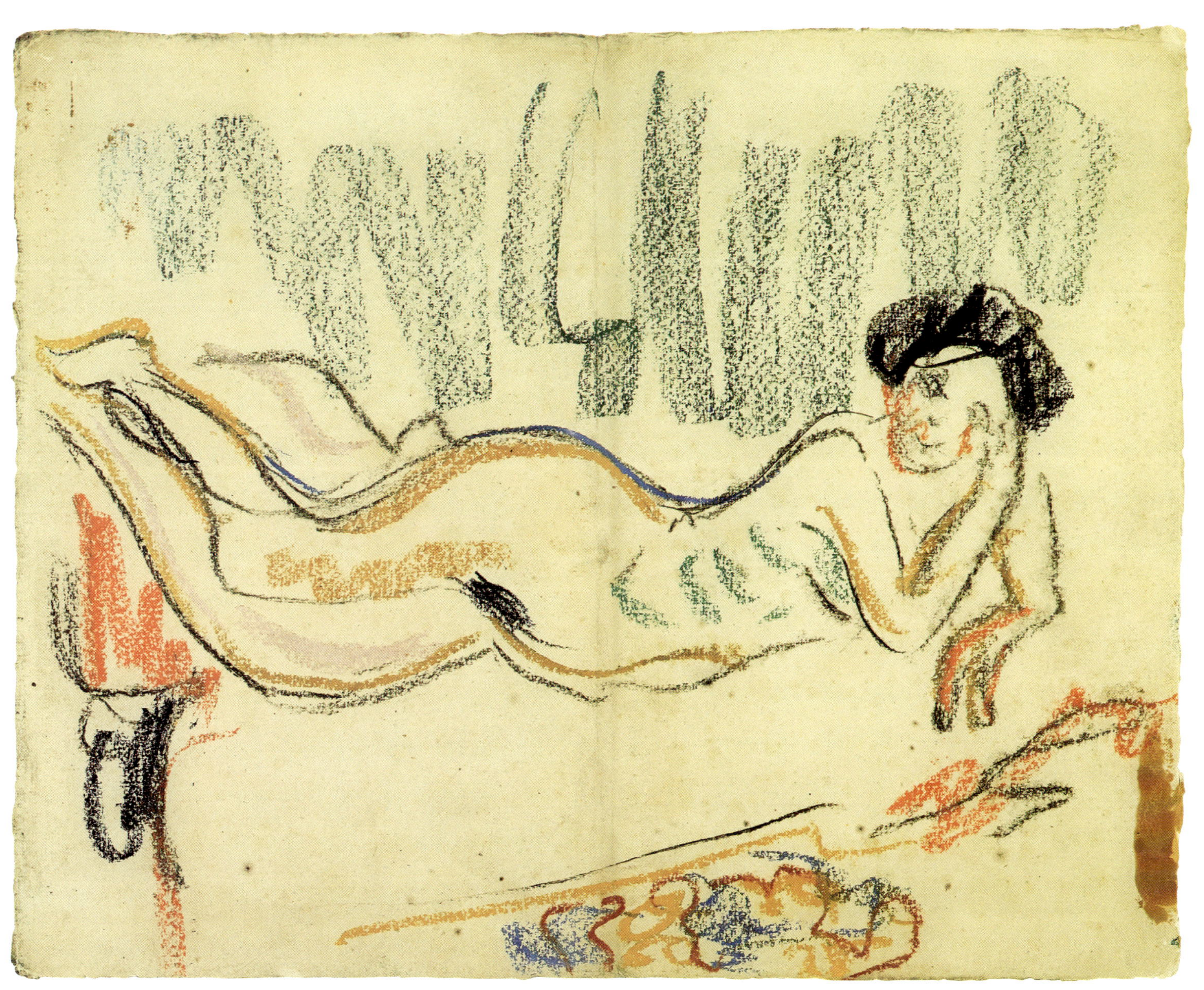

7 Ernst Ludwig Kirchner
RECLINING NUDE (DODO), 1908

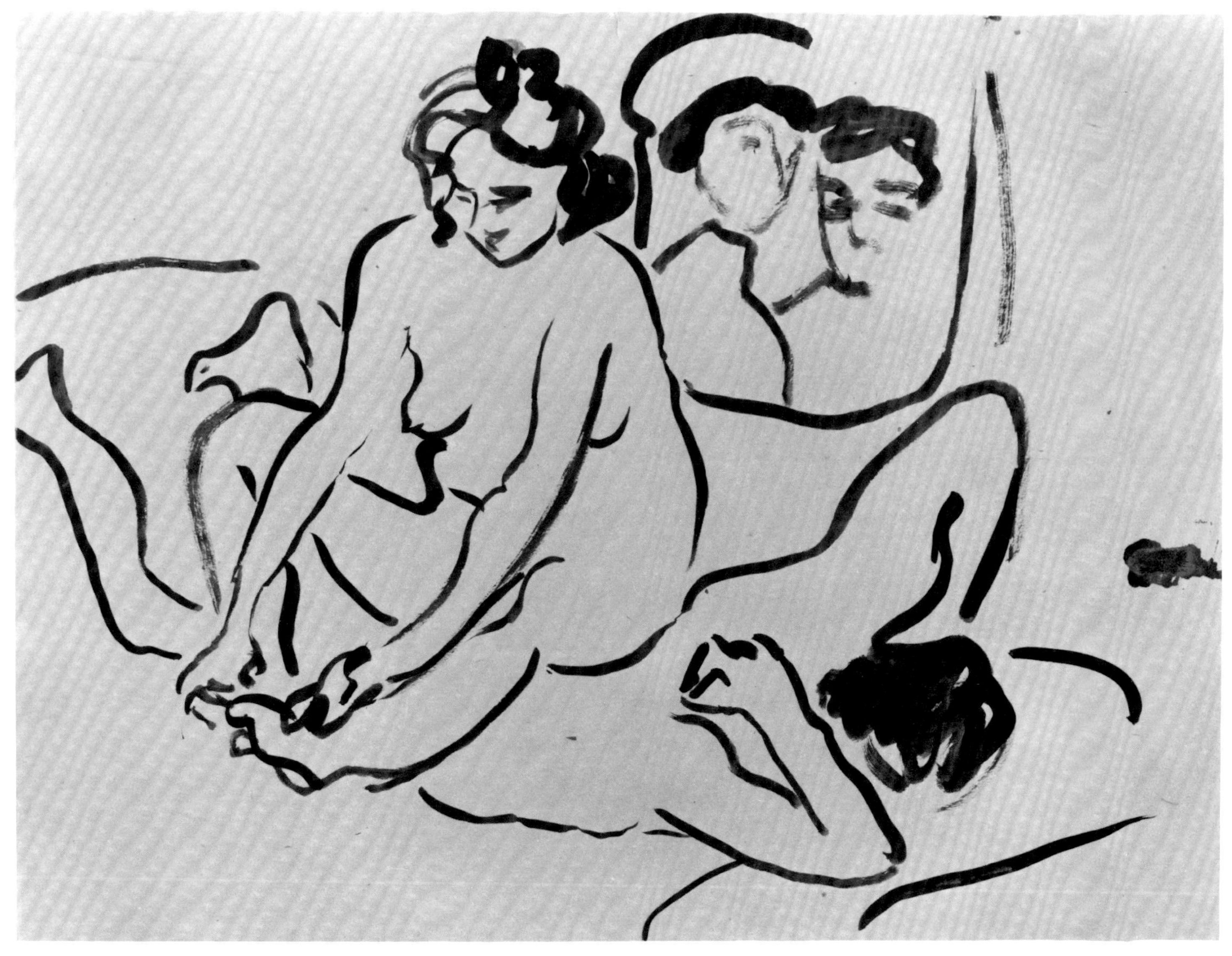

6 Ernst Ludwig Kirchner

NUDES ON A DIVAN, ca. 1908

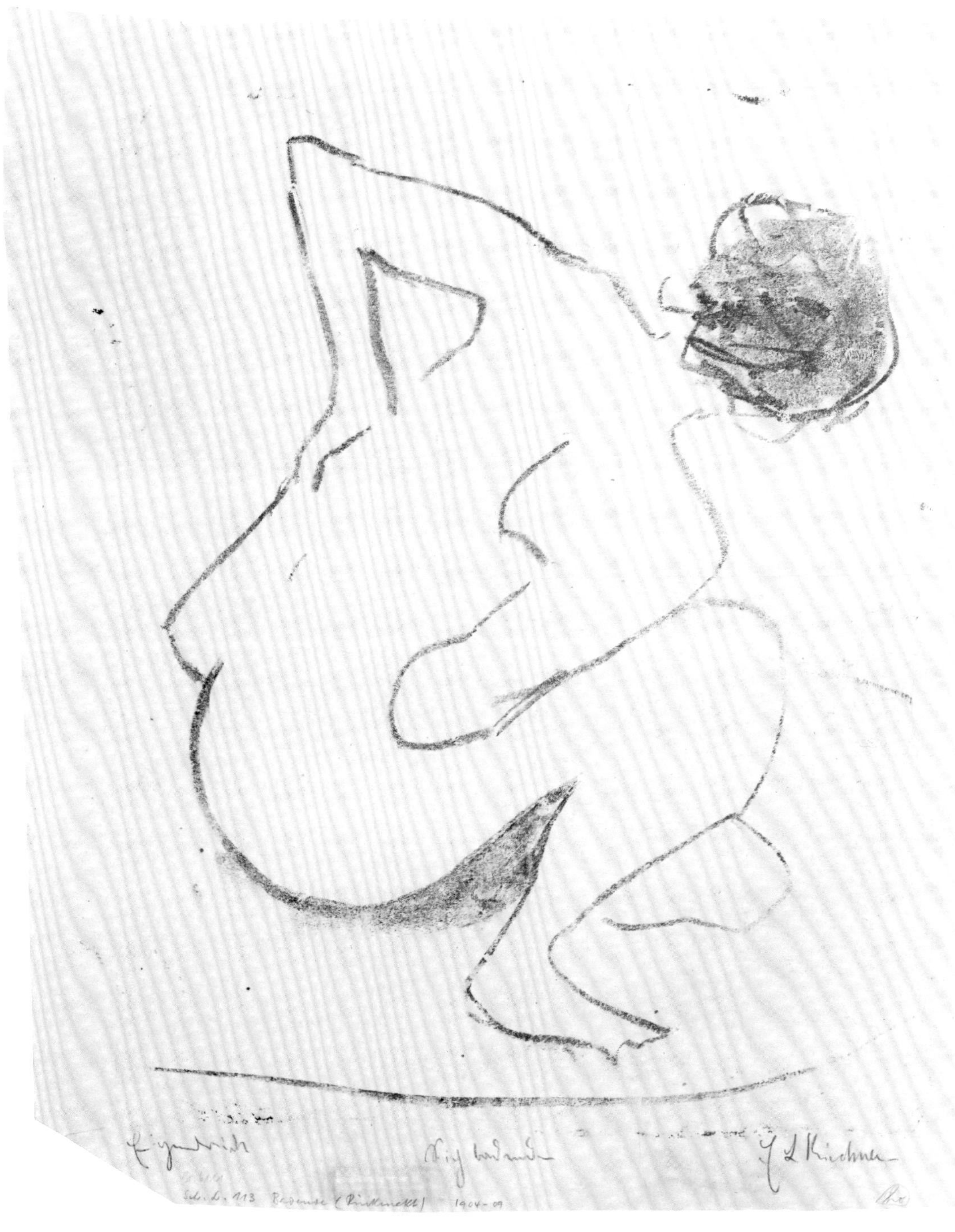

8 Ernst Ludwig Kirchner
WOMAN BATHING, 1909

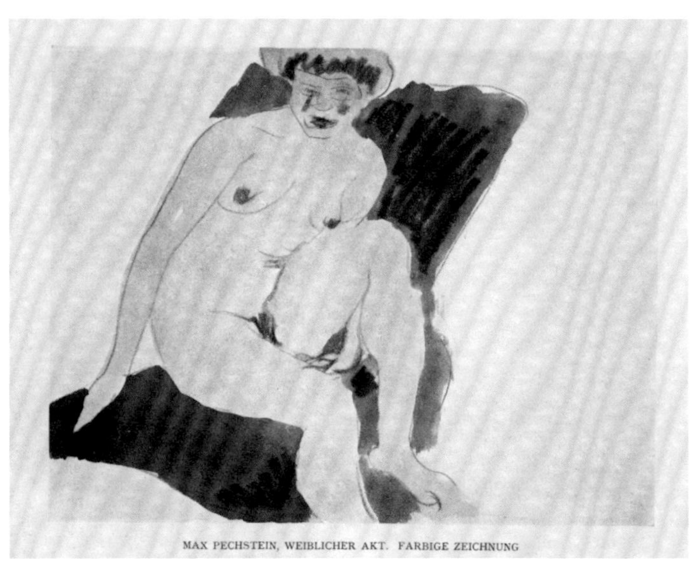

figure 15
Max Pechstein, *Female Nude*, from *Kunst und Künstler* XXII, 1924: 76.
By permission of Harvard College Library, Cambridge.

In 1908, Pechstein had become the first member of *Die Brücke* to explore freely drawn line: that spring, he traveled to Paris to exhibit his work in the Salon des Indépendants. There, he recalled, he "visited all the art exhibitions" and "began to change style, to fight Impressionism." Returning to Berlin in the summer, he recounted having "sketches, drawings, and designs flowing out of [his] hands."[162] Henri Matisse's student, Hans Purrmann, seems to have served as an intermediary between Pechstein and members of the Fauve circle.[163] A watercolor drawing from 1909 (fig. 15) confirms the impact of both Matisse's and Rodin's figural styles on Pechstein through their continuous contour lines, compressed and distorted anatomical proportions, and awkward and sexually expressive poses.[164]

figure 16
Max Pechstein, *Nude*, 1909, watercolor on brown paper, 13 1/4 x 17 1/4". National Gallery of Art, Washington, D.C. Rosenwald Collection.

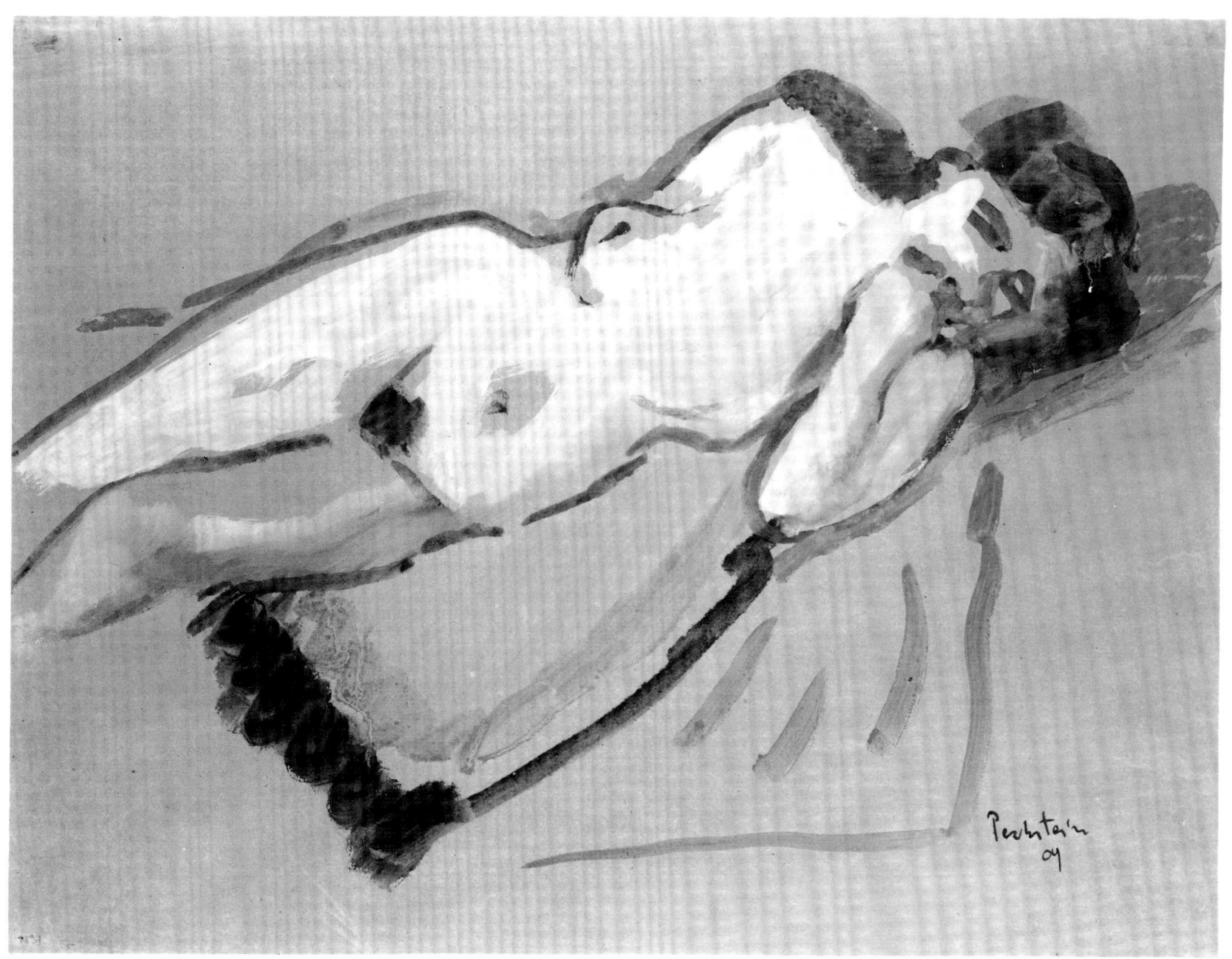
Pechstein
09

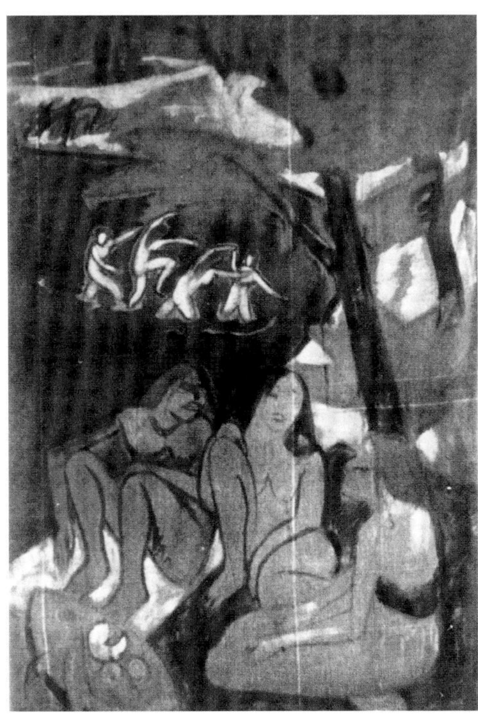

figure 17
Max Pechstein, *At the Seashore*, 1910/1911,
textile inks on muslin, 102 x 80". Staatliche Museum zu Berlin,
Preussischer Kulturbesitz, Nationalgalerie.

A drawing of a bathing figure (cat. no. 31; color plate), likely from the summer of 1910 when Pechstein worked outdoors at Moritzburg with Kirchner and Erich Heckel, and related to his ink-on-muslin *At the Seashore* (fig. 17), testifies to a closer relationship to Rodin's sketches. Pechstein's simplified, swooping lines—which mark both anatomy and trajectory—and his veil of watercolor wash recapitulate Rodin's technique while relocating the model from the contained environment of the studio to the open air. In this regard, Pechstein and the other members of *Die Brücke* projected Rodin's notion of woman-as-nature back onto nature itself.

31 Max Pechstein
BATHER, n.d.

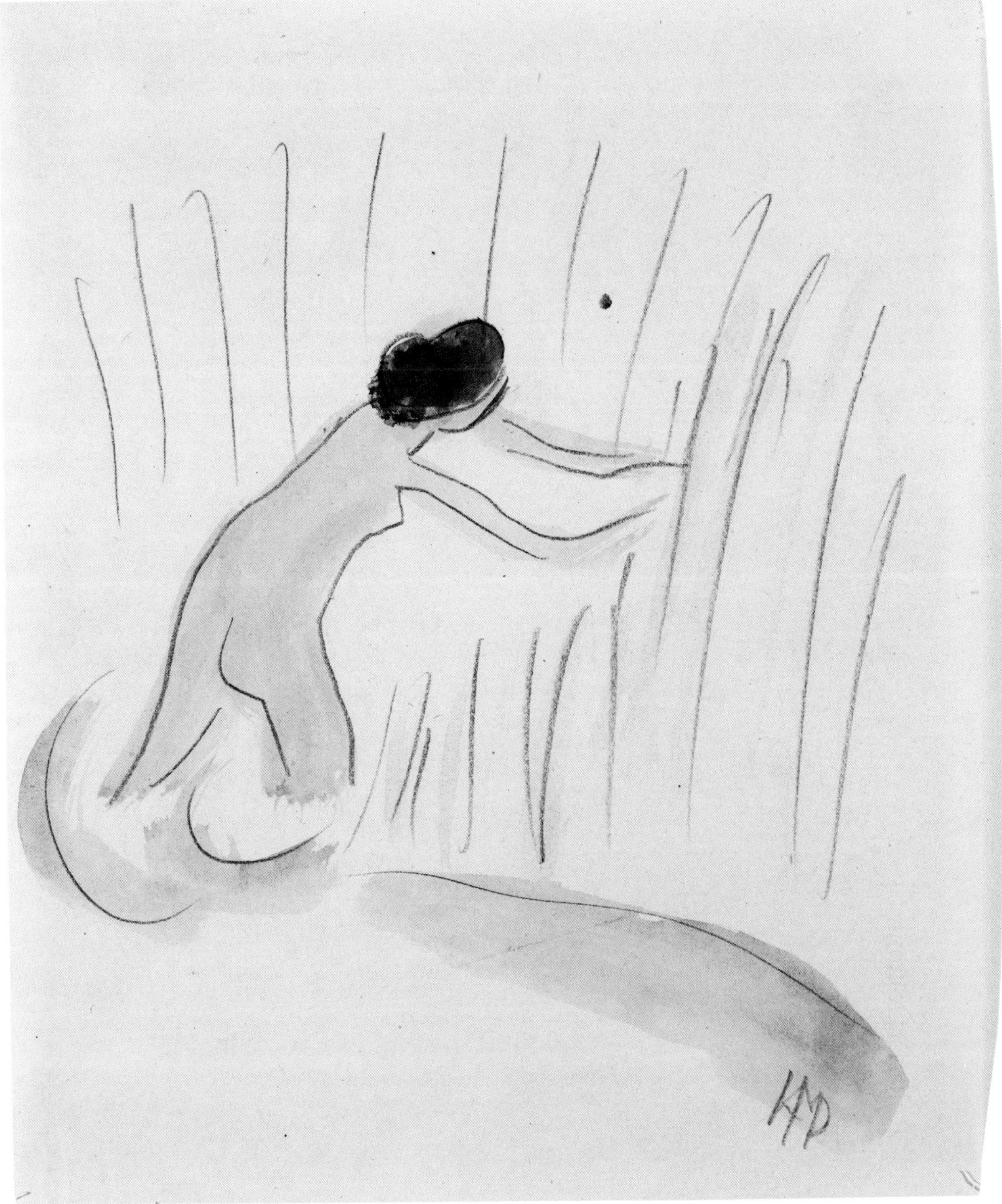

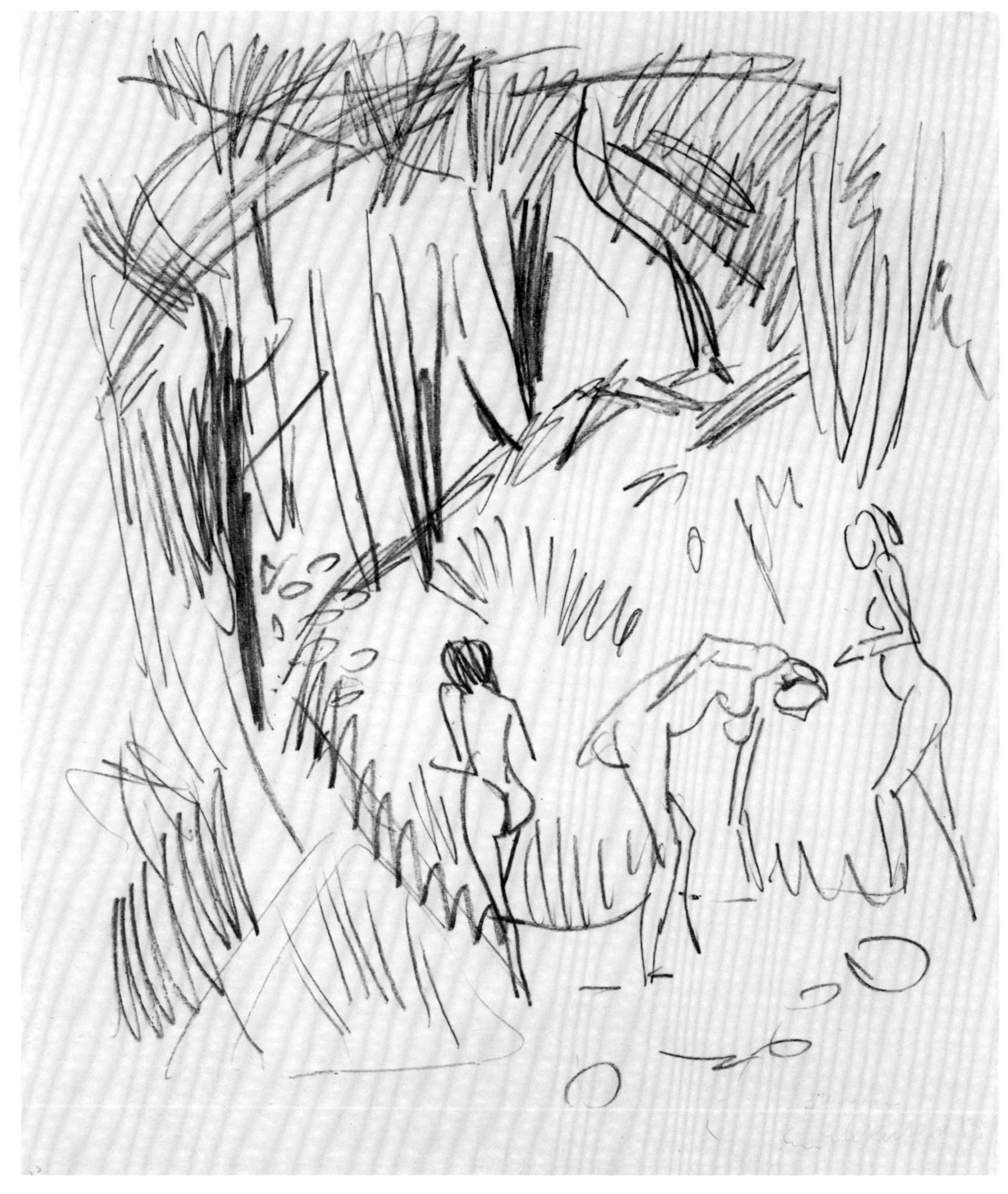

3 Erich Heckel

THREE FIGURES, 1913

Kirchner's BATHER ON THE BEACH (fig. 19; color plate), created at Fehmarn Island on the Baltic coast in 1912–1913, represents both a dialogue with Pechstein's figural style and a sustained interest in the naked body as an extension of nature. Like many of the *Brücke* artists' collective efforts at Moritzburg in the summer of 1910, this image represents a figure engulfed by and merging with nature, one of the central themes of Expressionism. Kirchner's naked model is a distant relative of the *Nachtkultur* and nature-worship images that were so popular in turn-of-the-century Germany.[165] In such works as Alois Kolb's *An die Schönheit* (fig. 18), the body is represented as intact and unified, its histrionic gestures signaling the desire for union with nature's vital forces. While Kolb's conventional image illustrates and narrates the immersion in nature, Kirchner's technique of gestural drawing enacts it. A sign for spontaneity and for emotional and scopic immersion, the gestural line here becomes a Vitalist device.[166] Kirchner's representation of the body no longer corresponds purely to the model's contours—the line describing the buttocks merely notes a cursory cleavage and then shoots off the body entirely, terminating in the space just to the right of the figure's hip. Tree, rock, and raft are signified by reduced geometric shapes. As technique and theme, gestural drawing accords with and discloses nature-based ecstasy.

Kirchner claimed that he discovered this convergence of subject and process by accident:

> *Through the speed of the work (moving, walking, not holding still until one was finished), abbreviations took place in the sketches—abbreviations which still rendered the intended image most accurately and clearly for others, often better than did the precise execution on the larger sheets. I was struck with astonishment; there was after all a form which could represent, say, a man or a movement exactly and for all that depart from the objective form in nature.... Was it perhaps possible in this manner to produce an art, understandable to all—an art in the language of symbolic form?*[167]

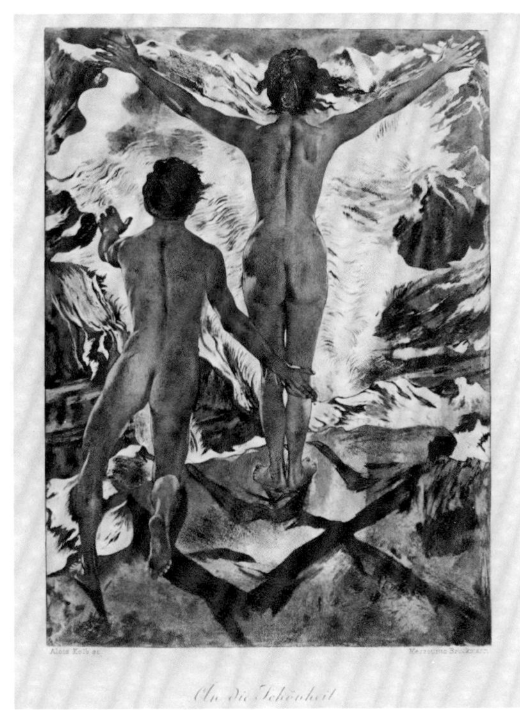

figure 18
Alois Kolb, *An die Schönheit*, from *Die Kunst* XIV, Munich, 1906, plate facing 1. By permission of Harvard College Library, Cambridge.

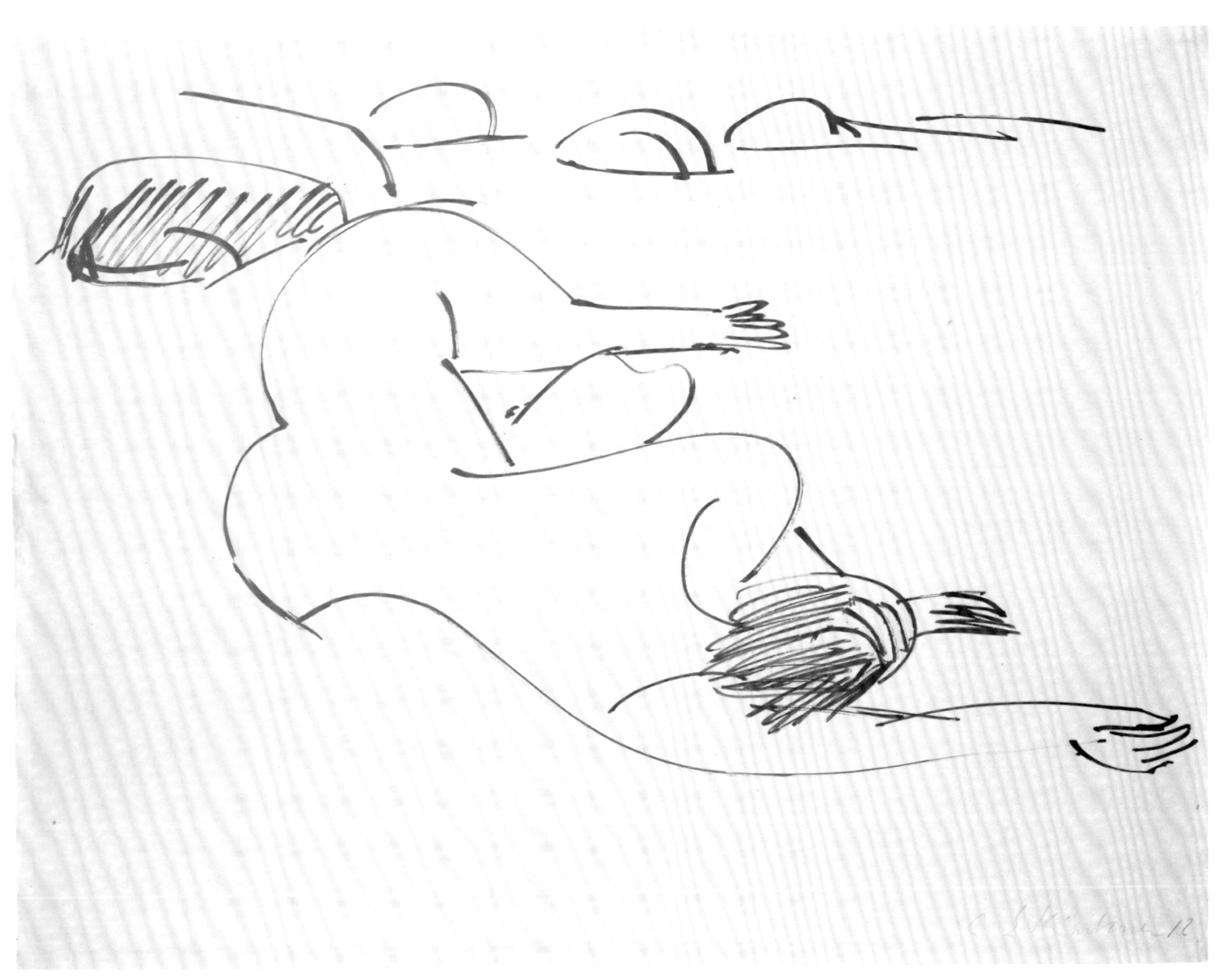

10 Ernst Ludwig Kirchner

BATHER LYING ON THE BEACH AMONG ROCKS, 1912

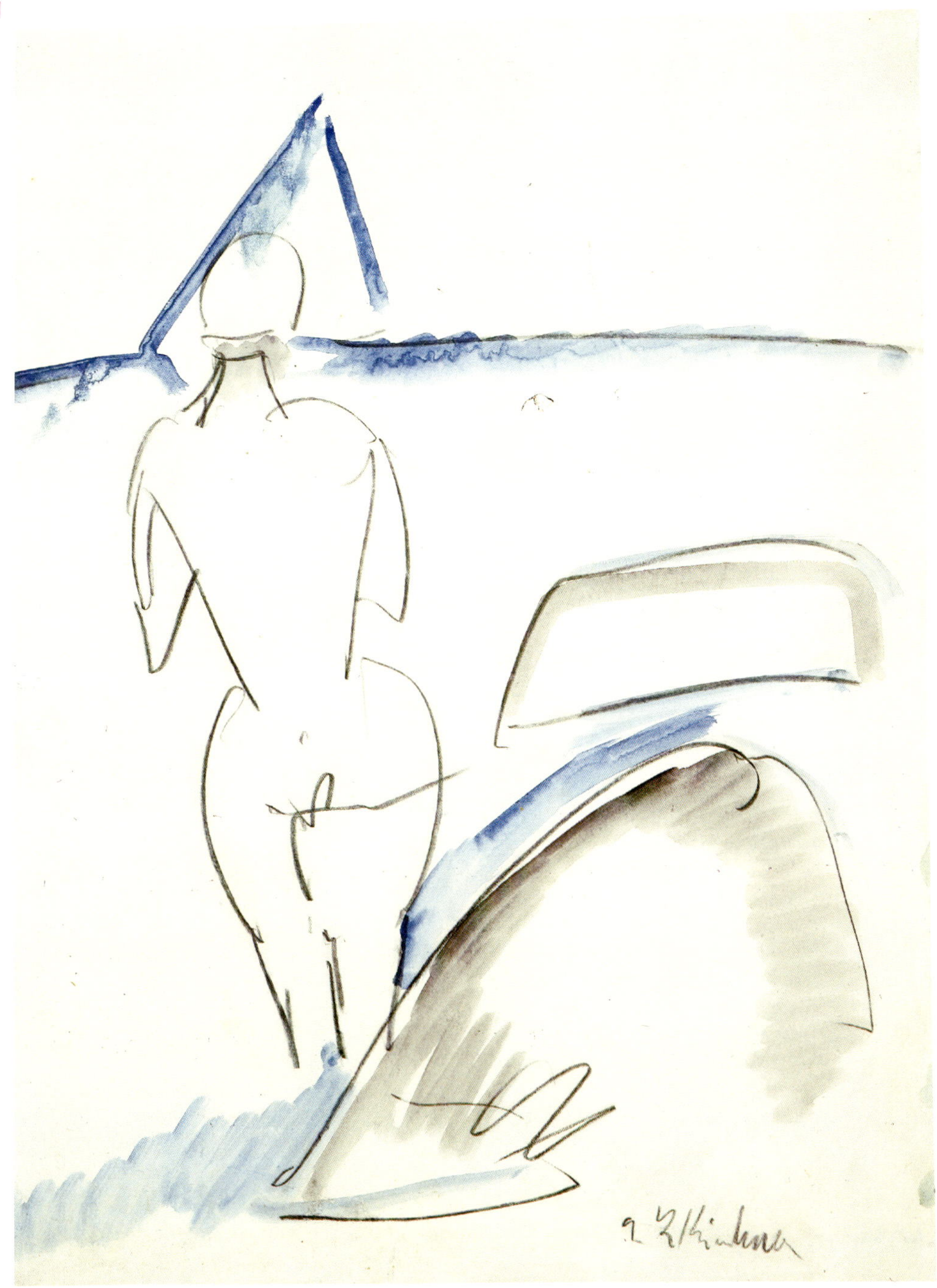

figure 19

Ernst Ludwig Kirchner, *Bather on the Beach*, 1912–13, black crayon with blue and gray wash, 17 1/6 x 12 1/2".
National Gallery of Art, Washington, D.C. Gift of Mr. and Mrs. Jacob Kaihen in honor of Charles Parkhurst.

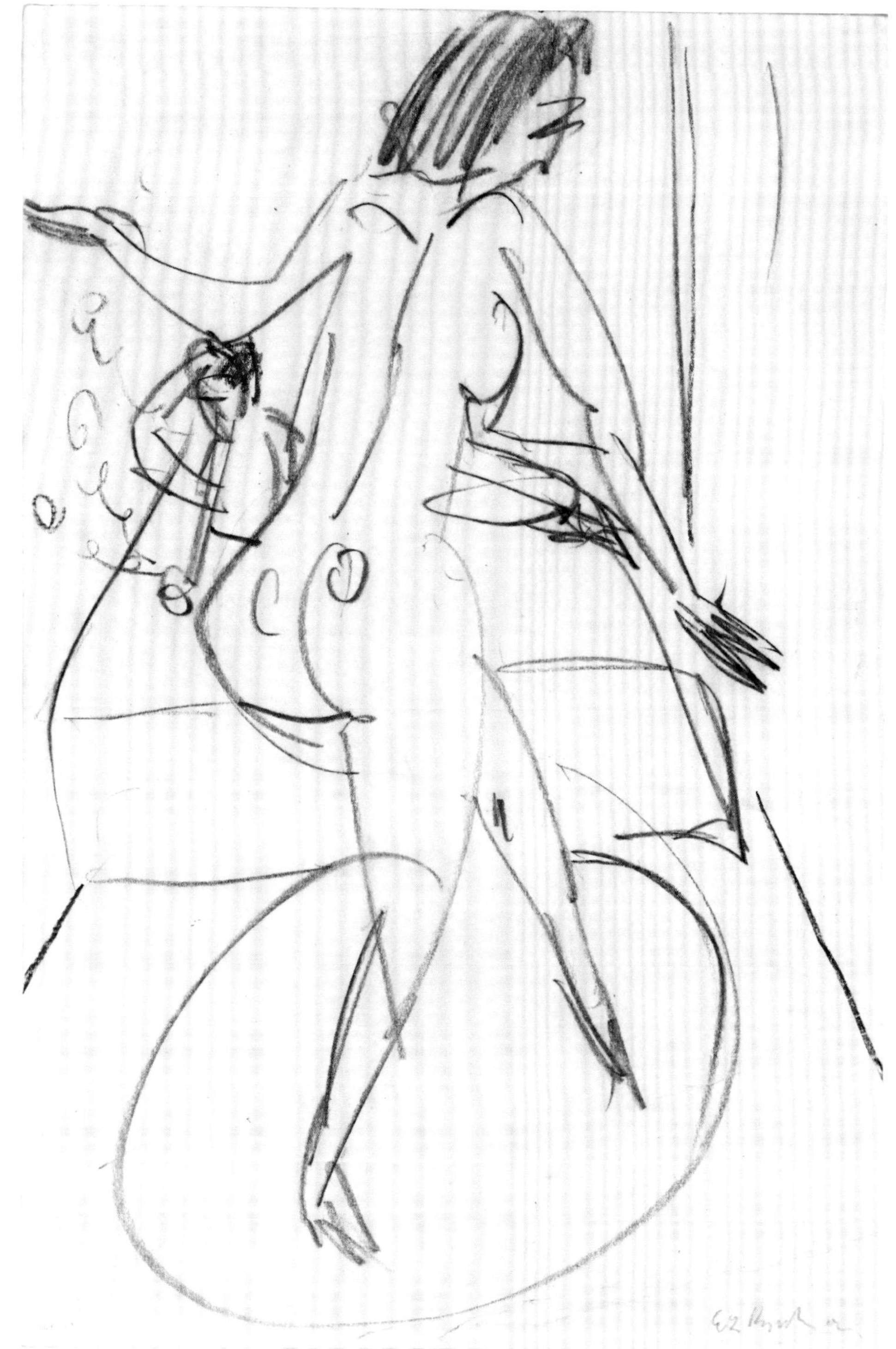

The rapid sketches to which Kirchner refers were created in his studio in 1908–1910 (cat. no. 5); in the open air at Moritzburg in 1909 and 1910, and at Fehmarn in 1908 and 1912–1913; and in urban streets and cabarets throughout the period. SMOKER AND DANCER from 1912 (cat. no. 9) records Kirchner's observation of a cabaret performer in a Berlin café as she is surveyed by another spectator. As her jagged feet stride across the circular sign for a spotlight, she presents the relocation of the erotic spectacle of the model from the studio to the public spaces of the city. This spectacle, recalls Kirchner, initiated his break from conventional drawing technique: "Every day the nude, and study of movement on the streets and in drinking halls. Out of the naturalistic surface with its variations I sought a surface specifically determined by the picture, and thus came to reject academically correct drawing."[168] As with the affinities between the French and Austrian avant-garde, the practice of gestural drawing as a modern invention was adopted in Berlin and Dresden just as Kirchner and his colleagues initiated their independent styles. The large exhibitions of Rodin's works in 1904, Klimt's drawings at the Arnold Gallery in Dresden in October 1907, and Matisse's drawings at the 1908 Berlin Secession; the publication and analysis of Rodin's drawings; and the reproduction of Kokoschka's drawings in *Der Sturm* after 1910 all supported the technical practices and theoretical orientations of the German artists.

9 Ernst Ludwig Kirchner
SMOKER AND DANCER, 1912

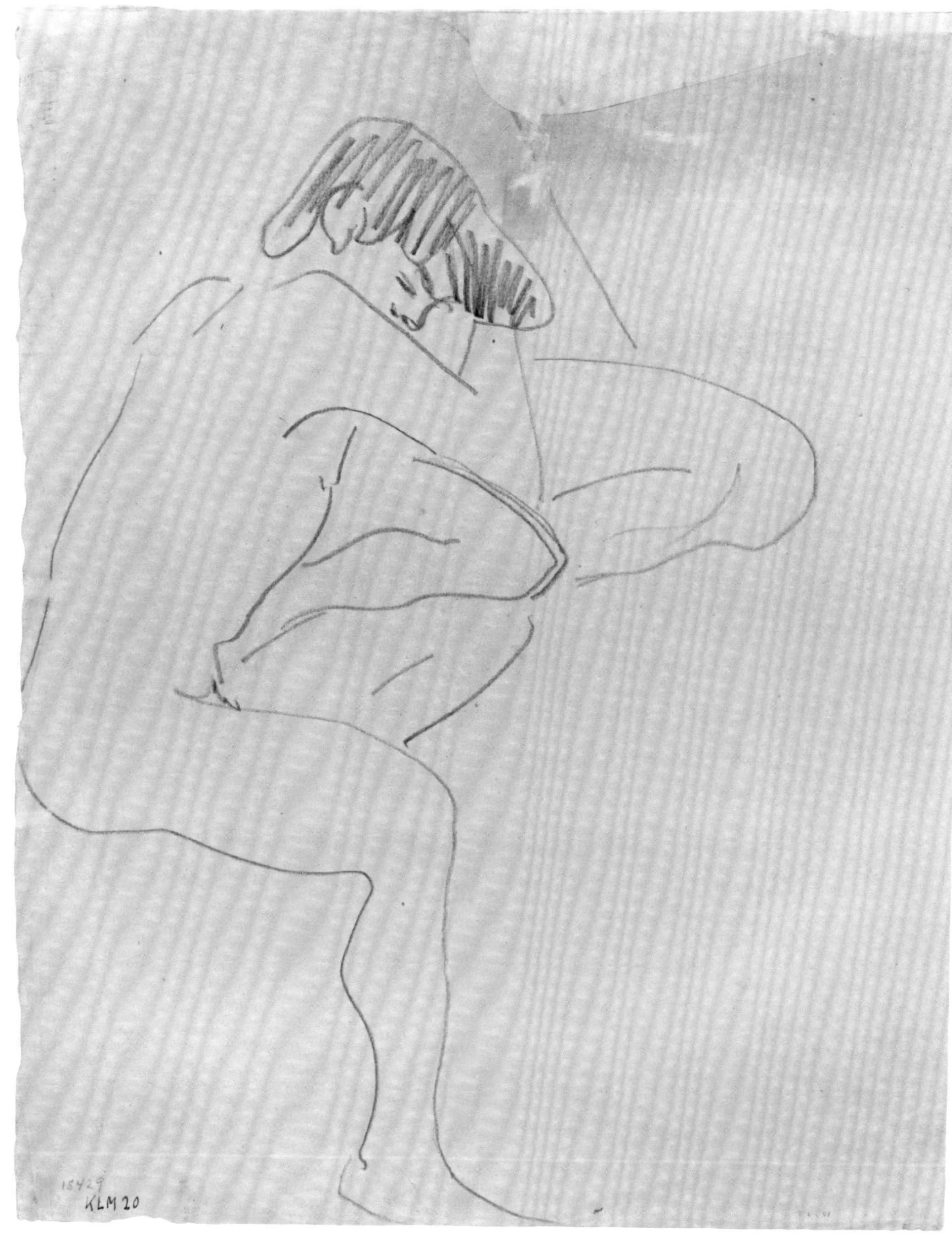

5 Ernst Ludwig Kirchner
COUPLE, ca. 1908 (recto)

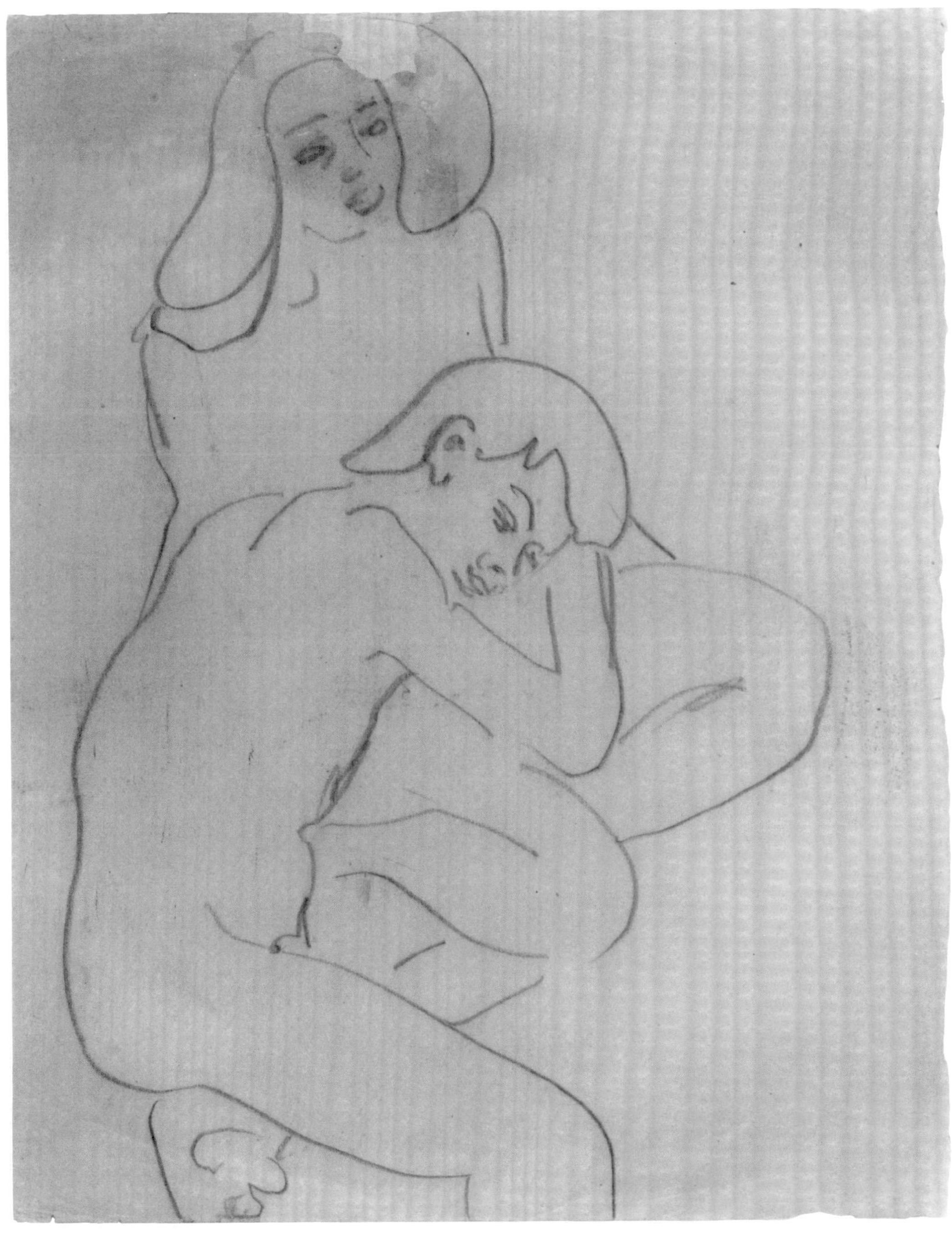

COUPLE, ca. 1908 (verso)

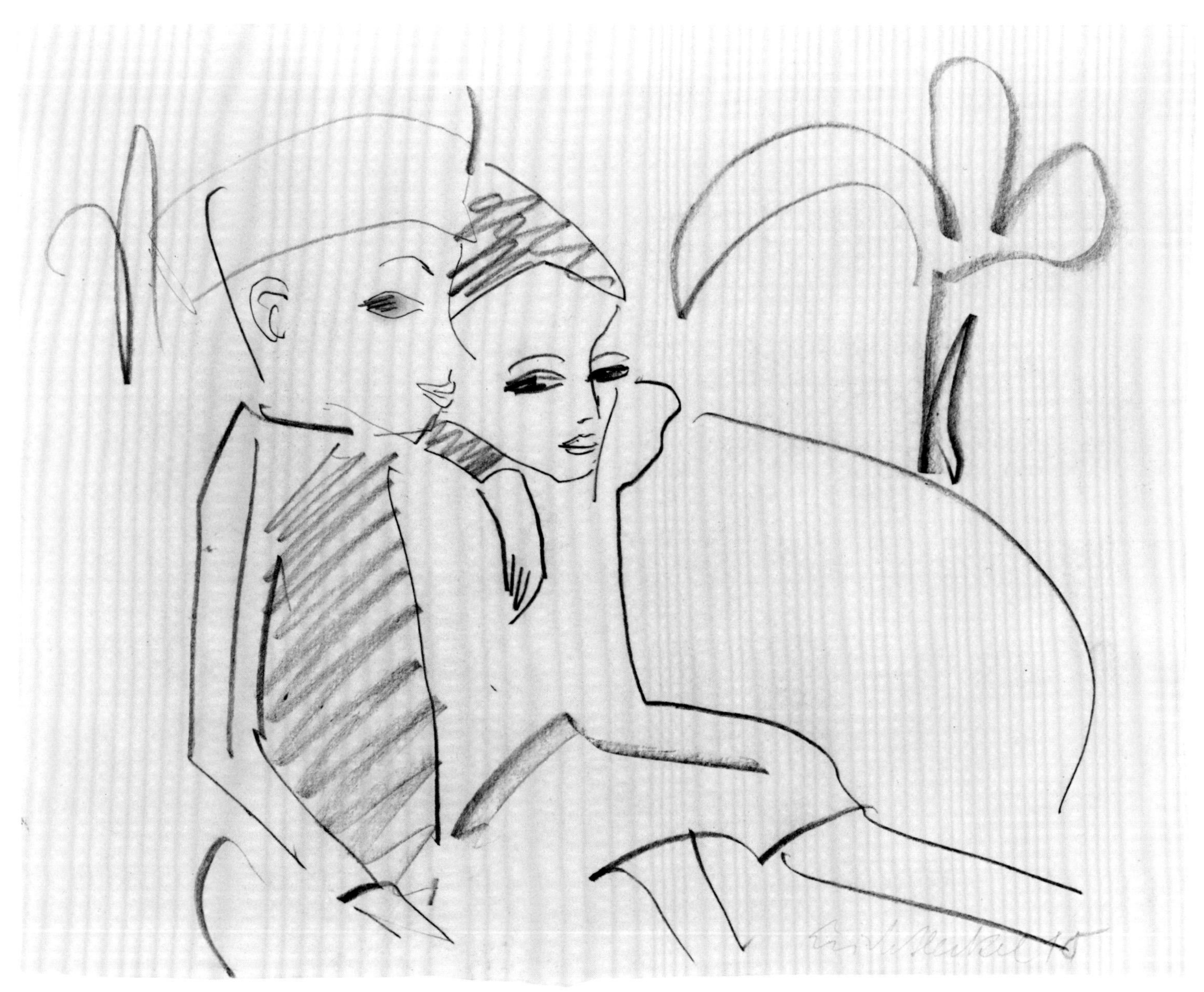

2 Erich Heckel

BROTHER AND SISTER, 1910

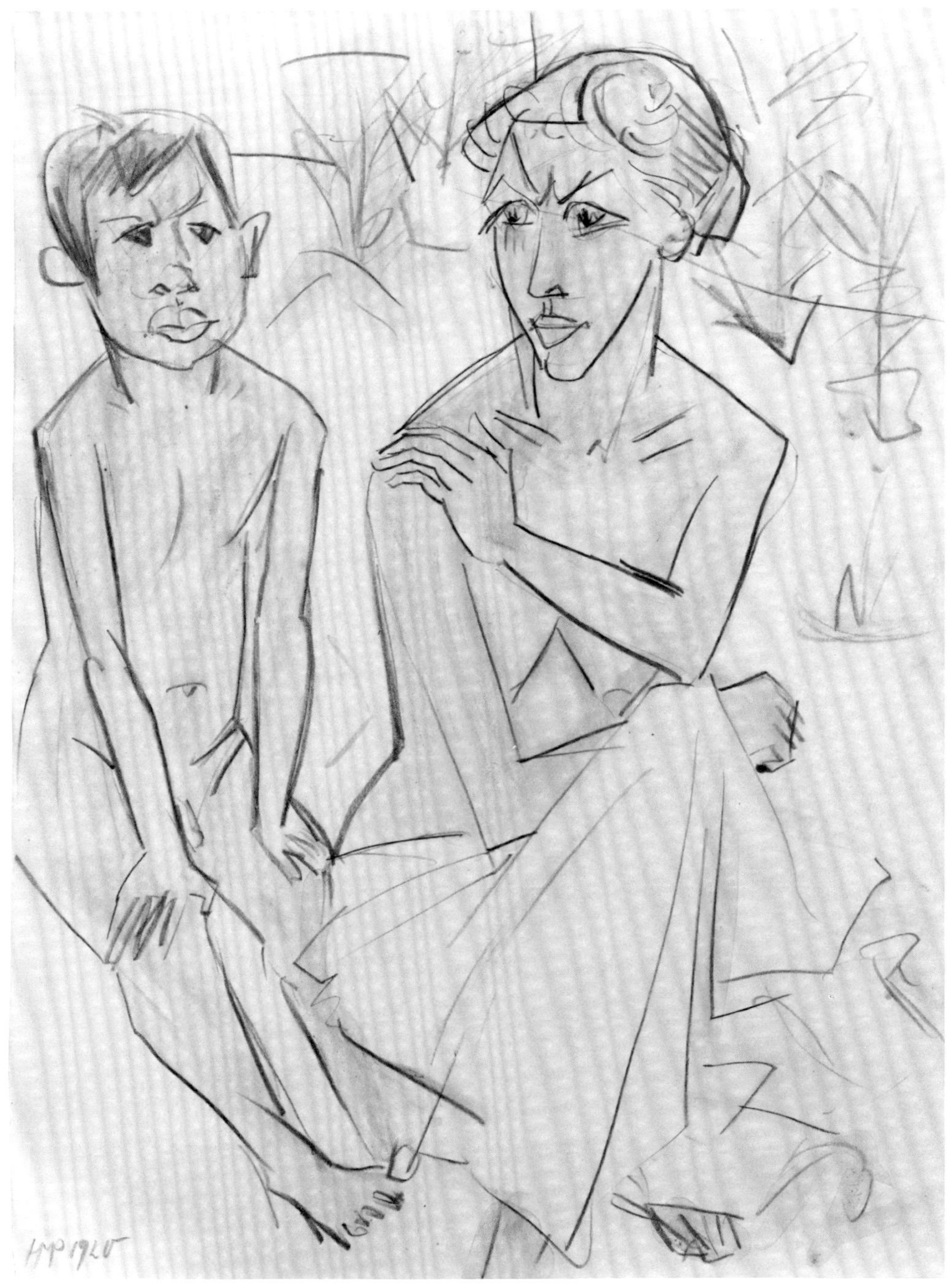

32 Max Pechstein
MOTHER AND SON, 1910

By 1910, through widespread diffusion of the French, Austrian, and German artists' work throughout Europe, gestural drawing emerged as a signature style of the avant-garde. It provided a notational system that held within it the kinesthetic responses of both artist and model—in Kirchner's words, a "language of symbolic form." With its emphasis on both the physical presence of the model and the suggestion of temporality, gestural drawing is analogous to both dance and dance notation: it collapses the body into a sign.[169] As in the revolutions in dance notation that occurred in the late nineteenth century, such as Friedrich Albert Zorn's influential 1887 *Grammatik der Tanzkunst* (fig. 20), gesture and direction are distilled into signs for the body.[170] Zorn, like the Berlin-based time-motion specialist Rudolf von Laban, examined gesture as a signifying practice analogous to a grammar. This idea had also begun to gain currency in the social sciences, which interpreted gesture as a key to mental disorder, kinship patterns, and non-verbal or pre-verbal communication.[171] There are important points of contact between these endeavors and the first generation of artists who employed gestural drawing.[172] The recording of gesture in the contexts of dance and communication, as in so many aspects of late nineteenth-century scientific culture,[173] posited gesture as a rational and measurable phenomenon. The grammar of dance is, in fact, interrelated with gestural drawing itself. Kirchner's SMOKER AND DANCER, as well as Klimt's, Kokoschka's, Schiele's, and Rodin's contacts with and representations of dance and ritualized gesture,[174] embeds dance within gestural technique and acknowledges both movement and drawing in relation to textual practices.

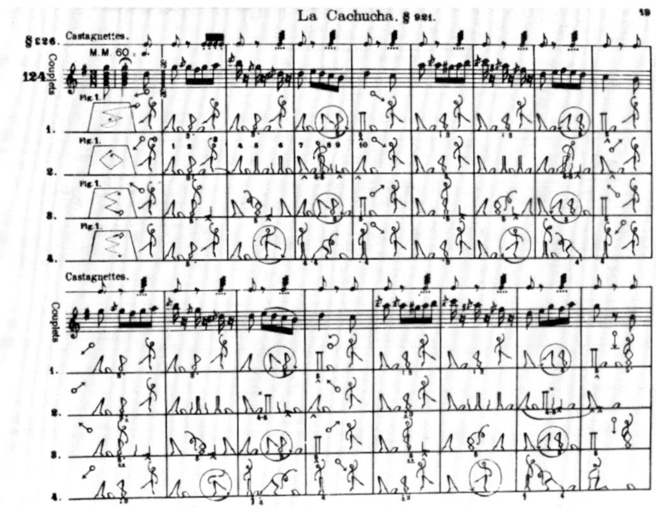

figure 20

Friedrich Albert Zorn, *Grammatik der Tanzkunst*, Leipzig, 1887, plate 19. By permission of Harvard College Library, Cambridge.

When Kirchner wrote of modern hieroglyphs, his reference was not specifically to the dynamic movement of models contained within his works, but to his condensation or synthesis of visual impressions into a signifying system, a text. Matisse and Kokoschka likewise spoke of gestural drawings as texts, Kokoschka as "journal entries,"[175] and Matisse as "plastic writing."[176] As these descriptions imply, through gestural drawing the body was inscribed in a new kind of writing. Whether in the reed pen drawings of Fernand Léger (cat. nos. 20 and 21), in which the arching lines of the body subsume the model's identity into a kind of pictogram, or in Schiele's highly individuated self-portrayals, the gestural line collapses form into contour, corporeality into trajectory. By reading the cursive text of the body, the spectator retraces the artist's perceptual and emotional possession of the model. Gestural drawing defines the body as the artist's autograph rather than merely perceived sensation through the synopsis of the body. For this reason, gestural drawings were received as "the most modern of the modern" of formal inventions by 1910.[177]

Gestural drawing was not just another new technique of early twentieth-century modernism, but a major paradigm shift in the history of figuration. Gestural drawings translated the figure into a sign in the same years as non-objectivity in painting was born. Perhaps, as suggested by André Masson, the practice of drawing itself had a bearing on the later emergence of an abstract figuration.[178] In the practice of early modernist gestural drawing, the writing of the body provided the cryptic language and empathic distillations through which the body would be reconfigured as an abstract cipher of figuration, a modern hieroglyph.

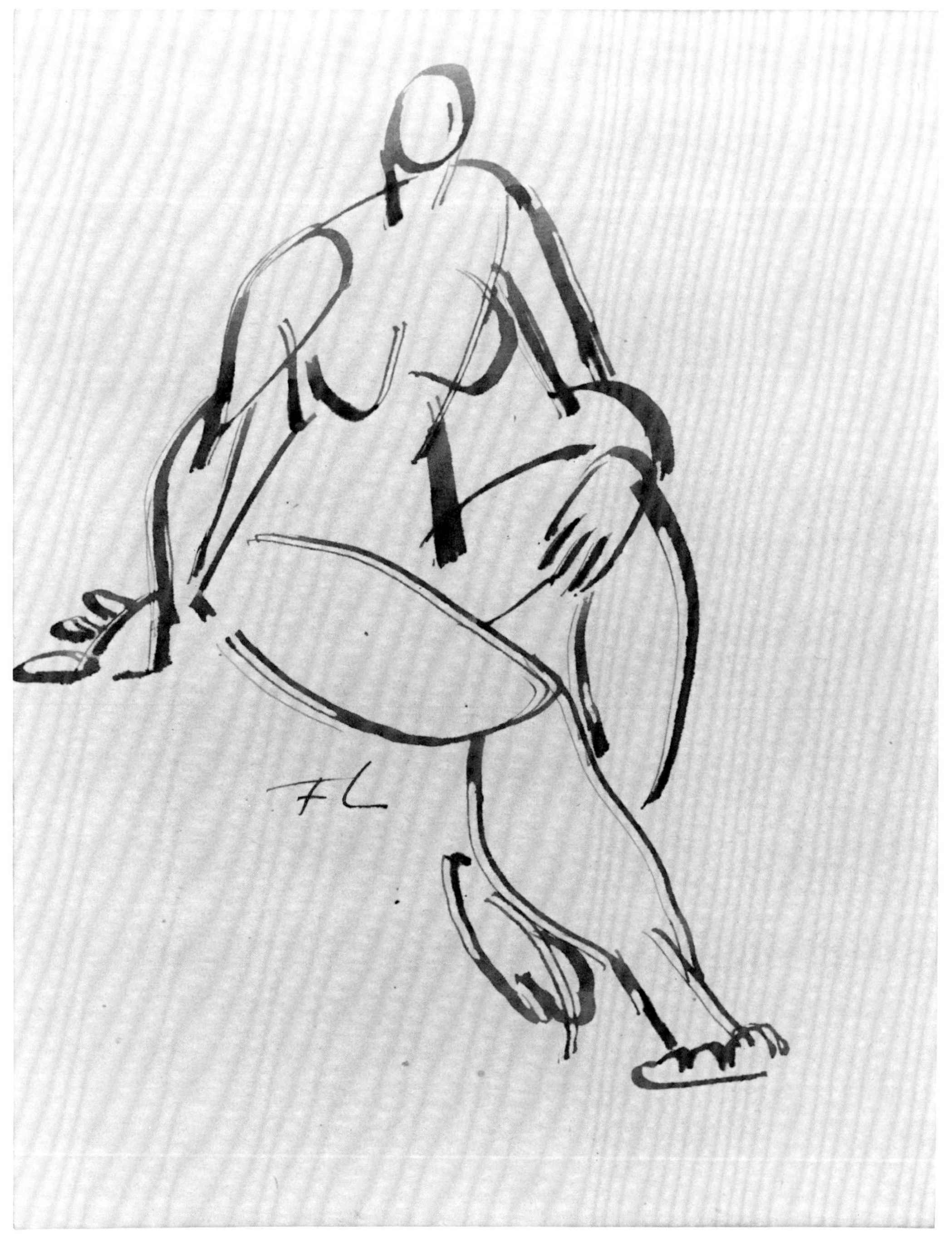

20 Fernand Léger
SEATED NUDE, ca. 1911

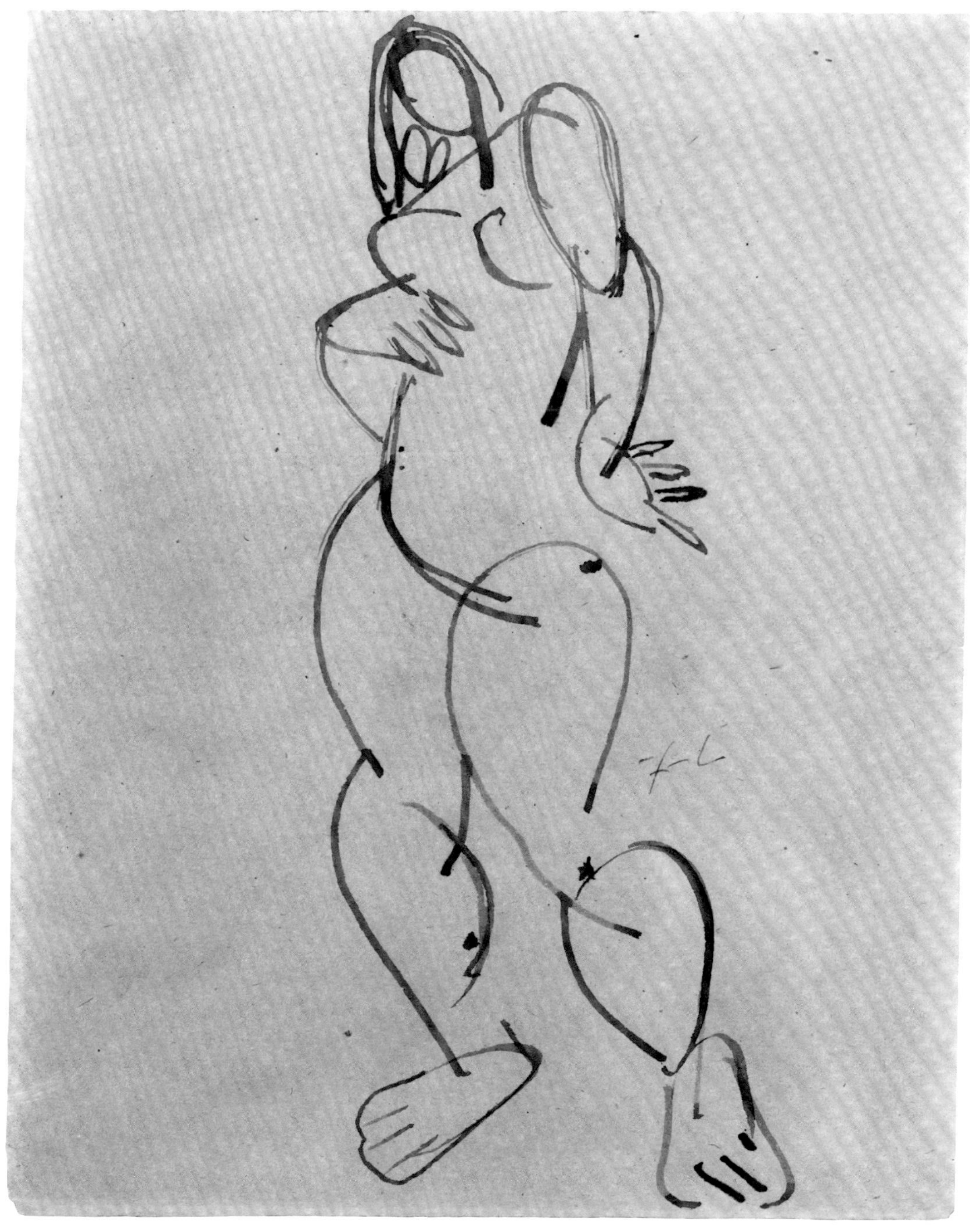

21 Fernand Léger

STANDING FEMALE FIGURE, 1911

ENDNOTES

1 Henri Matisse, quoted in Alfred H. Barr, Jr., *Matisse, His Art and His Public* (New York: Museum of Modern Art, 1951), 38.

2 On the history of the sketch esthetic, see Albert Boime, *The Academy and French Painting in the Nineteenth Century* (New Haven: Yale University Press [1971], 1986), and his *Strictly Academic: Life Drawing in the Nineteenth Century* (exh. cat., University Art Gallery, State University of New York at Binghamton, 1974).

3 See Kirk Varnedoe, "Rodin as a Draftsman: A Chronological Perspective," in Albert E. Elsen and J. Kirk T. Varnedoe, *The Drawings of Rodin* (exh. cat., National Gallery of Art, Washington, D.C., 1971), 25–120; Varnedoe's "Rodin's Drawings," in *Rodin Rediscovered*, ed. Albert E. Elsen (exh. cat., National Gallery of Art, Washington, D.C., 1981), 153–190; and Catherine Lampert, *Rodin: Sculpture and Drawings* (exh. cat., Hayward Gallery, London, 1986), especially chapter 4: "The Late Years."

4 Jacques Lipchitz, quoted in Kurt Valentin, *The Heritage of Auguste Rodin* (exh. cat., Buchholz Gallery, New York, 1950), unpaginated.

5 Rodin's statement was recorded by Antoine Bourdelle: quoted in Elisabeth Chase Geissbuhler, *Rodin: Later Drawings* (Boston: Beacon Press, 1963), 20.

6 Ernst Ludwig Kirchner et al., "*Die Brücke* Program," trans. in *German Expressionism: Documents from the End of the Wilhelmine Empire to the Rise of National Socialism*, ed. Rose-Carol Washton Long (New York: G. K. Hall & Co., 1993), 23.

7 Louis de Marsalle [E. L. Kirchner], "Zeichnungen von E. L. Kirchner," *Genius*, Munich, 1926: trans. in *Voices of German Expressionism*, ed. Victor H. Meisel (Englewood Cliffs, N.J.: Prentice-Hall, Inc., 1970), 22.

8 Ibid., 24.

9 Louis Aragon also seized upon the term hieroglyph to describe the way in which Henri Matisse repeatedly drew the image of a mouth until he had fully condensed and absorbed it: "He has become so familiar with it that he need not draw it, he writes it. He has developed his own hieroglyph for the mouth." Louis Aragon, *Henri Matisse. roman* (Paris: Gallimard, 1971), vol. 1, 106: quoted in Pierre Schneider, *Matisse*, trans. Michael Taylor and Bridget Strevens Romer (New York: Rizzoli, 1984), 576.

10 See endnote 106.

11 Charles Blanc, "Du style et de M. Ingres," *Gazette des Beaux-Arts* XIV (January 11, 1863), 15: quoted in Richard Shiff, *Cézanne and the End of Impressionism: A Study of the Theory, Technique, and Critical Evaluation of Modern Art* (Chicago: The University of Chicago Press, 1984), 82.

12 Yve-Alain Bois, "Matisse and 'Arche-Drawing'," in *Painting as Model* (Cambridge: M.I.T. Press, 1990), 3ff.

13 Scholars have acknowledged the decisive role that this technique played in the works of several individual artists included in the exhibition, and in relation to the overall concern with issues implicated in the notion of the avant-garde—directness, emphatic facture, spontaneity, and "primitivism." However, the technique itself, or rather the techniques that comprise gestural drawing, have not been examined as a generational phenomenon.

See, for example, Bois's examination of Matisse's "arche-drawing" as the break from divisionism and the foundation for his signature work. See also Albert E. Elsen, "Drawing and a New Sexual Intimacy," in *Egon Schiele: Art, Sexuality, and Viennese Modernism*, ed. Patrick Werkner (Palo Alto: The Society for the Promotion of Science and Scholarship, 1994), 5–31. My observations on Rodin's reputation, particularly in Germany and Austria, and on Egon Schiele's stylistic debt to Rodin parallel Elsen's invaluable essay, which I received only when the present manuscript was in its final stages of preparation.

Ruth Butler has recently called attention to the importance of Rodin's drawings for the younger generation: "It is the drawings that relate most pertinently to the initiatives of younger avant-garde artists at the beginning of the twentieth century." Ruth Butler, *Rodin: The Shape of Genius* (New Haven: Yale University Press, 1993), 436. In 1972, Albert E. Elsen acknowledged the parallelism among graphic styles at the turn of the century: "Artists as divergent as Matisse, Kokoschka, and Schiele looked long and knowingly at Rodin's many exhibited and published drawings and surely learned much from them." Elsen, "Rodin's Drawings and the Mastery of Abundance," in Elsen and Varnedoe, 24. Elsen's "Rodin's Drawings and the Art of Matisse," *Arts*, vol. 61, no. 7 (March 1987), 32–39, and his 1994 article on Schiele, flesh out this observation. On the notion of direct graphic techniques as "primitive," see for example Jill Lloyd, *German Expressionism: Primitivism and Modernity* (New Haven: Yale University Press, 1991), especially "Turning Away from History: The *Jugendstil* Renewal."

14 See Shiff.

15 Karl Schmidt-Rottluff, "The New Program" (originally published as "Das Neue Program," *Kunst und Künstler* XII, 1914, 299ff.): quoted in Meisel, 29.

16 Amédée Ozenfant, *Foundations of Modern Art* [1931] (New York: Dover Publications, Inc., 1952), 45 and 55. I would like to thank Kirk Varnedoe for calling this passage to my attention.

17 See Varnedoe, Elsen and Varnedoe, esp. 87ff., and "Rodin's Drawings," in Elsen, *Rodin Rediscovered*.

18 Anthony M. Ludovici, *Personal Reminiscences of Auguste Rodin* (Philadelphia: J. B. Lippincott Co., 1926), 134–135. This biography was written from notes made during Ludovici's term as Rodin's secretary in 1906.

19 Clément Janin, "Les Dessins de Rodin," *Les Maîtres Artistes* (October 15, 1903), 286–287: quoted in Varnedoe, Elsen and Varnedoe, 69–76.

20 The critical writings about Rodin published in response to his exhibitions are listed chronologically in Alain Beausire, *Quand Rodin Exposait* (Paris: Éditions du Musée Rodin, 1988), and are analyzed at length in Varnedoe, Elsen and Varnedoe, and in Lampert.

21 Judith Cladel, *Auguste Rodin, L'Oeuvre et l'homme* (Brussels: Van Oest, 1908). This observation was made by Varnedoe in Elsen and Varnedoe, 93.

22 Varnedoe, Elsen and Varnedoe, 98–99.

23 Ibid., 98.

24 Ibid. See also Howard C. Rice, "Glimpses of Rodin," in *Princeton University Library Chronicle* XXVII, no. 1 (Autumn 1965).

25 The author of the reproductions in *La Revue Blanche* was identified in Varnedoe, Elsen and Varnedoe, 116, note 111, as Jules-Léon Perrichon, "who did many subsequent wood block line reproductions of the later drawings."

26 Ludovici, 133.

27 Ibid., 134–135.

28 Varnedoe, Elsen and Varnedoe, 99.

29 A description of the drawings that Rodin exhibited in Brussels was published anonymously in "Rodin Dessinateur," *L'Écho de Paris* (May 10, 1899) and translated in Varnedoe, Elsen and Varnedoe, 116, note 112: "The author of *The Kiss* has exhibited in Brussels, besides a great number of sculptural works known in Paris, around a hundred original drawings which had never been out of his folios. These are, for the most part, curious studies from the studio, notations of the nude, taken in haste, to fix a pose of the model."

30 On the chronology and reconstructed content of these exhibitions, see Beausire.

31 Lampert, 137.

32 Camille Mauclair, "L'Art de M. Auguste Rodin," *Revue des Revues* (June 15, 1898), 597–599, 607: quoted in Varnedoe, Elsen and Varnedoe, 86–87.

33 Judith Cladel, *Auguste Rodin pris sur la vie* (Paris: Éditions de La Plume, 1903), 24: trans. in Varnedoe, Elsen and Varnedoe, 116, note 113.

34 Julius Meier-Graefe, *Modern Art, Being a Contribution to a New System of Aesthetics* [1904], trans. Florence Simmonds and George W. Chrystal (New York: Arno Press, 1968), vol. 2, 14.

35 Ibid.

36 Ibid., 10. On Meier-Graefe's rhetorical method, see my forthcoming "Julius Meier-Graefe, German Modernism, and the Genealogy of Genius," in *Studies in the History of Art*, ed. Françoise Forster-Hahn (Washington, D.C.: Center for Advanced Study in the Visual Arts).

37 Anne M. Wagner, "Rodin's Reputation," in *Eroticism and the Body Politic*, ed. Lynn Hunt (Baltimore: The Johns Hopkins University Press, 1991), 192.

38 Kirk Varnedoe, "Modes and Meanings in Rodin's Erotic Drawings," in *Rodin: Eros and Creativity*, ed. Rainer Crone and Siegfried Salzmann (Munich: Prestel-Verlag, 1992), 208–209.

39 See, for example, Philippe Sollers and Alain Kirili, *Rodin: Dessins érotiques* (Paris: Gallimard, 1987).

40 Ludovici, 140.

41 Arthur Symons, "Rodin," *The Fortnightly Review* CCCXXVI (June 1, 1902), 957.

42 Arthur Symons, "Les Dessins de Rodin," French trans. Henry D. Davray, *La Plume*, numéro exceptionnel, 3e fascicule (1900), 383: quoted in Wagner, 191. Wagner notes that Symons's article in *The Fortnightly Review* (as in endnote 41) does not include this statement.

43 Leo Steinberg, "The Algerian Women and Picasso at Large," in *Other Criteria: Confrontations with Twentieth-Century Art* (London and New York: Oxford University Press, 1976), 174.

44 Quoted in Paul Gsell, *Dix Dessins Inédites par Auguste Rodin* (Paris: Albert Besnard, 1921): trans. in Victoria Thorsen, "Symbolism and Conservatism in Rodin's Late Drawings," in Elsen and Varnedoe, 133.

45 "Drawing is the masculine sex of art and color the feminine sex." Charles Blanc, *Grammaire des arts du dessin* [1867] (Paris: V. J. Renouard, 1880), 21–22. This statement has been quoted and interpreted in Shiff, 83; Anne Middleton Wagner, *Jean-Baptiste Carpeaux: Sculptor of the Second Empire* (New Haven: Yale University Press, 1986), 31; and Norma Broude, *Impressionism: A Feminist Reading: The Gendering of Art, Science, and Nature in the Nineteenth Century* (New York: Rizzoli, 1991), 14.

46 Quoted in Steinberg, 191 (see endnote 43).

47 Martin Jay, "Scopic Regimes of Modernity," in *Vision and Visuality*, ed. Hal Foster (Seattle: The Bay Press, 1988), 8.

48 See, for example, Symons, 963 (endnote 41): "[Woman] turns up in herself in a hundred attitudes, turning always upon the central pivot of her sex, which emphasizes itself with a fantastic and frightful monotony.... It is a machine in movement, a monstrous, devastating machine, working mechanically, and possessed by the one rage of the animal."

49 Auguste Rodin, *Art: Conversations with Paul Gsell* [1911], trans. Jacques de Caso and Patricia B. Saunders (Berkeley: University of California Press, 1984), 13.

50 Like others before me, I question the "spontaneousness" of the women who masturbated or engaged in partnered sexual activity while Rodin watched and sketched. See Wagner, "Rodin's Reputation," for a discussion of this activity and its reception.

51 Quoted in Albert E. Elsen, *Rodin* (London: Secker and Warburg, 1974), 154, note 3, and in Petra ten-Doesschate Chu, "Lecoq de Boisbaudran and Memory Drawing: A Teaching Course between Idealism and Naturalism," in *The European Realist Tradition*, ed. Gabriel P. Weisberg (Bloomington: Indiana University Press, 1982), 284.

52 Elsen discusses the contrast between Rodin's studio practice and traditional modeling within the academy in "Rodin's Drawings and the Mastery of Abundance," in *The Drawings of Rodin*, 17–18. See also Alain Kirili, "The Scandal of Rodin and His Models," in Crone and Salzmann, 210–213.

53 Rodin to Antoine Bourdelle, quoted and discussed in Geissbuhler, 20, and retrans. in Varnedoe, Elsen and Varnedoe, 84.

54 Auguste Rodin, "The Dancers of King Sisowath of Cambodia," in *Auguste Rodin: Drawings and Watercolors*, ed. Ernst-Gerhard Güse, trans. John Gabriel and Michael Taylor (New York: Rizzoli, 1984), 271–272.

55 Rodin, *Conversations with Paul Gsell*, 11–12. This approach to natural drawing, to the direct confrontation of bodies in motion, was identified by Rodin as a consequence of his training under Horace Lecoq de Boisbaudran.

56 Ludovici, 122.

57 Lampert, 175.

58 Rainer Maria Rilke, *Auguste Rodin*, trans. Jessie Lemont and Hans Trausil (New York: Sunrise Turn, Inc., 1919), 45–46.

59 See Butler, *The Shape of Genius*, on Rodin's models. Butler provides the most comprehensive study of Rodin's models to date, mentioning them by name (cf. 436). She also quotes from an unsigned 1903 article reporting that, among professional models, Rodin's studio conditions were considered among the best in Paris: "Life of an Artist's Model in Paris: A Transcript from the Experiences of One Who Poses for Painters and Sculptors," *New York Tribune* (January 25, 1903): quoted on 436.

60 Cécile Goldscheider, in *Rodin inconnu* (exh. cat., Éditions du Musée Rodin, Paris, 1962), 40, reports that Rodin was fascinated by the French cancan, and that the presence of dancers from the Moulin-Rouge and the Moulin de la Galette can be seen in his work.

61 Butler, *The Shape of Genius*, 436.

62 Jules Lemaître, "Philosophie de la danse," *Revue Illustrée*, no. 17 (August 15, 1900), 22. He writes: "Oriental dance is, in essence, a *solo* and a spectacle." Non-Western dance was, like other forms of Orientalism, highly popular in turn-of-the-century Paris. Foreign traveling troupes performed regularly, and French dancers such as Cléo de Mérode (born in Paris to Belgian parents) gave "Oriental" dance performances in costume. On Mérode, see Chassaigne de Néronde, "Cléo de Mérode," *Revue Illustrée*, no. 17 (August 15, 1900); on the concept of Orientalism, see Edward W. Said, *Orientalism* (New York: Random House, 1978).

63 George Bois, "Le sculpteur Rodin et les danseuses Cambodgiennes," *L'Illustration* (July 28, 1906), 64.

64 Ludovici, 131–132.

65 George Bois, 65.

66 Varnedoe made this observation in Elsen and Varnedoe, 98.

67 On Duncan, Fuller, and St. Denis and the naturalizing of dance, see Mary Clarke and Clement Crisp, *The History of Dance* (New York: Crown Publishers, Inc., 1981), 213–220.

68 Isadora Duncan, *My Life* (New York: Boni and Liveright, 1927), 85.

69 See Irma Duncan, *The Technique of Isadora Duncan* (New York: Kamin Publishers, 1937). The author outlines the fundamentals of Duncan's method, placing them in opposition to the conventions of ballet: "The limitations of the ballet should be obvious, even to the layman. The five fundamental positions of the feet, on which its technique is founded, are in opposition to all natural laws, and since the body is essentially a natural instrument it should not be made to function by other than natural means": ix.

70 Hugo von Hofmannsthal, quoted in Clarke and Crisp, 220 (see endnote 67).

71 Rodin, in a letter (January 19, 1908) quoted and trans. in Loïe Fuller, *Fifteen Years of a Dancer's Life with Some Account of Her Distinguished Friends* (London: Herbert Jenkins Ltd., 1913), 124.

72 Albert E. Elsen, "Rodin's Drawings and the Art of Matisse," *Arts*, vol. 61, no. 7 (March 1987), 32–39.

73 Ibid., 34.

74 Ibid., 35. Elsen writes: "I propose that as one of his drawing modes from 1900 on, Matisse adopted Rodin's technique of continuous or instantaneous drawing, or that he combined this technique with occasional glances at the paper, in order to preserve his concentration, the immediacy of his perception, and an unimpeded flow of the sensations the model inspired."

75 Ibid.

76 Barr, 52.

77 Matisse showed Rodin several of his drawings, and Rodin is reported to have said, "Fuss over it, fuss over it. When you have fussed over it two weeks more, come back and show it to me again." Matisse did not return. In André Gide, *Journal* (New York, 1947), vol. 1, 175: trans. in Barr, 52, note 1. Matisse recalled, ca. 1937: "I was taken to Rodin's studio in the rue de l'Université by one of his students who wanted to show my drawings to his master. Rodin received me kindly and seemed relatively interested. He told me that I had a 'facility of hand,' which wasn't true. And he recommended that I do more carefully worked drawings and that I show them to him again. I never went back. . . ." Matisse, "On Rodin," in *Rodin in Perspective*, ed. Ruth Butler (Englewood Cliffs, N.J.: Prentice-Hall, Inc., 1980), 149. As Schneider proposes in *Matisse*, 264, and Elsen, "Rodin's Drawings and the Art of Matisse," 34, confirms, Matisse probably made more than one visit to Rodin's studio.

78 Barr, 52. For Bourdelle's commentaries on Rodin's figure drawings, see Geissbuhler.

79 Matisse's German student Hans Purrmann recalls that Matisse learned about Rodin's working methods from "Bevilaqua." See Hans Purrmann, *Schriften*, ed. Barbara and Erhard Göpel (Wiesbaden: Lines Verlag, 1961), 126. See also Albert E. Elsen, *The Sculpture of Henri Matisse* (New York: Harry N. Abrams, Inc., 1972), 29.

80 Roger Marx, "Cartons d'artistes—Auguste Rodin," *L'Image* (September 1897), 293–299; and "Les Pointes-sèches de M. Rodin," *Gazette des Beaux-Arts* XXVII, no. 1 (1902), 204–208.

81 Barr, 43.

82 See, for example, Maurice Denis's reference to Rodin at the beginning of his review of the 1905 Salon d'Automne in *L'Ermitage* (November 15, 1905), quoted in Barr, 63.

83 A number of other artists rented spaces there as well, including Isadora Duncan, Jean Cocteau, and Rainer Maria Rilke. Cocteau describes the milieu in *Paris Album 1900–1914* (London: W. A. Allen, 1956), 131–135.

84 Schneider, 545–547.

85 Bois, 22. Bois calls this "arche-drawing" by analogy to Derrida's concept of arche-writing.

86 Barr, 98, describes this painting as "virtually a drawing."

87 Victor Carlson, *Matisse as Draughtsman* (exh. cat., The Baltimore Museum of Art, Baltimore, 1971), 15.

88 Henri Matisse, "Notes of a Painter on His Drawing" [1939], in Jack D. Flam, *Matisse on Art* (New York: E.P. Dutton, 1978), 81.

89 Riva Castleman reports that these lithographs were executed on lithographic transfer paper and were based on the same model and done at approximately the same time. The transfer lithographs were printed on Auguste Clot's presses in Paris. See Castleman, "Nude," in *Matisse in the Collection of The Museum of Modern Art*, ed. John Elderfield (New York: The Museum of Modern Art, 1978), 48–49.

90 Henri Matisse, quoted in Aragon, *Matisse*, vol. 1, 234, and cited in Bois, 45.

91 James Huneker, writing for the *New York Sun*, described these lines as "virile and masterly." Quoted in *Camera Work: A Critical Anthology*, ed. Jonathan Green (New York: Aperture, 1973), 175.

92 William Lieberman, *Henri Matisse: Fifty Years of His Graphic Art* (New York: Braziller, 1956), 19, note 3.

93 Castleman, in Elderfield, 50. Castleman notes that this drawing, in reduced scale, was used by Matisse to illustrate Pierre Reverdy, *Les Jockeys camoflés* (Paris, 1918).

94 Shiff, 58.

95 Ibid., 59.

96 Ludovici, 137.

97 For a close reading of this text, see Roger Benjamin, *Matisse's "Notes of a Painter": Criticism, Theory, and Context, 1891–1908* (Ann Arbor: U.M.I. Research Press, 1987). Benjamin and Shiff note that the theme of creative distortion also runs through George Desvallières's original introduction to "Notes of a Painter."

98 Sarah Stein, "Sarah Stein's Notes," in Flam, 43.

99 Jean Moréas, "Un Manifeste littéraire: Le Symbolisme," *Le Figaro* (September 18, 1886), quoted in Shiff, 44.

100 Eugène Véron, *Aesthetics*, trans. W. H. Armstrong (London: Chapman & Hall, 1879), 125.

101 Ibid., 251.

102 Ibid., 257.

103 William James, *The Principles of Psychology*, vol. 1 (New York: Henry Holt and Company, 1890), 607.

104 Ibid., 611.

105 Véron in turn criticized academic painting because of its stasis: 252–253. For the same reason, he dismissed photography as a faulty system of representation because it could not account for the passage of time. This observation was repeated by the artist and theorist Adolf von Hildebrand in *The Problem of Form in Painting and Sculpture*, trans. Max Meyer and Robert Morris Ogden [1932] (New York: Garland Publishing, Inc., 1978). He writes that the perceiving eye is a superior means of capturing movement because "we are not instantaneous cameras for observing Nature, but beings who combine ideas and who use isolated perceptions only for the purpose of weaving them into an ideational content": 109–110. Correspondingly, Matisse later stated: "... when we surprise the movement by means of a snapshot, the resultant image reminds us of nothing that we have seen. Movement seized while it is going on is only intelligible to us if we do not isolate the present sensation from either the one which precedes it, or the one which follows it." See Benjamin, 189.

Benjamin in turn discusses Matisse's view of the snapshot in the light of Rodin's interest in the chronophotography of Muybridge and Marey: 190. On this, see Aaron Scharf, *Art and Photography* (Hammersmith: Penguin Books, 1974), 218–225. In conversation with Paul Gsell, Rodin stated: "... it is the artist who is truthful and it is photography which lies, for in reality time does not stop, and if the artist succeeds in producing the impression of a movement which takes several moments for accomplishment, his work is certainly much less conventional than the scientific image, where time is abruptly suspended": 224–225.

106 See, for example, Flam, 33. Much has been written about the parallels between Henri Bergson's writings about time and perception and Matisse's theories. Bergson's notion of *durée*, that discrete moments of time can only be known through observation, was expressed in *Time and Free Will* (1889), *Matter and Energy* (1896), and, most famously, in *Creative Evolution* (1907). See Marta Braun's discussion of Bergson's philosophy of time and the perception of matter in *Picturing Time: The Work of Etienne-Jules Marey (1830–1904)* (Chicago: The University of Chicago Press, 1992). Stephen Kern notes the general influence of Bergson's ideas and cites the Dutch critic Ernst Te Peerdt's *The Problem of Instants of Time in Painting and Drawing* (1899) as one of many treatises that attempted a direct application of the issue of temporality to artistic practice. Stephen Kern, *The Culture of Time and Space 1880–1918* (Cambridge: Harvard University Press, 1983), 22.

107 Matisse, "Notes of a Painter," in Flam, 37.

108 Quoted by Stein, in Flam, 43 (see endnote 98).

109 Hildebrand, 21.

110 Ibid., 22–23.

111 On the parallels between Hildebrand and Riegl's theories of perception, see Margaret Iversen, *Alois Riegl: Art History and Theory* (Cambridge: The M.I.T. Press, 1993), 9.

112 Hildebrand, 14.

113 Ibid., 123.

114 Quoted in Ludovici, 138.

115 Hildebrand, 55.

116 A discussion of gestalt psychology in regard to Klimt and Vienna is provided in Werner Hofmann, *Gustav Klimt*, trans. Inge Goodman (Greenwich: New York Graphic Society, 1971), 36–41.

117 Ernst Mach, *Contributions to the Analysis of the Sensations* [1885], trans. C. M. Williams (Chicago: The Open Court Publishing Company, 1897).

118 Ernst Mach, "Why Has Man Two Eyes?" in *Popular Scientific Lectures*, trans. Thomas J. McCormack (Chicago: The Open Court Publishing Company, 1910), 69.

119 Hermann von Helmholtz, *Physiologischen Optik*, 3 vols. (Hamburg and Leipzig: Verlag von Leopold Voss, 1910). This foundational study was first published in its complete form in 1867. A second edition was issued posthumously in 1896.

120 More direct recordings of movement are found in Matisse's dance notations from the 1930s, in which a few lines synthesize the rapid movements of dancers. See, for example, Schneider, 577. See also Jack D. Flam, *Matisse: The Dance* (exh. cat., National Gallery of Art, Washington, D.C., 1993).

121 Hermann Bahr, *Expressionismus* (Munich: Delphin-Verlag, 1920), 74–75.

122 Ibid., 82.

123 Ibid., 83.

124 Oskar Kokoschka, "On the Nature of Visions," trans. Heidi Medlinger and John Thwaites, in Edith Hoffmann, *Kokoschka: Life and Work* (London: Faber and Faber, 1947), 285.

125 Kokoschka, quoted in Ludwig Goldschneider, *Kokoschka* (London: Phaidon Press, 1963), 7.

126 Described in Steven Steinlein, "Ludwig Heinrich Jungnickel-München," *Deutsche Kunst und Dekoration* XVII (November 1905), 118, and cited in Jane Kallir, *Austria's Expressionism* (exh. cat., The Galerie St. Etienne, New York, 1981), 30. Kallir notes, "Kokoschka claimed to have instituted this avant-garde teaching method himself, but the above article, written the year he entered the Kunstgewerbeschule, clearly indicates that Roller was responsible."

127 J. P. Hodin, *Oskar Kokoschka: The Artist and His Time* (Greenwich: New York Graphic Society, 1966), 62. Kokoschka informed Hodin that his impulse to attend the Kunstgewerbeschule was stimulated by his desire to "make something real—a carpet, a book, or a poster, but at the academy only 'art' was recognized." He positions his study of nude bodies in motion within this context as "something real."

128 *Oskar Kokoschka*, ed. Richard Calvocoressi (exh. cat., Tate Gallery, London, 1986), 193. Calvocoressi described a class at the Kunstgewerbeschule as a "rather conventional life class" in which students drew detailed pencil sketches from nude models. Within his own evening classes, however, Kokoschka introduced the practice of drawing rapidly from figures in motion. He repeated this technique at his own "School of Seeing" in Salzburg. On Kokoschka's teaching, see Georg Eisler, "Kokoschka as Teacher: A Personal View," in the same publication, 45.

129 Alice Strobl and Alfred Weidinger have recently called attention to Rodin's influence on Kokoschka in "Oskar Kokoschka: Early Graphic Works," *Oskar Kokoschka, Works on Paper: The Early Years, 1897–1917* (exh. cat., Solomon R. Guggenheim Museum, New York, 1994), 20. This catalogue became available during the final preparation of this essay.

130 Frank Whitford records: "Many of Kokoschka's sketches were made after models whom the artist found in the working-class districts of Vienna. Almost all of them were children forced to live in squalor and the privations of a city which could not keep pace with its spectacular growth." Frank Whitford, *Egon Schiele* (New York and Toronto: Oxford University Press, 1981), 56.

131 Elsen, "Drawing and a New Sexual Intimacy," in Werkner, *Egon Schiele*, 132, note 10. The drawings are identified by Claudie Judrin, "La diffusion des dessins du vivant de Rodin," in *Musée Rodin. Inventaire des dessins*, vol. 1 (Paris: Éditions du Musée Rodin, 1984), xlvii, note 33. Strobl and Weidinger, 20, indicate that Kokoschka saw the 1908 exhibition and that "Rodin's work showed Kokoschka a much looser, freer way of handling line and thus allowed him to break away from a conservative, academic drawing style."

132 Rainer Maria Rilke, "The Rodin-Book," in *Selected Works*, vol. 1, trans. G. Craig Houston (London: The Hogarth Press, 1954), 145–146.

133 See, for example, Meier-Graefe (as in endnote 34), and Roger Marx in *Pan* (November 1897).

134 Alessandra Comini, *Egon Schiele's Portraits* (Berkeley: University of California Press, 1974), 38.

135 See Peter Vergo, *Art in Vienna 1898–1918: Klimt, Kokoschka, Schiele, and their Contemporaries* (London: Phaidon Press, 1975), 26–28.

136 Butler, *Rodin in Perspective*, 127.

137 Kirk Varnedoe, *Vienna 1900: Art, Architecture, and Design* (exh. cat., The Museum of Modern Art, New York, 1986), 182.

138 See Comini, 200, note 36.

139 Ibid., 62.

140 Jane Kallir, "Egon Schiele: An Introduction," in *Egon Schiele* (exh. cat., National Gallery of Art, Washington, D.C., 1994), 12, and 15, note 3. On the history and reception of the University paintings, see Vergo, 49–61.

141 Undated typescript in the Bibliothek der Stadt Wien, cited in Vergo, 60.

142 Klimt provided both artists entree into the Werkstätte. See Egon Schiele, "Klimt's Generosity of Spirit was Genuine," in *Gustav Klimt: Drawings*, ed. Serge Sabarsky (Mt. Kisko: Moyer Bell Limited, 1983), 15–16.

143 Kokoschka stated in 1962: "I was an admirer of Klimt, and when I was twenty he bought some of my drawings. Mine looked a little like his, because they too were austerely linear, without shading—the lines not as spare as his, but broken and less uniform. Yet in one major aspect they were quite different: Klimt always showed his nudes standing or seated, always completely at rest; while I then drew only nudes *in action*, the movements caught in a flash—I learned that from the Japanese. I actually met and spoke to Klimt only once, at the first *Kunstschau*. I never visited his studio." Quoted in Goldscheider, 9.

144 Berta Zuckerkandl-Szeps's memories of Klimt: quoted in Hodin, 161 (see endnote 127).

145 Kokoschka, letter to Erwin Lang from Vienna in late 1907, trans. in Olda Kokoschka and Alfred Marnau, *Oskar Kokoschka: Letters 1905–1976* (London: Thames and Hudson, 1992), 15.

146 Quoted in Whitford, 62. This statement was later published in 1914 in the Berlin journal *Die Aktion*.

147 Wilhelm Worringer, *Abstraction and Empathy: A Contribution to the Psychology of Style* [1908] (New York: International Universities Press, 1967).

148 Letter from Schiele to Leopold Czihaczek (September 1, 1911): quoted in Patrick Werkner, "Body Language, Form and Idea in Austrian Expressionist Painting," in *Egon Schiele and His Contemporaries: Austrian Painting and Drawing from 1900 to 1930 from the Leopold Collection, Vienna*, ed. Klaus Albrecht Schröder and Harald Szeemann (Munich: Prestel-Verlag, 1989), 35.

149 Quoted in Ludovici, 138.

150 Quoted by Stein, in Flam, 43.

151 Quoted in Whitford, 132–133.

152 Schiele, in a letter to Arthur Roessler (1910): quoted in Comini, 38.

153 Quoted in Whitford, 58–59.

154 The story is recounted in Whitford, 110–119.

155 Philip Seely Larson, "Drawing Styles and Graphic Detail in *Brücke* Art, 1905–1920" (Ph.D. diss., Columbia University, 1971), 49.

156 For a discussion of Rodin's reception in 1904, see Ernst-Gerhard Güse, "Auguste Rodin und Deutschland," in *Auguste Rodin: Zeichnungen und Aquarelle*, ed. Ernst-Gerhard Güse (exh. cat., Westfälisches Landesmuseum für Kunst und Kulturgeschichte Münster, 1984).

157 J. A. Schmoll gen. Eisenwerth, "Rodin's Late Drawings and Watercolors," in *Auguste Rodin: Drawings and Watercolors*, ed. Ernst-Gerhard Güse (New York: Rizzoli, 1984), 214–215 and 226. See also Volker Wahl, "Die Jenaer Ehrenpromotion von Auguste Rodin und der 'Rodin-Skandal' zu Weimer 1905/06," 58–67, and Claude Keisch, "Chronologie des Weimarer 'Rodin-Skandals'," in *Auguste Rodin: Plastik, Zeichnungen, Graphik*, ed. Claude Keisch (Staatliche Museen zu Berlin/D.D.R., Nationalgalerie, 1979).

158 Eisenwerth, 226. Kaiser Wilhelm II is reported to have impugned both Rodin's reputation and the morality of Germans by stating in 1907 that Rodin's international reputation was a mystery to him and that "no one in France would consider looking at the drawings now on show at the Berlin Secession, but the good Berliners are all eyes and think them admirable...." See Jules Huret's description of the attacks on Rodin in *Le Figaro*, March 26, 1907. See also J. A. Schmoll gen. Eisenwerth, "Rodin und Kaiser Wilhelm II," in *Rodin-Studien: Persönlichkeit, Werke, Wirkung, Bibliographie* (Munich: Prestel-Verlag, 1983), 329–346.

159 See endnotes 48, 58, and 132.

160 See, for example, Donald E. Gordon, "Kirchner in Dresden," *Art Bulletin*, vol. 48 (1966), 335–366.

161 Larson, 81.

162 Max Pechstein, *Erinnerungen* (Wiesbaden: Limes Verlag, 1960), 28, 32, and 33.

163 Gabrielle Linnebach, "La Brücke et le fauvisme," in *Paris/Berlin: Rapports et contrastes France–Allemagne 1900–1933* (exh. cat., Centre National d'Art et de Culture Georges Pompidou, Paris, 1978), 70.

164 This drawing was reproduced in *Kunst und Künstler* XXII (1924), 76. Its current location is unknown.

165 Jill Lloyd provides a summary of the back-to-nature and nudism movements in Germany, and examines how the *Brücke* Moritzburg works related to them, in *German Expressionism* (as in endnote 13), 102–110. See also George Mosse, *Nationalism and Sexuality: Middle-Class Morality and Sexual Norms in Modern Europe* (Madison: The University of Wisconsin Press, 1985).

166 Vitalism is a term describing a neo-Darwinian philosophical movement and, in turn, a range of social responses to the notion of nature as a unified realm, in which all life is connected through a vital fluid. Based in part on the writings of Ernest Haeckel, whose book *Riddle of the Universe* (1899) was in its eighth edition by 1905, Vitalism proposed a direct link between human society and all living things. As a popularized idea, Vitalism was monistic, anti-urban, and nationalistic. An issue of the journal *Jugend* was dedicated to Haeckel on his seventieth birthday. On Vitalism as a popular movement see Fritz Stern, *The Politics of Cultural Despair: A Study in the Rise of Germanic Philosophy* (Berkeley: University of California Press, 1961), 123–124.

167 Kirchner in a letter to Dr. Carl Hagemann (June 30, 1937), trans. in Donald E. Gordon, *Ernst Ludwig Kirchner* (Cambridge: Harvard University Press, 1968), 19.

168 Letter to Botho Gräf (September 21, 1916), trans. in Gordon, 20.

169 Paul Klee, who assimilated formative lessons from his confrontation with Rodin's drawings in 1904–1907, recognized in the drawings a pictorial collapse of the figure: "Above all Rodin with caricatures of nudes!—caricatures!—a species unknown before him. The greatest I saw among them stupendously brilliant. Contours are drawn with a few pencil lines, a flesh tone is put down in watercolor with a loaded brush, and drapery is indicated by another, a greenish color, for instance. That is all, and the effect is monumental." Klee's meandering-line figure drawings from these years (fig. 21) redirect Rodin's technique from the observation of silhouette toward linear excursions across the surfaces of figures. Quoted in Marcel Franciscono, *Paul Klee: His Work and Thought* (Chicago: The University of Chicago Press, 1991), 78ff.

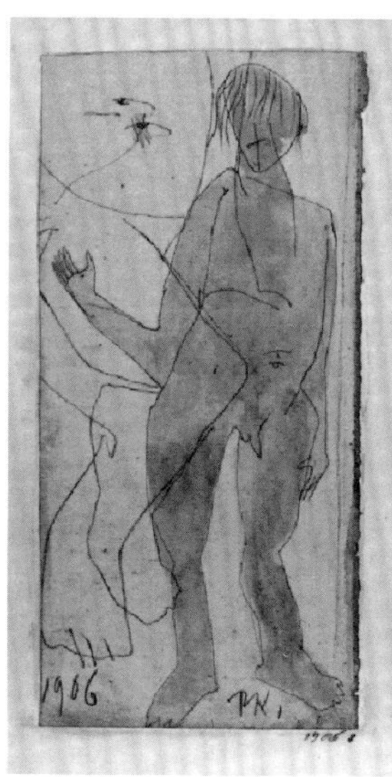

figure 21
Paul Klee, *Nude Youth*, 1905/08, pencil and watercolor on paper, 6 1/2 x 3 1/8". Paul Klee-Stiftung, Kunstmuseum Bern.

170 Ann Hutchinson, "A Brief History of Dance Notation," in *Tracking, Tracing, Marking, Pacing (Movement Drawings)* (exh. cat., Pratt Institute, New York, 1982), unpaginated. See also Vladimir Stepanov, *Alphabet des mouvements du corps humain* (Paris: M. Zouckermann [Librairie P. Vigot], 1892), which provided the sign system that was later adapted by Nijinsky.

171 See, for example, Archibald H. Sayce, *Introduction to the Science of Language*, 2 vols. (London: K. C. Paul & Co., 1880), esp. vol. 1, 81–82; Charles Darwin, *The Expression of Emotions in Men and Animals* (London: J. Murray, 1872); and such studies as Garrick Mallery, *Sign Language Among North American Indians Compared with that Among Other Peoples and Deaf-Mutes* [1881] (The Hague and Paris: Mouton, 1972), which attempt to analyze gestural language as a "primitive" form of communication.

172 See, for example, Werkner's discussion of Schiele's interest in the pathology of gesture and movement, 36–37, and Comini's comprehensive analysis of Schiele's interest in gestural language, esp. 134–135.

173 For a survey of approaches to the rationalization of motion and gesture, see Braun.

174 On this, see Werkner.

175 Kokoschka's correspondence, cited by Paul Westheim in the introduction to *Kokoschka Drawings*, ed. Ernest Rathenau (London: Thames and Hudson, 1962), 7.

176 Matisse, "Notes of a Painter on his Drawing" [1939], in Flam, 81.

177 The phrase was applied to Matisse's drawings by Eduard Steichen in 1910: "Drawings by Henri Matisse are the most modern of the moderns—his drawings are the same to him and his painting as Rodin's are to his sculpture.... Some are more finished than Rodin's, more of a study of *form* than *movement*—abstract to the limit." Undated letter from Steichen to Stieglitz, quoted in Barr, 113.

It is significant that Rodin's first exhibited works at Stieglitz's Gallery 291 were his drawings. Fifty-eight drawings, selected by Eduard Steichen, were exhibited by Stieglitz in January 1908 as the gallery's first display of advanced European art. Their seismographic linearity was viewed within the New York art world as the pinnacle of modernist touch, and their erotic content was understood to be evidence of a genuine, unhampered subjectivity. A sampling of New York reviews of Rodin's exhibition at Gallery 291 are provided in *Camera Work*, ed. Green. See especially J.N. Laurvik, from the *Times*, 144–145.

The affinity that Steichen recognized between Rodin's and Matisse's work was subsequently reflected in the New York press. James Huneker, writing in the *New York Sun*, repeated the descriptions of Rodin's work that had appeared in the wake of his Gallery 291 exhibition as "agility of line, velocity in its notation and an uncompromising attitude in the presence of the human machine," and then expressed the opinion that Matisse's graphic work exceeded Rodin's in its surety, its extraction of human energies, its sexual content, and its deployment of direct line: "Compared to these memoranda of the gutter and brothel the sketches of Rodin (once exhibited in this gallery) are academic, are meticulous." Huneker, in Green, 175.

178 In 1954, echoing Ozenfant, André Masson commented that the gestural touch of this first generation of modernists held within it the seeds of significant later developments: "Never were any drawings more freely executed than those Rodin drew from the model. These lines are truly 'lines of life'; his areas of color, movement itself. Their wonderful transparency is one with their joyous strength. When they first appeared they caused great surprise. Too often today, in the light of these drawings, our intrepidity seems marked with dull heaviness, sullen aggressiveness, or grossness coldly systematic...." André Masson, *Auguste Rodin* (exh. cat., Curt Valentin Gallery, New York, 1954).

CATALOGUE OF THE EXHIBITION

All artists represented in the exhibition are listed alphabetically. Works of art are arranged chronologically under their authors' names. Measurements are given in both inches and centimeters, with height preceding width. The page number on which a reproduction appears is indicated at the end of the entry.

ANDRÉ DERAIN (1880–1954), FRENCH

1 NUDE, n.d.
charcoal on paper
17 1/2 x 16 1/8 in. (44.4 x 41 cm)
Solomon R. Guggenheim Museum, New York
Gift of Alexander Liberman, 1978
page 36

ERICH HECKEL (1883–1970), GERMAN

2 BROTHER AND SISTER, 1910
black crayon on white paper
11 x 13 5/8 in. (27.5 x 34.6 cm)
Busch-Reisinger Museum, Harvard University Art Museums, Cambridge, Massachusetts: Loeb Fund and Friends of the Busch-Reisinger Museum
page 94

3 THREE FIGURES, 1913
graphite on wove paper
18 1/4 x 15 5/16 in. (46.4 x 38.9 cm)
National Gallery of Art, Washington, D.C.
Rosenwald Collection, 1950.17.307 (New York venue only)
page 86

ERNST LUDWIG KIRCHNER (1880–1938), GERMAN

4 MODEL ON A DIVAN, ca. 1908
charcoal on paper
17 5/8 x 13 5/8 in. (44.7 x 34.6 cm)
Davis Museum and Cultural Center, Wellesley College
Anonymous extended loan
page 78

5 COUPLE, ca. 1908 (recto and verso)
pencil on paper
17 1/2 x 13 1/2 in. (44.4 x 34.3 cm)
Davis Museum and Cultural Center, Wellesley College
Anonymous extended loan
pages 92 (recto) and 93 (verso)

6 NUDES ON A DIVAN, ca. 1908
brush and ink on paper
13 1/2 x 17 5/8 in. (34.3 x 44.8 cm)
Davis Museum and Cultural Center, Wellesley College
Anonymous extended loan
page 80

7 RECLINING NUDE (DODO), 1908
colored crayon on gray cardboard
14 1/4 x 17 1/8 in. (35.5 x 44 cm)
Francey and Dr. Martin L. Gecht, Chicago
page 79

8 WOMAN BATHING, 1909
lithograph
15 1/2 x 12 3/4 in. (39.4 x 32.4 cm)
The Fogg Art Museum, Harvard University Art Museums,
Cambridge, Massachusetts: George R. Nutter Fund
and William M. Prichard Fund
page 81

9 SMOKER AND DANCER, 1912
graphite and black crayon on cream wove paper
22 x 14 3/8 in. (55.9 x 36.5 cm)
The Detroit Institute of Arts: Founders Society Purchase,
John S. Newberry Fund
page 90

10 BATHER LYING ON THE BEACH AMONG ROCKS, 1912
reed pen and black ink
18 1/8 x 23 3/16 in. (46.1 x 58.9 cm)
National Gallery of Art, Washington, D.C.
Ailsa Mellon Bruce Fund, 1984.18.1 (New York venue only)
page 88

GUSTAV KLIMT (1862–1918), AUSTRIAN

11 STRIDING FIGURE WITH ARMS RAISED TO THE RIGHT, n.d.
pencil on paper
22 x 14 5/8 in. (56 x 37.3 cm)
Private collection
page 61

12 GIRL SEATED IN A CHAIR, ca. 1904
charcoal on Japanese paper
21 5/8 x 13 3/4 in. (55 x 34.9 cm)
Solomon R. Guggenheim Museum, New York
page 62

13 LADY WITH A FAN, n.d.
charcoal on brown paper
18 x 12 1/4 in. (45.7 x 31.1 cm)
Busch-Reisinger Museum, Harvard University Art Museums, Cambridge, Massachusetts: Purchase in memory of Louis W. Black
page 63

14 SEATED NUDE, n.d.
graphite on paper
22 x 14 7/16 in. (55.9 x 36.7 cm)
The Snite Museum of Art, University of Notre Dame, Indiana
60.47.2
page 58

15 SEATED NUDE WITH ARMS CROSSED, 1910–12
graphite on paper
21 11/16 x 13 13/16 in. (55 x 35.1 cm)
The University of Iowa Museum of Art, Iowa City, Iowa
1977.5
page 59

16 STUDY OF A MALE FIGURE, n.d.
charcoal on Japanese paper
16 x 12 in. (40.6 x 30.5 cm)
Davis Museum and Cultural Center, Wellesley College
Gift of Professor John McAndrew, 1957.10
page 60

17 RECLINING NUDE, n.d.
graphite on paper
14 5/8 x 22 1/16 in. (37.2 x 56.1 cm)
Davis Museum and Cultural Center, Wellesley College
Gift of Mrs. Sarah d'Harnoncourt (Class of 1925), 1984.12
page 65

OSKAR KOKOSCHKA (1886–1980), AUSTRIAN

18 NUDE YOUTH SEEN FROM THE BACK, 1906–07 (possibly 1905)
pencil, light red and gray wash on paper
17 3/8 x 11 15/16 in. (44.1 x 30.4 cm)
Allen Memorial Art Museum, Oberlin College, Ohio
Elisabeth Lotte Franzos Bequest, 1958 (Wellesley venue only)
page 54

19 SEATED WOMAN, 1912–13
gouache and crayon on buff wove paper
11 5/8 x 13 7/8 in. (29.5 x 35.3 cm)
Solomon R. Guggenheim Museum, New York
page 56

FERNAND LÉGER (1881–1955), FRENCH

20 SEATED NUDE, ca. 1911
reed pen and ink on tan paper, mounted on cardboard
12 3/16 x 9 1/8 in. (31 x 23.2 cm)
The University of Michigan Museum of Art, Ann Arbor
1948/1.273
page 98

21 STANDING FEMALE FIGURE, 1911
brown ink on tan wove paper
12 7/8 x 9 9/16 in. (32.7 x 24.3 cm)
The Fogg Art Museum, Harvard University Art Museums, Cambridge, Massachusetts: Anonymous Gift
page 99

HENRI MATISSE (1869–1954), FRENCH

22 AT THE SEASIDE (BATHER), ca. 1905
watercolor and pencil on paper
5 3/4 x 9 5/8 in. (14.6 x 24.5 cm)
The Metropolitan Museum of Art, New York
Alfred Stieglitz Collection, 1949
page 39

23 PENSIVE NUDE IN A FOLDING CHAIR, 1906
lithograph
14 3/4 x 10 5/8 in. (37.5 x 27 cm)
The Museum of Modern Art, New York
Given in memory of Leo and Nina Stein
253.50
page 42

24 CROUCHING NUDE WITH EYES LOWERED, 1906
transfer lithograph
17 3/4 x 11 1/16 in. (45.1 x 28.1 cm)
The Baltimore Museum of Art: The Cone Collection, formed by
Dr. Claribel Cone and Miss Etta Cone of Baltimore, Maryland
BMA 1950.12.133
page 51

25 BACK VIEW OF A NUDE WITH NECKLACE, 1906
transfer lithograph
17 3/4 x 10 15/16 in. (45 x 27.9 cm)
The Baltimore Museum of Art: Blanche Adler Memorial Fund
BMA 1958.116
page 40

26 UNTITLED (SEATED NUDE), ca. 1906
ink on paper
10 5/8 x 8 1/4 in. (27 x 21 cm)
The Phillips Collection, Washington, D.C.
Gift of Marjorie Phillips, 1984
page 49

27 ÉTUDE DE NUE (LE GRAND BOIS), 1906
woodcut on laid paper
22 3/4 x 18 1/16 in. (57.8 x 46.2 cm)
The Baltimore Museum of Art: The Cone Collection, formed by
Dr. Claribel Cone and Miss Etta Cone of Baltimore, Maryland
BMA 1950.12.236
page 47

28 ÉTUDE DE NUE (PETIT BOIS NOIR), 1906
woodcut on laid paper
18 x 11 1/4 in. (45.8 x 28.7 cm)
The Baltimore Museum of Art: The Cone Collection, formed by
Dr. Claribel Cone and Miss Etta Cone of Baltimore, Maryland
BMA 1950.12.235
page 46

29 SEATED NUDE (PETIT BOIS CLAIR), 1906
woodcut
13 1/2 x 10 1/2 in. (34.3 x 26.7 cm)
Davis Museum and Cultural Center, Wellesley College
Gift of Tower Court Students, 1956.28
page 45

30 NUDE WITH BRACELETS, ca. 1909
pen and ink on paper
12 5/8 x 8 7/8 in. (32.1 x 22.5 cm)
The Metropolitan Museum of Art, New York
Alfred Stieglitz Collection, 1949
page 52

MAX PECHSTEIN (1881–1955), GERMAN

31 BATHER, n.d.
graphite and watercolor on paper
8 x 6 7/16 in. (20.3 x 16.4 cm)
Busch-Reisinger Museum, Harvard University Art Museums, Cambridge, Massachusetts: Gift of Louis W. Black
page 85

32 MOTHER AND SON, 1910
pencil with wash on paper
14 1/2 x 11 5/8 in. (37 x 27.2 cm)
Philadelphia Museum of Art: Gift of Lessing J. Rosenwald
page 95

AUGUSTE RODIN (1840–1917), FRENCH

33 UNTITLED, n.d.
pencil and watercolor on paper
9 1/2 x 12 in. (24.1 x 30.5 cm)
Philadelphia Museum of Art
page 25

34 L'ABANDONNÉE, ca. 1900
graphite on paper
7 9/16 x 11 7/8 in. (19.4 x 30.4 cm)
The Metropolitan Museum of Art, New York: Rogers Fund, 1910
page 35

35 STANDING NUDE WOMAN WITH STUDY OF FEET AT LOWER RIGHT CORNER, n.d.
graphite and watercolor on paper
14 1/4 x 8 3/4 in. (36 x 22.5 cm)
Philadelphia Museum of Art: Gift of Jules E. Mastbaum
page 22

36 WOMAN SEATED, FACING RIGHT, n.d.
pencil on paper
7 3/4 x 11 1/2 in. (19.5 x 29.1 cm)
Philadelphia Museum of Art: Gift of Jules E. Mastbaum
page 23

37 RECLINING WOMAN, CLOTHED, n.d.
graphite and watercolor on paper
7 15/16 x 12 1/4 in. (19.8 x 31.1 cm)
Philadelphia Museum of Art: Gift of Jules E. Mastbaum
page 18

38 KNEELING MALE NUDE, n.d.
graphite and watercolor on paper
7 7/8 x 12 1/4 in. (20 x 31 cm)
Philadelphia Museum of Art: Gift of Jules E. Mastbaum
page 15

39 SKETCH OF NUDE WOMAN, n.d.
graphite and watercolor on off-white paper
7 1/2 x 11 11/16 in. (19.1 x 29.7 cm)
The Fogg Art Museum, Harvard University Art Museums, Cambridge, Massachusetts: Transferred from Houghton Library, Gift of Mme A. Aubert
page 20

40 STANDING WOMAN SEEN FROM BEHIND, n.d.
pencil and watercolor on paper
12 1/2 x 9 3/4 in. (31.8 x 24.8 cm)
Philadelphia Museum of Art: Gift of Jules E. Mastbaum
page 26

41 MONTAGE SHEET WITH THREE CUT-OUT FIGURES, ca. 1900–05
collage, watercolor, and pencil on paper
22 1/8 x 28 5/8 in. (56.2 x 72.7 cm)
Graphic Arts Collection, Rare Books and Special Collections, Princeton University Library
page 27

42 CAMBODIAN DANCING GIRL, 1906
watercolor over pencil on paper
11 5/16 x 7 3/4 in. (28.7 x 19.7 cm)
Museum of Fine Arts, Boston: Bequest of John T. Spaulding
48.851
page 32

EGON SCHIELE (1890–1918), AUSTRIAN

43 SEATED NUDE, ca. 1910
graphite on brown wove paper
21 1/8 x 15 in. (53.6 x 38.1 cm)
Busch-Reisinger Museum, Harvard University Art Museums, Cambridge, Massachusetts: Anonymous Gift
page 69

44 THE KISS, 1911
pencil on paper
22 x 14 3/4 in. (55.9 x 37.5 cm)
The Metropolitan Museum of Art, New York
Bequest of Scofield Thayer, 1982
page 70

45 FEMALE NUDE WITH HANDS CLASPED BEHIND HEAD, 1911
pencil on paper
19 x 12 3/8 in. (48.3 x 31.4 cm)
Indiana University Art Museum, Bloomington, Indiana
Jane and Roger Wolcott Memorial and Gift of Dr. Otto Kallir
page 71

46 STANDING SEMI-NUDE FROM THE BACK, 1912
pencil on paper
17 x 11 15/16 in. (43.1 x 30.4 cm)
Indiana University Art Museum, Bloomington, Indiana
Gift of Serge Sabarsky
page 72

47 WOMAN AND GIRL EMBRACING, 1918
charcoal on paper
18 1/4 x 11 3/4 in. (46.3 x 29.8 cm)
The Metropolitan Museum of Art, New York
Bequest of Scofield Thayer, 1982
page 73

48 SEATED NUDE WITH ORANGE HEADBAND, 1913
watercolor and pencil
19 3/16 x 12 1/8 in. (48.7 x 30.8 cm)
Francey and Dr. Martin L. Gecht, Chicago
page 66

49 SEATED NUDE IN SHOES AND STOCKINGS, 1918
charcoal on paper
18 1/4 x 11 3/4 in. (46.4 x 29.8 cm)
The Metropolitan Museum of Art, New York
Bequest of Scofield Thayer, 1982
page 76

SELECTED BIBLIOGRAPHY

Bahr 1920
Bahr, Hermann. *Expressionismus*. Munich: Delphin-Verlag, 1920.

Barr 1951
Barr, Alfred H., Jr. *Matisse: His Art and His Public*. New York: The Museum of Modern Art, 1951.

Beausire 1988
Beausire, Alain. *Quand Rodin Exposait*. Paris: Éditions du Musée Rodin, 1988.

Benjamin 1987
Benjamin, Roger. *Matisse's "Notes of a Painter": Criticism, Theory, and Context, 1891–1908*. Ann Arbor: U.M.I. Research Press, 1987.

Bergson 1911
Bergson, Henri. *Matter and Memory*. Translated by Nancy Margaret Paul and W. Scott Palmer. London: George Allen & Unwin Ltd., 1911.

Boime 1974
Boime, Albert. *Strictly Academic: Life Drawing in the Nineteenth Century* (exhibition catalogue). Binghamton: University Art Gallery, State University of New York, 1974.

Boime 1986
Boime, Albert. *The Academy and French Painting in the Nineteenth Century*. New Haven: Yale University Press [1971], 1986.

Bois 1906
Bois, George. "Le sculpteur Rodin et les danseuses Cambodgiennes." *L'Illustration* (July 28, 1906): 64–65.

Bois 1990
Bois, Yve-Alain. *Painting as Model*. Cambridge: M.I.T. Press, 1990.

Braun 1992
Braun, Marta. *Picturing Time: The Work of Etienne-Jules Marey (1830–1904)*. Chicago: University of Chicago Press, 1992.

Broude 1991
Broude, Norma. *Impressionism: A Feminist Reading: The Gendering of Art, Science, and Nature in the Nineteenth Century*. New York: Rizzoli, 1991.

Bryson 1983
Bryson, Norman. *Vision and Painting: The Logic of the Gaze*. New Haven: Yale University Press, 1983.

Butler 1980
Butler, Ruth, ed. *Rodin in Perspective*. Englewood Cliffs, N.J.: Prentice-Hall, Inc., 1980.

Butler 1993
Butler, Ruth. *Rodin: The Shape of Genius*. New Haven: Yale University Press, 1993.

Carlson 1971
Carlson, Victor. *Matisse as Draughtsman* (exhibition catalogue). Baltimore: The Baltimore Museum of Art, 1971.

Chu 1982
Chu, Petra ten-Doesschate. “Lecoq de Boisbaudran and Memory Drawing: A Teaching Course between Idealism and Naturalism.” In *The European Realist Tradition*. Edited by Gabriel P. Weisberg. Bloomington: Indiana University Press, 1982: 242–289.

Cladel 1908
Cladel, Judith. *Auguste Rodin, L’Oeuvre et l’homme*. Brussels: Van Oest, 1908.

Comini 1974
Comini, Alessandra. *Egon Schiele’s Portraits*. Berkeley: University of California Press, 1974.

Crone and Salzmann 1992
Crone, Rainer, and Siegfried Salzmann, eds. *Rodin: Eros and Creativity*. Munich: Prestel-Verlag, 1992.

Driesbach 1978
Driesbach, Jan Tolhurst. “Three Drawings by Egon Schiele,” *Indiana University Art Museum Bulletin*. Bloomington, 1978: 60–77.

Dujardin-Beaumetz 1992
Dujardin-Beaumetz, François. *Entretiens avec Rodin*. Paris: Paul Dupont, 1992.

Duncan 1982
Duncan, Carol. “Virility and Domination in Early Twentieth-Century Vanguard Painting.” In *Feminism and Art History: Questioning the Litany*. Edited by Norma Broude and Mary D. Garrard. New York: Harper and Row, 1982: 293–313.

Duncan 1927
Duncan, Isadora. *My Life*. New York: Boni and Liveright, 1927.

Duthuit-Matisse and Duthuit 1983
Duthuit-Matisse, Marguerite, and Claude Duthuit. *Henri Matisse: L’Oeuvre gravé*. Paris: Imprimerie Union, 1983.

Elderfield 1978
Elderfield, John. *Matisse in the Collection of The Museum of Modern Art*. New York: The Museum of Modern Art, 1978.

Elderfield 1984
Elderfield, John. *The Drawings of Henri Matisse* (exhibition catalogue, Hayward Gallery). London: Thames and Hudson, 1984.

Elderfield 1992
Elderfield, John. *Henri Matisse: A Retrospective* (exhibition catalogue, The Museum of Modern Art). New York: Harry N. Abrams, Inc., 1992.

Elsen 1963
Elsen, Albert E. *Rodin* (exhibition catalogue, The Museum of Modern Art). New York: Doubleday, 1963.

Elsen 1965
Elsen, Albert E. *Auguste Rodin: Readings on His Life and Work*. Englewood Cliffs, N.J.: Prentice-Hall, Inc., 1965.

Elsen and Varnedoe 1971
Elsen, Albert E., and J. Kirk T. Varnedoe. *The Drawings of Rodin* (exhibition catalogue, National Gallery of Art, Washington, D.C.). New York: Praeger Publishers, 1971.

Elsen 1972
Elsen, Albert E. *The Sculpture of Henri Matisse*. New York: Harry N. Abrams, Inc., 1972.

Elsen 1972
Elsen, Albert E. "Drawing and the True Rodin." *Artforum*, vol. 10, no. 6 (February 1972): 64–69.

Elsen 1981
Elsen, Albert E., ed. *Rodin Rediscovered* (exhibition catalogue). Washington, D.C.: National Gallery of Art, 1981.

Elsen 1987
Elsen, Albert E. "Rodin's Drawings and the Art of Matisse." *Arts*, vol. 61, no. 7 (March 1987): 32–39.

Fagus 1900
Fagus, Félicien. "Discours sur la mission de Rodin," *La Revue Blanche* XXII (March–June–July–August 1900): 241–252.

Flam 1978
Flam, Jack D. *Matisse on Art*. New York: E.P. Dutton, 1978.

Franciscono 1991
Franciscono, Marcel. *Paul Klee: His Work and Thought*. Chicago: The University of Chicago Press, 1991.

Fuller 1913
Fuller, Loïe. *Fifteen Years of a Dancer's Life with Some Account of Her Distinguished Friends*. Introduction by Anatole France. London: Herbert Jenkins Ltd., 1913.

Geissbuhler 1963
Geissbuhler, Elisabeth Chase. *Rodin: Later Drawings*. Interpretations by Antoine Bourdelle. Boston: Beacon Press, 1963.

Goldscheider 1962
Goldscheider, Cécile. *Rodin inconnu* (exhibition catalogue). Paris: Éditions du Musée Rodin, 1962.

Gordon 1968
Gordon, Donald E. *Ernst Ludwig Kirchner*. Cambridge: Harvard University Press, 1968.

Green 1973
Green, Jonathan, ed. *Camera Work: A Critical Anthology*. New York: Aperture, 1973.

Güse 1984
Güse, Ernst-Gerhard, ed. *Auguste Rodin: Drawings and Watercolors*. Translated by John Gabriel and Michael Taylor. New York: Rizzoli, 1984.

Hildebrand 1978
Hildebrand, Adolf von. *The Problem of Form in Painting and Sculpture* [1893]. Translated by Max Meyer and Robert Morris Ogden [1932]. New York: Garland Publishing, Inc., 1978.

Hodin 1966
Hodin, J. P. *Oskar Kokoschka: The Artist and His Time*. Greenwich: New York Graphic Society, 1966.

Hoffman 1936
Hoffman, Malvina. *Heads and Tales*. New York: Charles Scribner's Sons, 1936.

Hofmann 1971
Hofmann, Werner. *Gustav Klimt*. Translated by Inge Goodman. Greenwich: New York Graphic Society, 1971.

Iversen 1993
Iversen, Margaret. *Alois Riegl: Art History and Theory*. Cambridge: The M.I.T. Press, 1993.

Judrin 1984–1992
Judrin, Claudie. *Musée Rodin. Inventaire des dessins*. 6 vols. Paris: Éditions du Musée Rodin, 1984–1992.

Kallir 1981
Kallir, Jane. *Austria's Expressionism* (exhibition catalogue, The Galerie St. Etienne). New York: Rizzoli, 1981.

Kallir 1990
Kallir, Jane. *Egon Schiele: The Complete Works*. New York: Harry N. Abrams, Inc., 1990.

Kallir 1994
Kallir, Jane. *Egon Schiele* (exhibition catalogue, National Gallery of Art, Washington, D.C.). With an essay by Alessandra Comini. New York: Harry N. Abrams, 1994.

Kokoschka and Marnau 1992
Kokoschka, Olda, and Alfred Marnau, eds. *Oskar Kokoschka: Letters 1905–1976*. Foreword by E. H. Gombrich. London: Thames and Hudson, 1992.

Lampert 1986
Lampert, Catherine. *Rodin: Sculpture and Drawings* (exhibition catalogue, Hayward Gallery). London: Arts Council of Great Britain, 1986.

Larson 1971
Larson, Philip Seely. "Drawing Styles and Graphic Detail in *Brücke* Art, 1905–1920." Ph.D. diss., Columbia University, 1971.

Long 1993
Long, Rose-Carol Washton, ed. *German Expressionism: Documents from the End of the Wilhelmine Empire to the Rise of National Socialism*. New York: G. K. Hall & Co., 1993.

Ludovici 1926
Ludovici, Anthony M. *Personal Reminiscences of Auguste Rodin*. Philadelphia: J. B. Lippincott Co., 1926.

MacDonald 1970
MacDonald, Stuart. *The History and Philosophy of Art Education*. New York: American Elsevier Publishers, 1970.

Martin 1983
Martin, Marianne. *Art and Dance: Images of the Modern Dialogue 1890–1980* (exhibition catalogue). Boston: Institute of Contemporary Art, 1983.

Mauclair 1898
Mauclair, Camille. "L'Art de M. Auguste Rodin." *Revue des Revues* (June 15, 1898): 591–610.

Meisel 1970
Meisel, Victor H., ed. *Voices of German Expressionism*. Englewood Cliffs, N.J.: Prentice-Hall, Inc., 1970.

Novotny and Dobai 1975
Novotny, Fritz, and Johannes Dobai. *Gustav Klimt, with a Catalogue Raisonné of His Paintings*. Boston: New York Graphic Society, 1975.

Ozenfant 1952
Ozenfant, Amédée. *Foundations of Modern Art* [1931]. New York: Dover Publications, Inc., 1952.

Pechstein 1960
Pechstein, Max. *Erinnerungen*. Edited by Leopold Reidemeister. Wiesbaden: Limes Verlag, 1960.

Poggioli 1968
Poggioli, Renato. *The Theory of the Avant-Garde*. Cambridge: Harvard University Press, 1968.

Rilke 1919
Rilke, Rainer Maria. *Auguste Rodin*. Translated by Jessie Lemont and Hans Trausil. New York: Sunrise Turn, Inc., 1919.

Rodin 1984
Rodin, Auguste. *Art: Conversations with Paul Gsell*. Translated by Jacques de Caso and Patricia B. Saunders. Berkeley: University of California Press, 1984.

Scharf 1974
Scharf, Aaron. *Art and Photography*. Hammersmith: Penguin Books, 1974.

Schneider 1984
Schneider, Pierre. *Matisse*. Translated by Michael Taylor and Bridget Strevens Romer. New York: Rizzoli, 1984.

Schorske 1980
Schorske, Carl E. *Fin-de-Siècle Vienna: Politics and Culture*. New York: Random House, 1980.

Schröder and Szeemann 1989
Schröder, Klaus Albrecht, and Harald Szeemann. *Egon Schiele and His Contemporaries: Austrian Painting and Drawing from 1900 to 1930 from the Leopold Collection, Vienna*. Munich: Prestel-Verlag, 1989.

Shiff 1984
Shiff, Richard. *Cézanne and the End of Impressionism: A Study of the Theory, Technique, and Critical Evaluation of Modern Art*. Chicago: The University of Chicago Press, 1984.

Strobl 1980–1989
Strobl, Alice. *Gustav Klimt: Die Zeichnungen.* 4 vols. Salzburg: Verlag Galerie Welz, 1980–1989.

Strobl and Weidinger 1994
Strobl, Alice, and Alfred Weidinger. *Oskar Kokoschka, Works on Paper: The Early Years, 1897–1917* (exhibition catalogue). New York: Solomon R. Guggenheim Museum, 1994.

Valentin 1950
Valentin, Kurt. *The Heritage of Auguste Rodin* (exhibition catalogue). New York: Buchholz Gallery, 1950.

Varnedoe 1986
Varnedoe, Kirk. *Vienna 1900: Art, Architecture, and Design* (exhibition catalogue, The Museum of Modern Art). Greenwich: New York Graphic Society, 1986.

Vergo 1975
Vergo, Peter. *Art in Vienna 1898–1918: Klimt, Kokoschka, Schiele, and their Contemporaries*. London: Phaidon Press, 1975.

Wagner 1991
Wagner, Anne M. "Rodin's Reputation." In *Eroticism and the Body Politic*. Edited by Lynn Hunt. Baltimore: The Johns Hopkins University Press, 1991: 191–242.

Werkner 1994
Werkner, Patrick, ed. *Egon Schiele: Art, Sexuality, and Viennese Modernism*. Palo Alto: The Society for the Promotion of Science and Scholarship, 1994.

Westheim 1962
Westheim, Paul. Introduction to *Kokoschka Drawings*. Edited by Ernest Rathenau. London: Thames and Hudson, 1962.

Whitford 1981
Whitford, Frank. *Egon Schiele*. New York and Toronto: Oxford University Press, 1981.

INDEX

PHOTOGRAPHY CREDITS

Allen Memorial Art Museum, Oberlin College, Oberlin, Ohio: cat. no. 18

The Art Institute of Chicago, Chicago, Illinois: fig. 6

The Baltimore Museum of Art, Baltimore, Maryland: cat. nos. 24, 25, 27, 28

The Barnes Foundation, Merion Station, Pennsylvania: fig. 8

The Cleveland Museum of Art, Cleveland, Ohio: fig. 13

Davis Museum and Cultural Center, Wellesley College, Wellesley, Massachusetts: fig. 5; photographs by Greg Heins: cat. nos. 4, 5 (recto and verso), 6, 16, 17, 29

The Detroit Institute of Arts, Detroit, Michigan: cat. no. 9

Graphische Sammlung Albertina, Vienna, Austria: fig. 12

Harvard College Library, Cambridge, Massachusetts: figs. 1, 4, 9, 10, 15, 18, 20

Harvard University Art Museums, Cambridge, Massachusetts: cat. nos. 2, 8, 13, 21, 31, 39, 43

Indiana University Art Museum, Bloomington, Indiana: photographs by Michael Cavanagh and Kevin Montague: cat. nos. 45, 46; fig. 14

Kunstmuseum Bern, Bern, Switzerland: fig. 21

The Metropolitan Museum of Art, New York: cat. nos. 22, 30, 34, 44, 47, 49

Musée Rodin, Paris, France: photograph by Bauche: fig. 2; photograph by Bruner-Dvorak: fig. 3

Museum of Fine Arts, Boston, Massachusetts: cat. no. 42

The Museum of Modern Art, New York: cat. no. 23; figs. 7, 11

Nationalgalerie, Berlin, Germany: fig. 17

National Gallery of Art, Washington, D.C.: cat. nos. 3, 10; fig. 16; photograph by Dean Beasom: fig. 19

Philadelphia Museum of Art, Philadelphia, Pennsylvania: cat. nos. 11, 32, 36, 37, 38, 40; photographs by Lynn Rosenthal: cat. nos. 33, 35

The Phillips Collection, Washington, D.C.: photograph by Edward Owen: cat. no. 26

Princeton University Libraries, Princeton, New Jersey: cat. no. 41

The Snite Museum of Art, University of Notre Dame, Notre Dame, Indiana: cat. no. 14

The Solomon R. Guggenheim Foundation, New York: photograph by David Heald: cat. no. 12; photographs by Robert E. Mates: cat. nos. 1, 19

The University of Iowa Museum of Art, Iowa City, Iowa: cat. no. 15

The University of Michigan Museum of Art, Ann Arbor, Michigan: cat. no. 20

This publication was designed by
Anita Meyer, plus design inc., Boston
production coordinated by Susan McNally
typeset in Meta+
by Moveable Type Inc., Toronto
and edited by
Nancy DuVergne Smith and Lucy Flint-Gohlke,
and by Jim Roberts, Moveable Type Inc.
2,000 copies were printed on
Potlatch Karma 80 lb text and Mohawk Ultrafelt 100 lb cover
in Worcester by Mercantile Printing Company, Inc.

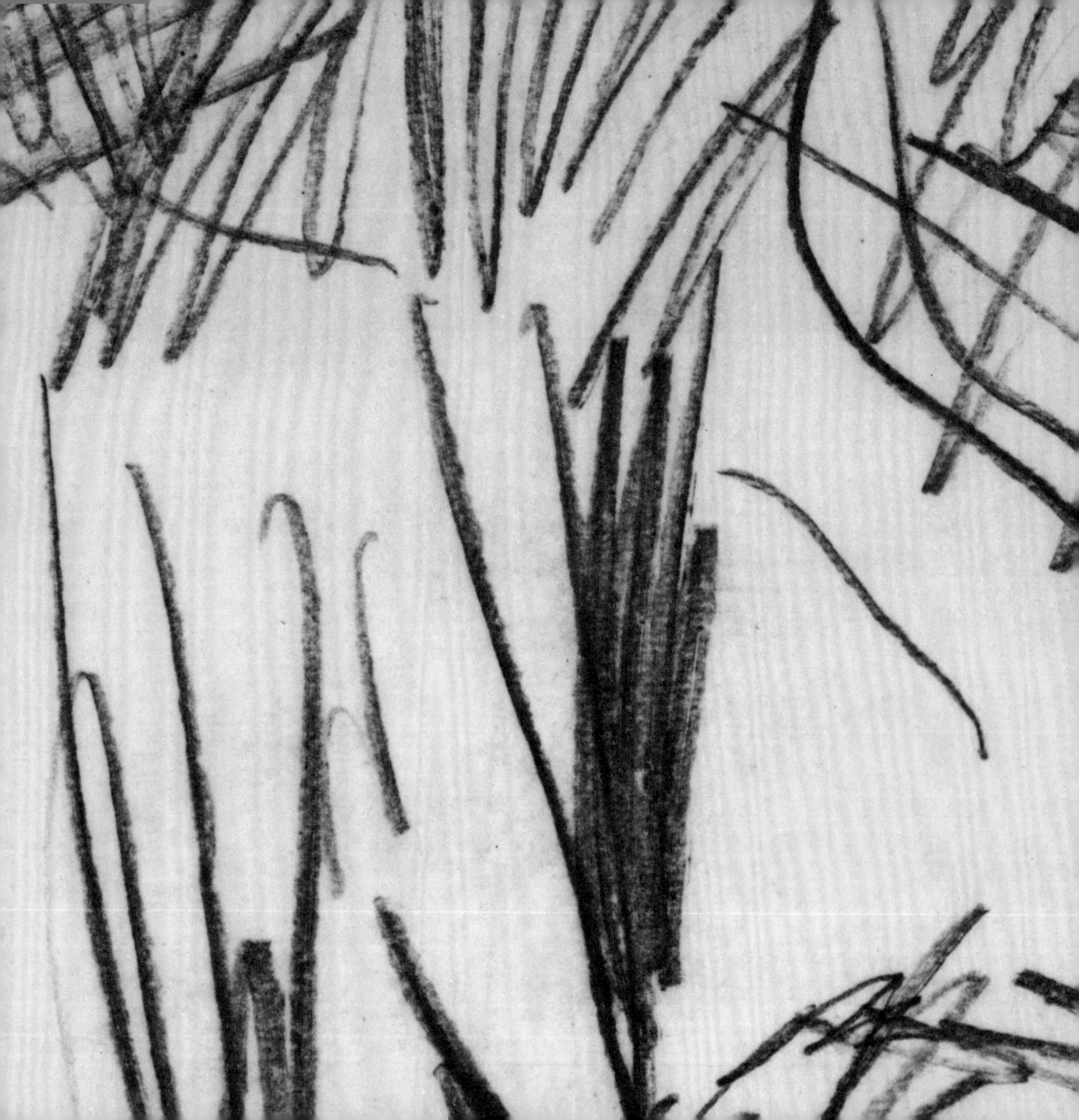